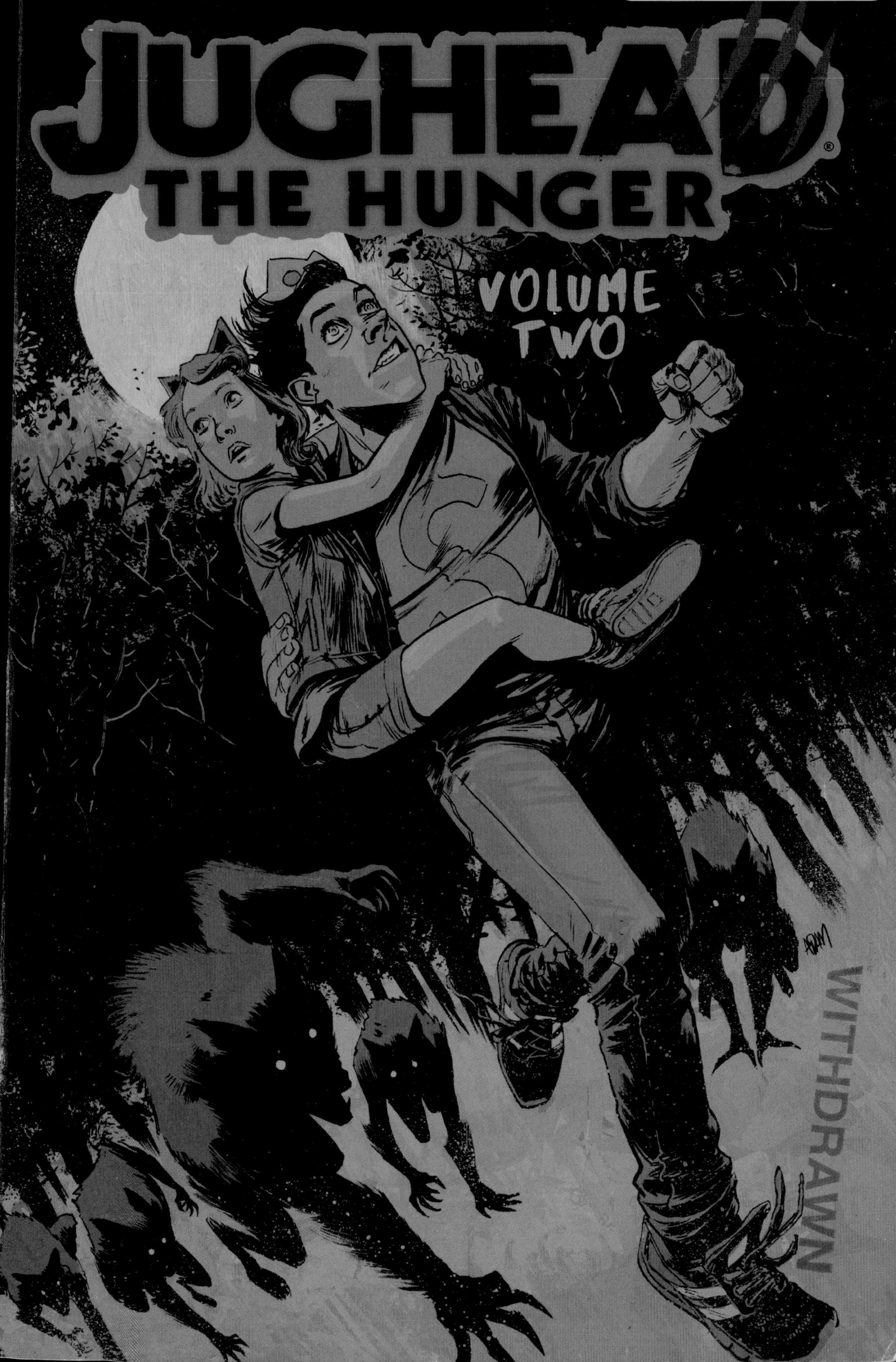
JUGHEAD®
THE HUNGER
VOLUME TWO

JUGHEAD
THE HUNGER

SCRIPT:
Frank Tieri

ART:
Pat & Tim Kennedy
Joe Eisma

INKS:
Bob Smith
Jim Amash
Ryan Jampole

COLORS:
Matt Herms
Andre Szymanowicz
Kelsey Shannon

LETTERS:
Jack Morelli

EDITORS:
Alex Segura
Jamie Lee Rotante

ASSOCIATE EDITOR:
Stephen Oswald
ASSISTANT EDITOR:
Vincent Lovallo

GRAPHIC DESIGN:
Kari McLachlan

EDITOR-IN-CHIEF
Victor Gorelick

PUBLISHER
Jon Goldwater

PREVIOUSLY...

ARCHIE ANDREWS, along with the werewolf hunters BETTY COOPER and her cousin BO COOPER, have been hot on the trail of their best friend/part-time werewolf JUGHEAD JONES. They've followed him to the circus where he was taking respite, but he had to flee after the brutal murder of ABBEY, a beloved carnival worker.

The death toll continued to rise as Jughead battled with his animalistic urges when he was confronted with something new: the knowledge that he is not the only one of his kind... his cousin, BINGO WILKIN, is also a werewolf. Previously believed to be dead, Bingo faked his own death so he could continue to evade Betty and her werewolf-hunting clan. Now, Jughead and Bingo must work together to stay alive.

Meanwhile, a meeting with Betty's mysterious aunt ELENA COOPER and a brush with murder has left Archie frazzled. But what none of them know is that REGGIE MANTLE is leading a whole new horde of werewolves back in RIVERDALE...

ISSUE FOUR

COVER ART Adam Gorham

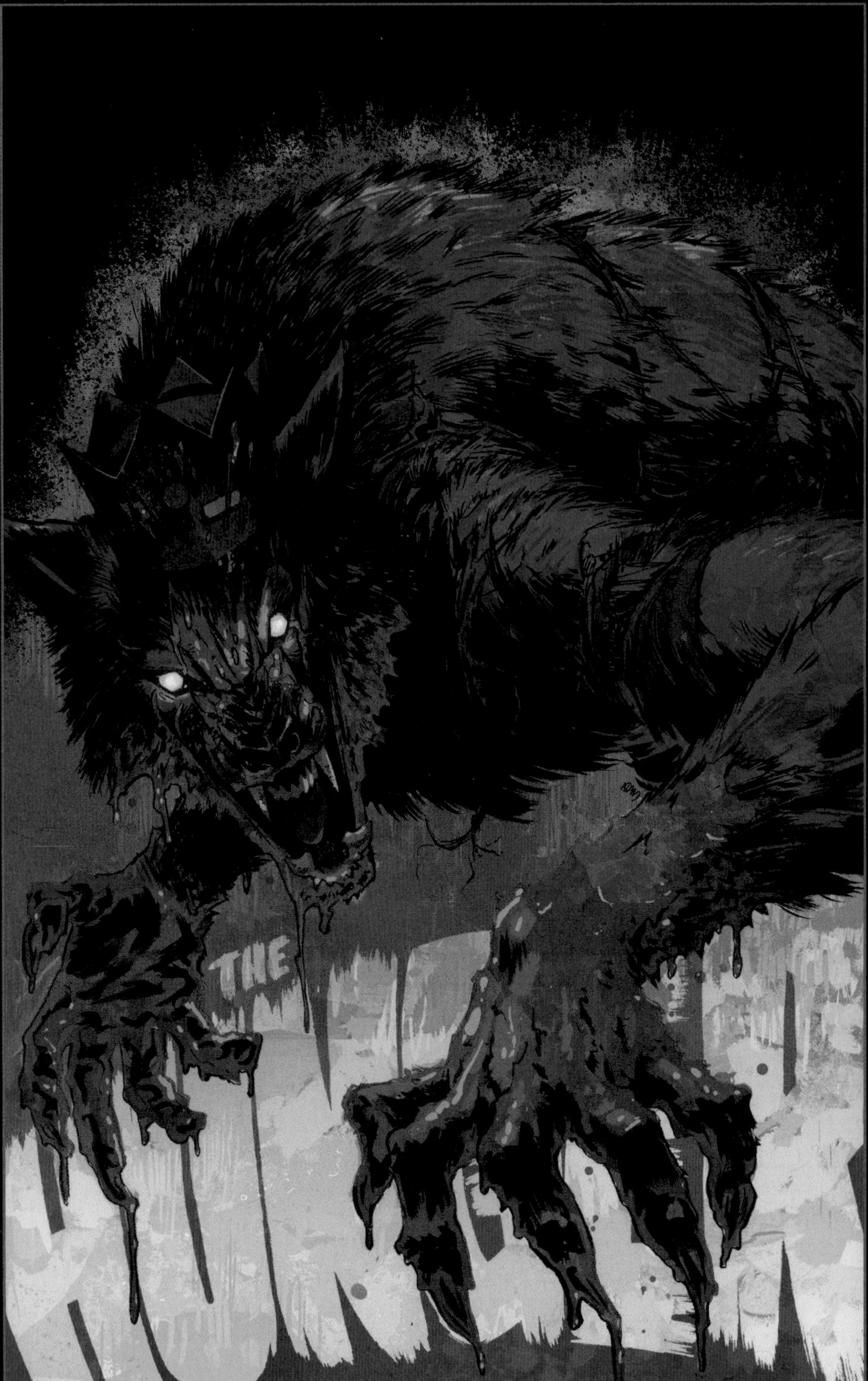
THE

STORY Frank Tieri ART Pat & Tim Kennedy (p. 1-10) Joe Eisma (p. 11-20)
COLORS Matt Herms INKS Bob Smith (p. 1-10) LETTERING Jack Morelli

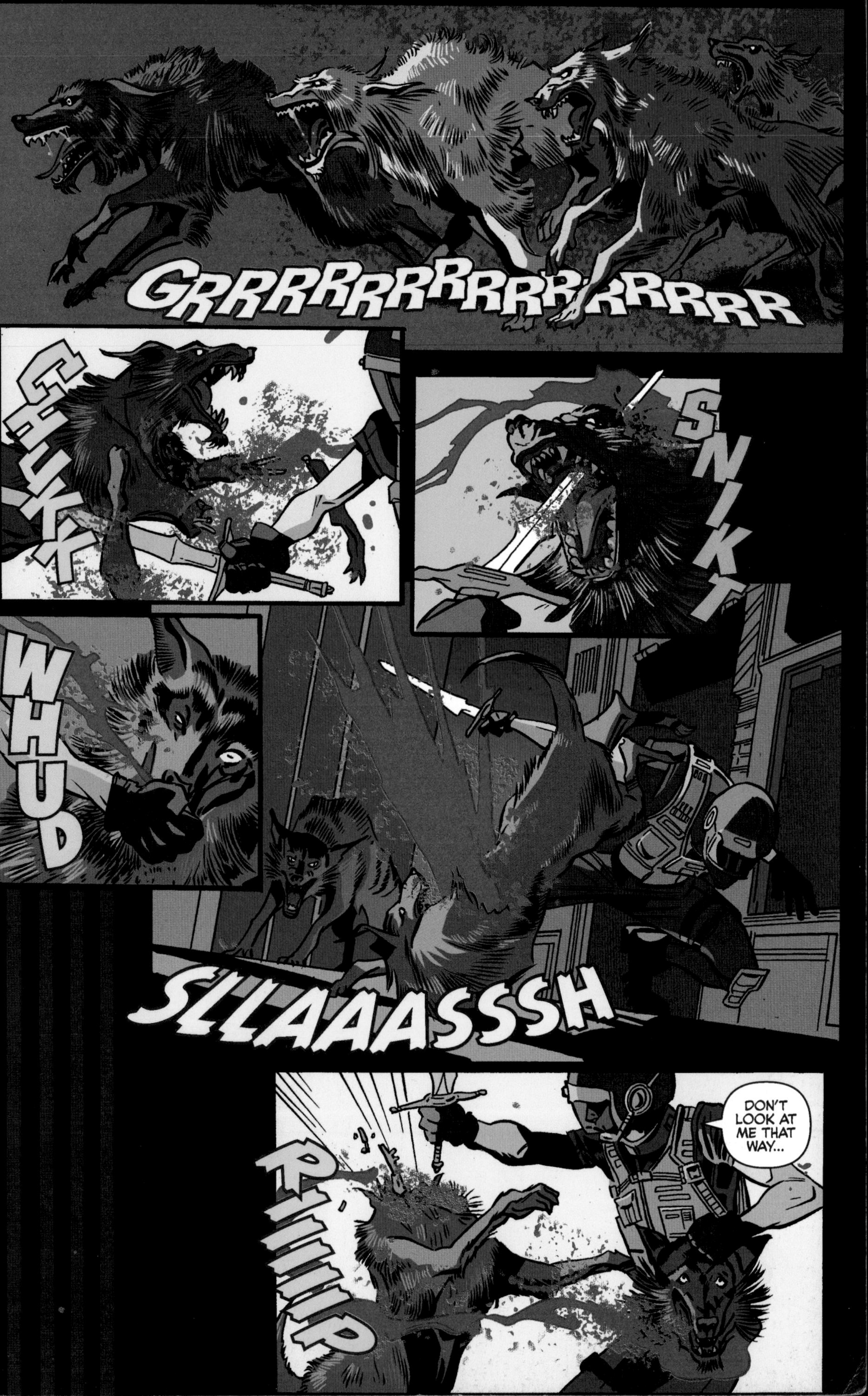
GRRRRRRRRRRRRRRR
CHUKK
SNIKT
WHUD
SLLAAASSSH
RIIIIIP
DON'T LOOK AT ME THAT WAY...

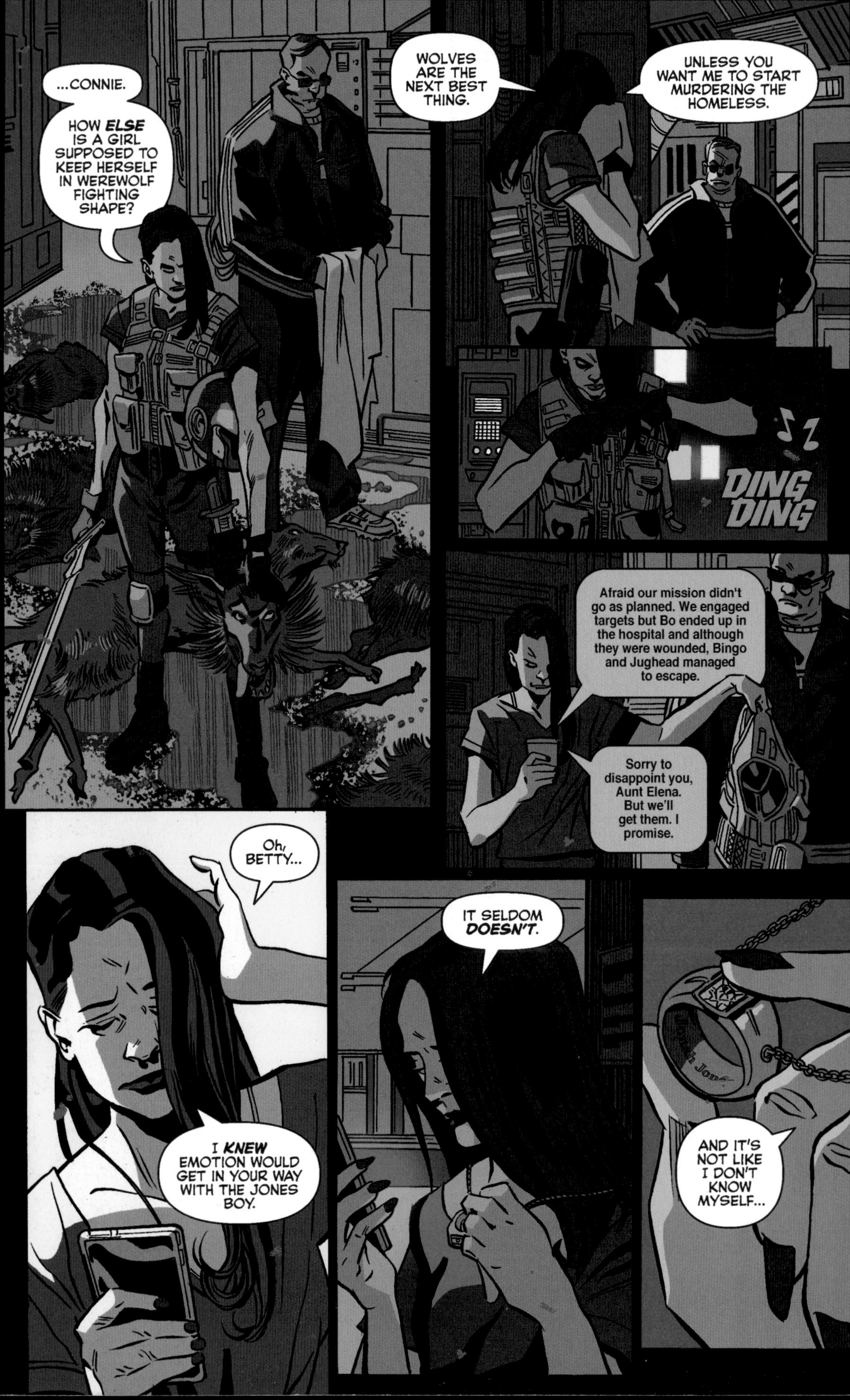
...CONNIE.
HOW *ELSE* IS A GIRL SUPPOSED TO KEEP HERSELF IN WEREWOLF FIGHTING SHAPE?
WOLVES ARE THE NEXT BEST THING.
UNLESS YOU WANT ME TO START MURDERING THE HOMELESS.
DING DING
Afraid our mission didn't go as planned. We engaged targets but Bo ended up in the hospital and although they were wounded, Bingo and Jughead managed to escape.
Sorry to disappoint you, Aunt Elena. But we'll get them. I promise.
Oh, BETTY...
I *KNEW* EMOTION WOULD GET IN YOUR WAY WITH THE JONES BOY.
IT SELDOM *DOESN'T*.
AND IT'S NOT LIKE I DON'T KNOW MYSELF...

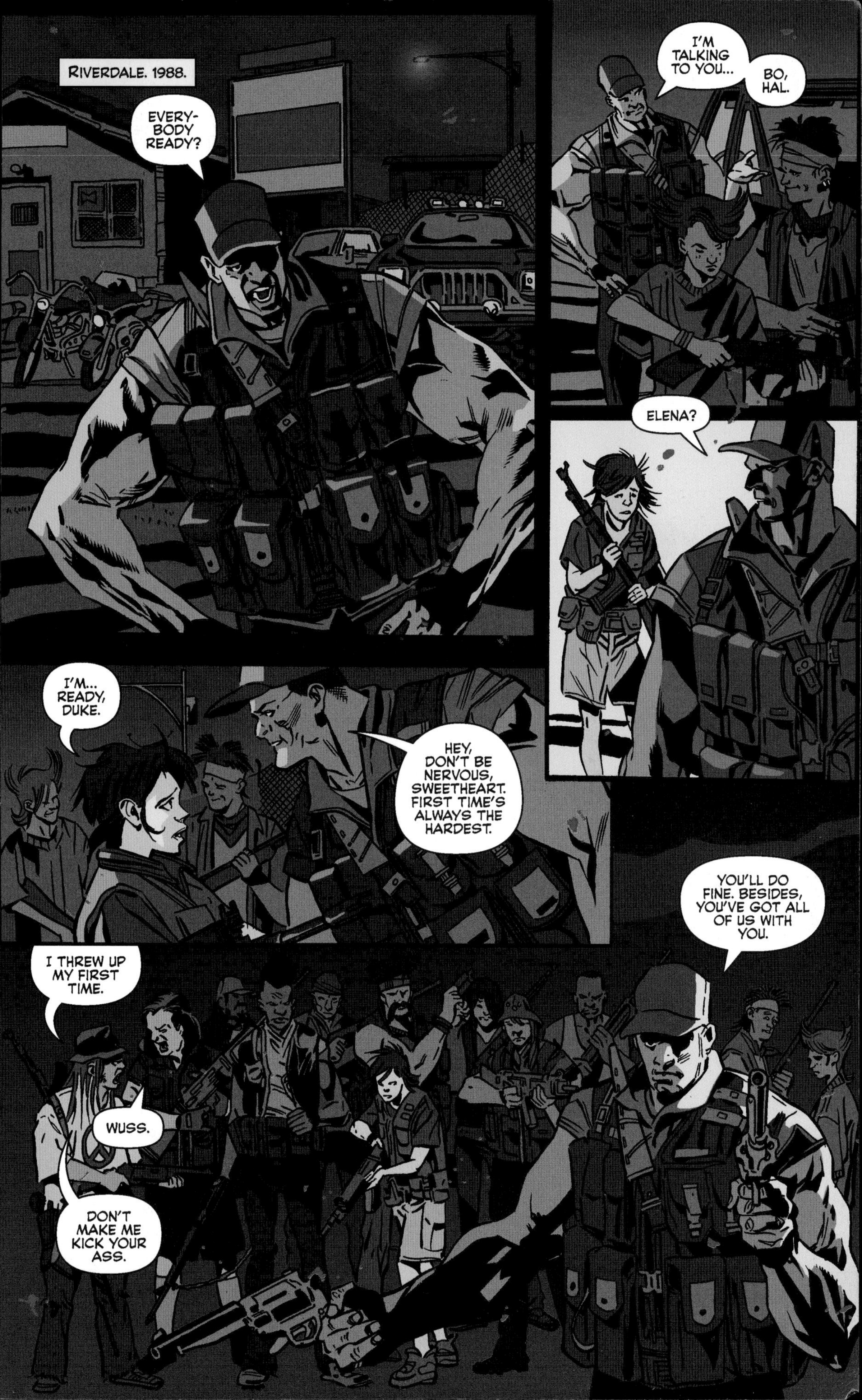
RIVERDALE. 1988.
EVERY-BODY READY?
I'M TALKING TO YOU...
BO, HAL.
ELENA?
I'M... READY, DUKE.
HEY, DON'T BE NERVOUS, SWEETHEART. FIRST TIME'S ALWAYS THE HARDEST.
YOU'LL DO FINE. BESIDES, YOU'VE GOT ALL OF US WITH YOU.
I THREW UP MY FIRST TIME.
WUSS.
DON'T MAKE ME KICK YOUR ASS.

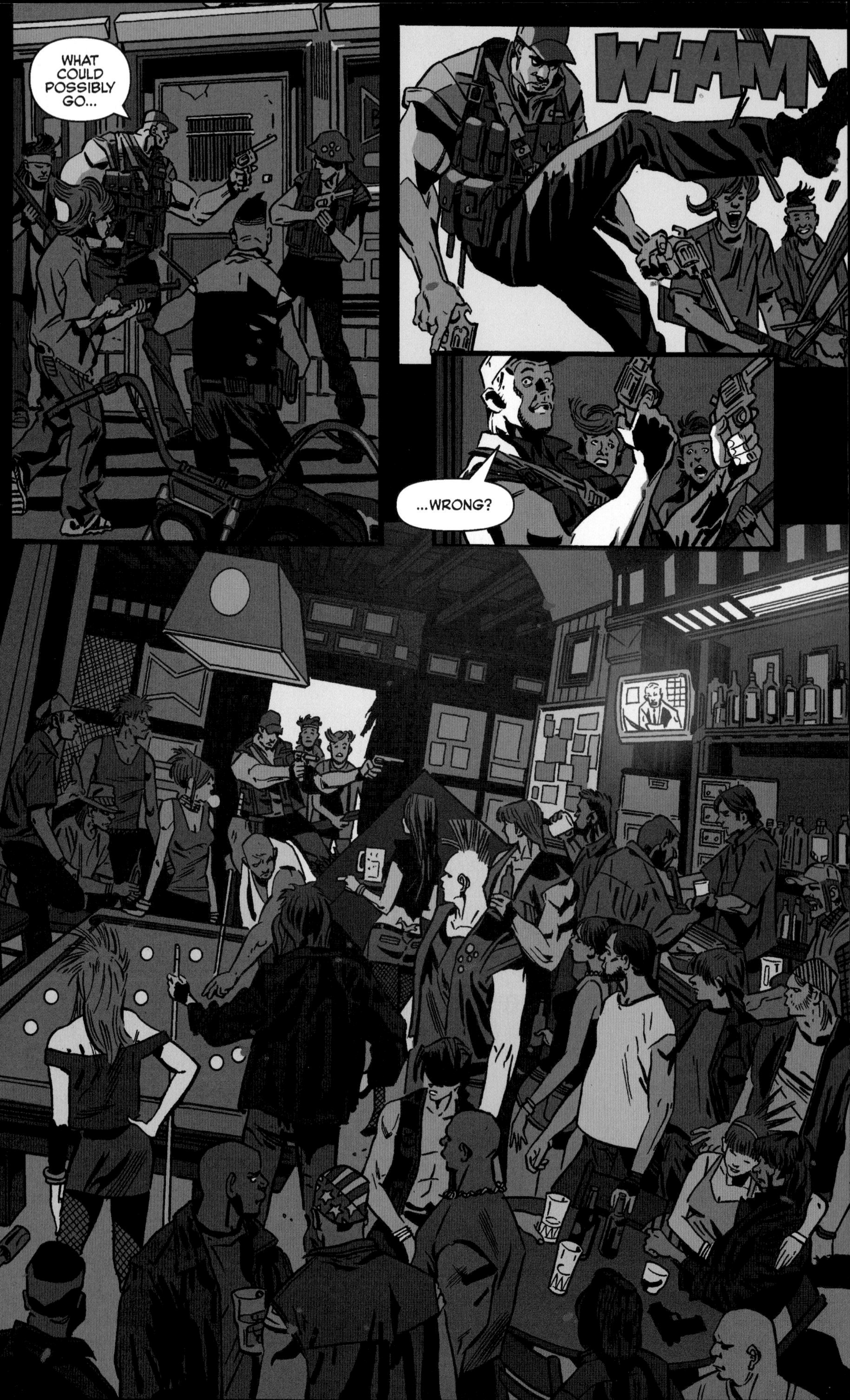
WHAT COULD POSSIBLY GO...
WHAM
...WRONG?

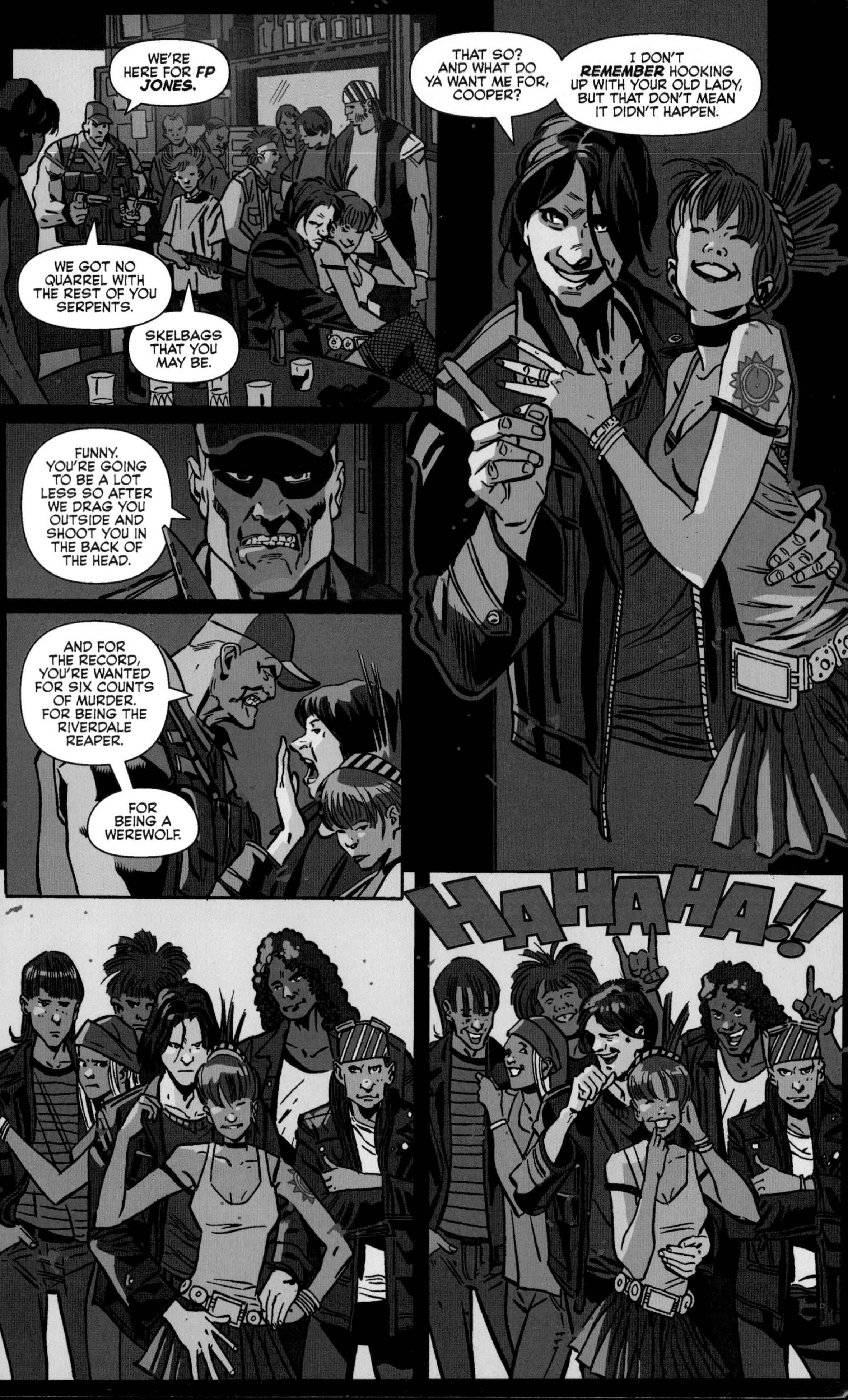
WE'RE HERE FOR **FP JONES.**
WE GOT NO QUARREL WITH THE REST OF YOU SERPENTS.
SKELBAGS THAT YOU MAY BE.
THAT SO? AND WHAT DO YA WANT ME FOR, COOPER?
I DON'T **REMEMBER** HOOKING UP WITH YOUR OLD LADY, BUT THAT DON'T MEAN IT DIDN'T HAPPEN.
FUNNY. YOU'RE GOING TO BE A LOT LESS SO AFTER WE DRAG YOU OUTSIDE AND SHOOT YOU IN THE BACK OF THE HEAD.
AND FOR THE RECORD, YOU'RE WANTED FOR SIX COUNTS OF MURDER. FOR BEING THE RIVERDALE REAPER.
FOR BEING A WEREWOLF.
HAHAHA!!

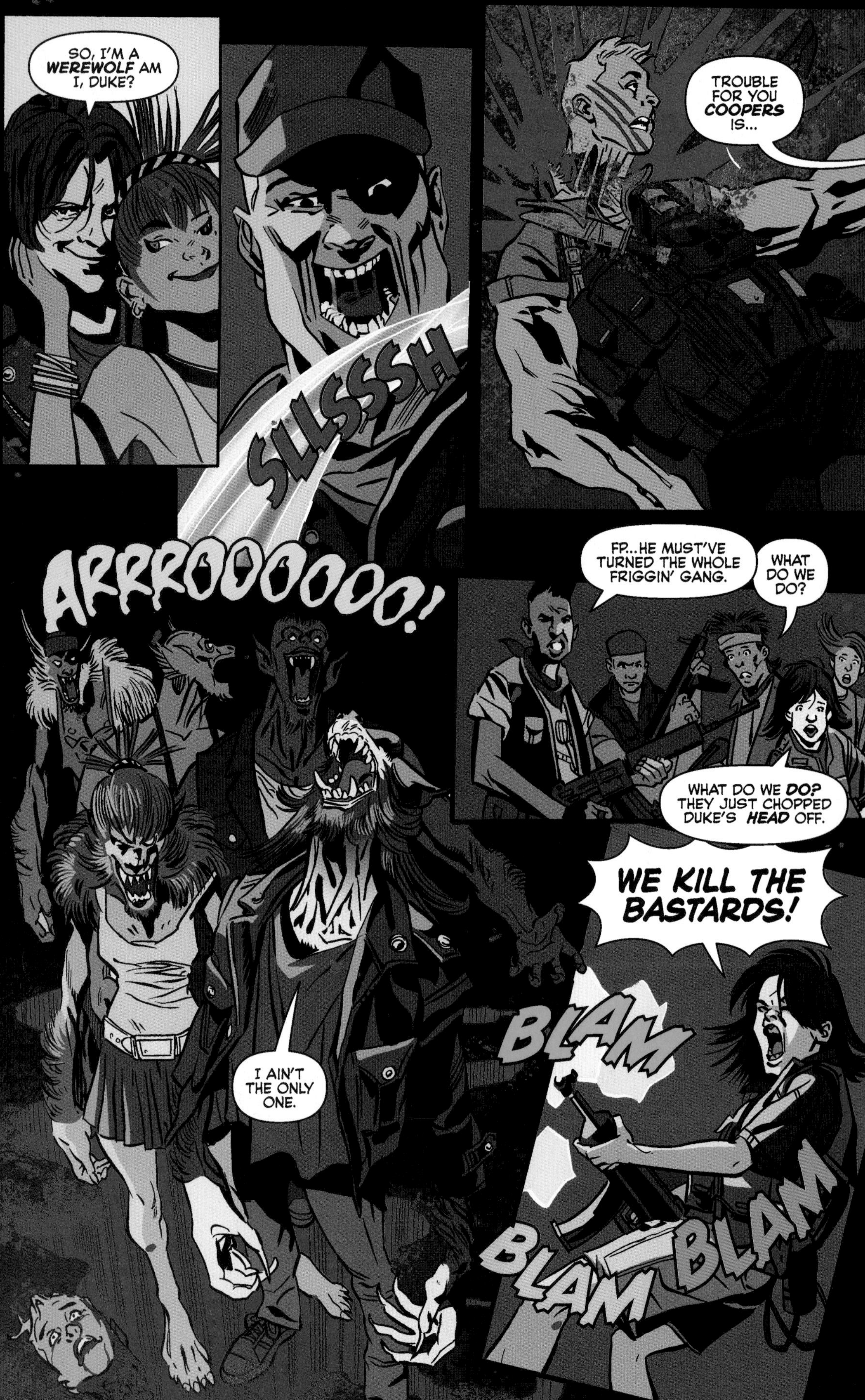
SO, I'M A WEREWOLF AM I, DUKE?
SLLSSSH
TROUBLE FOR YOU COOPERS IS...
ARRROOOOOOO!
I AIN'T THE ONLY ONE.
FP...HE MUST'VE TURNED THE WHOLE FRIGGIN' GANG.
WHAT DO WE DO?
WHAT DO WE DO? THEY JUST CHOPPED DUKE'S HEAD OFF.
WE KILL THE BASTARDS!
BLAM
BLAM
BLAM

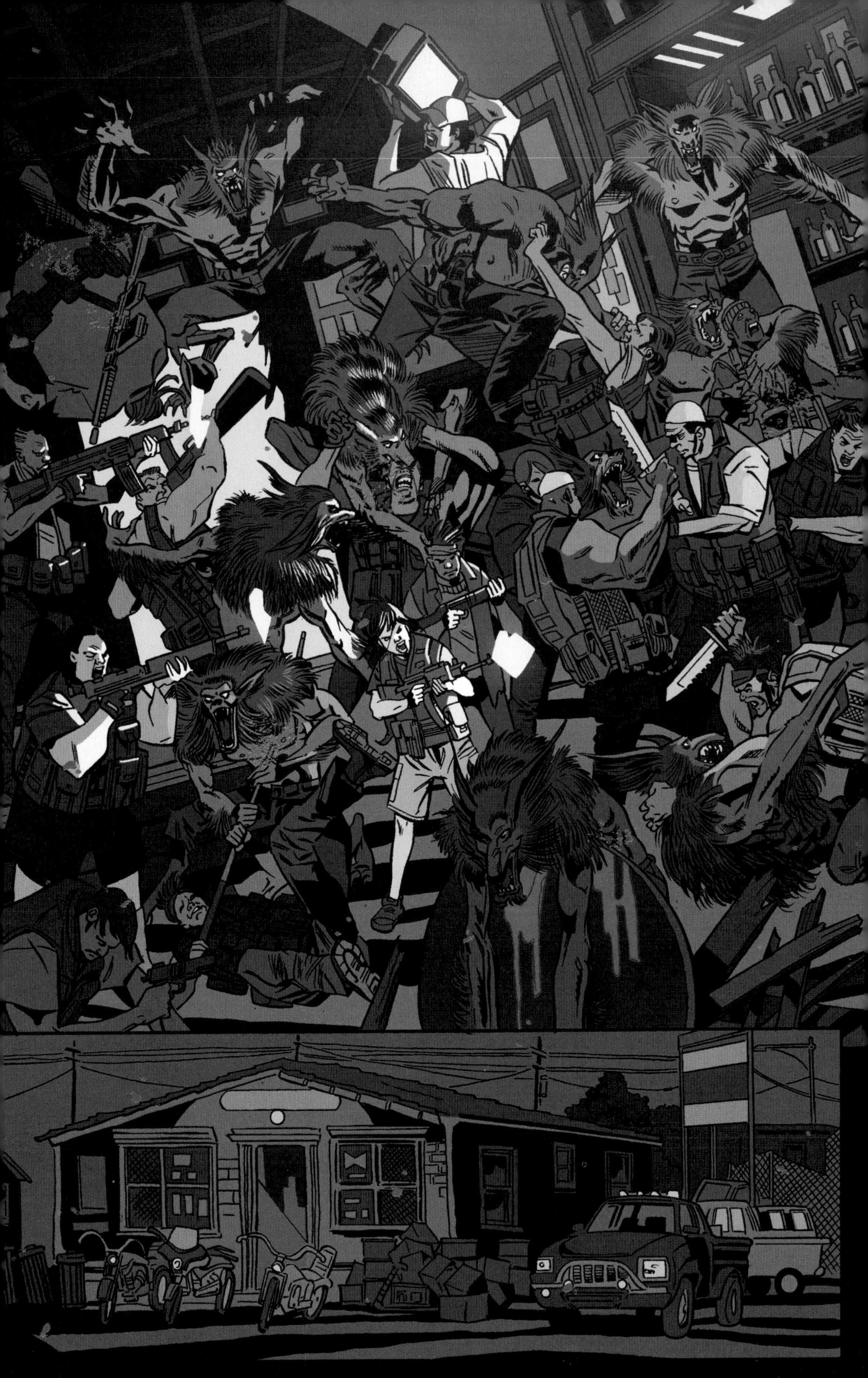

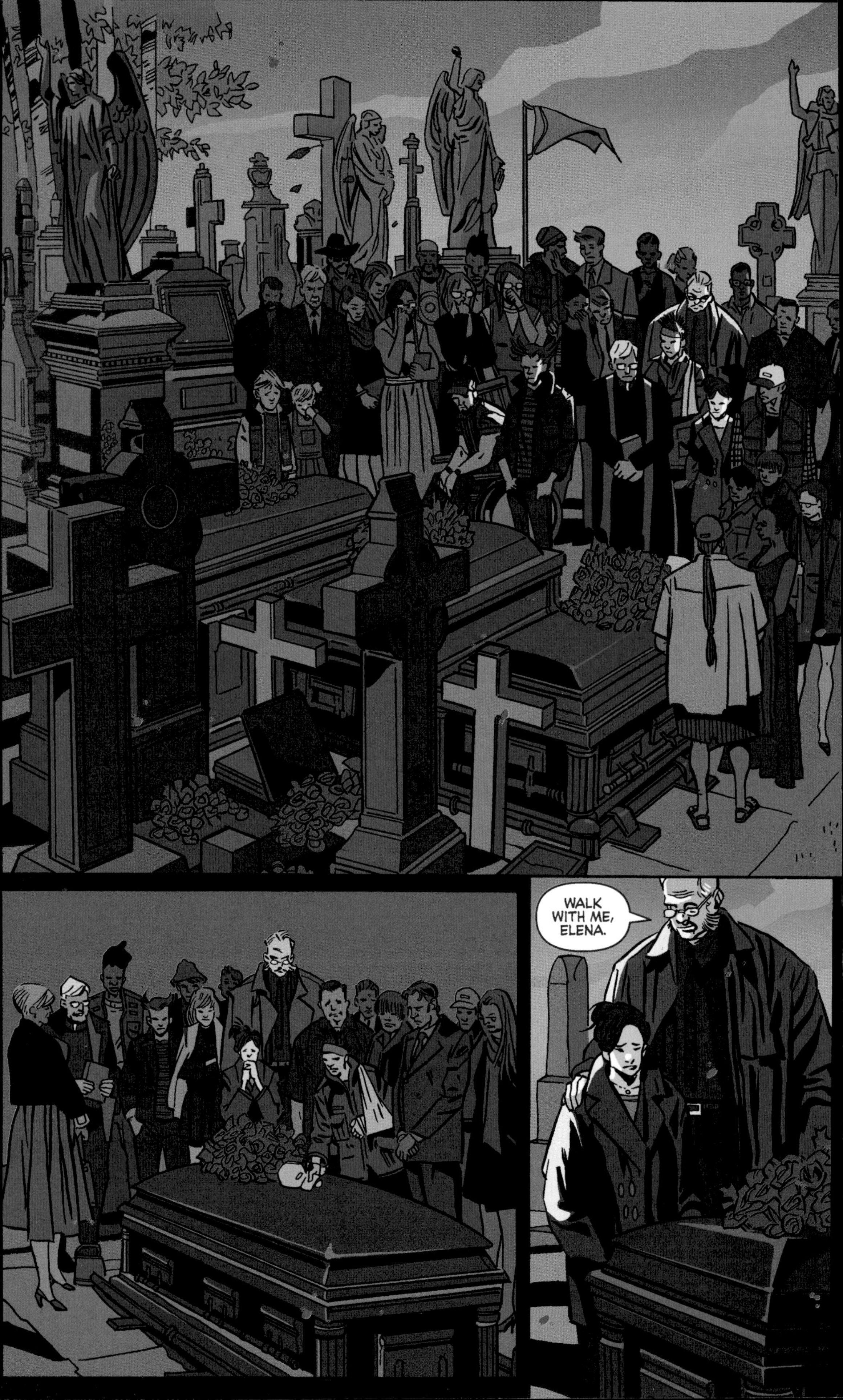
WALK WITH ME, ELENA.

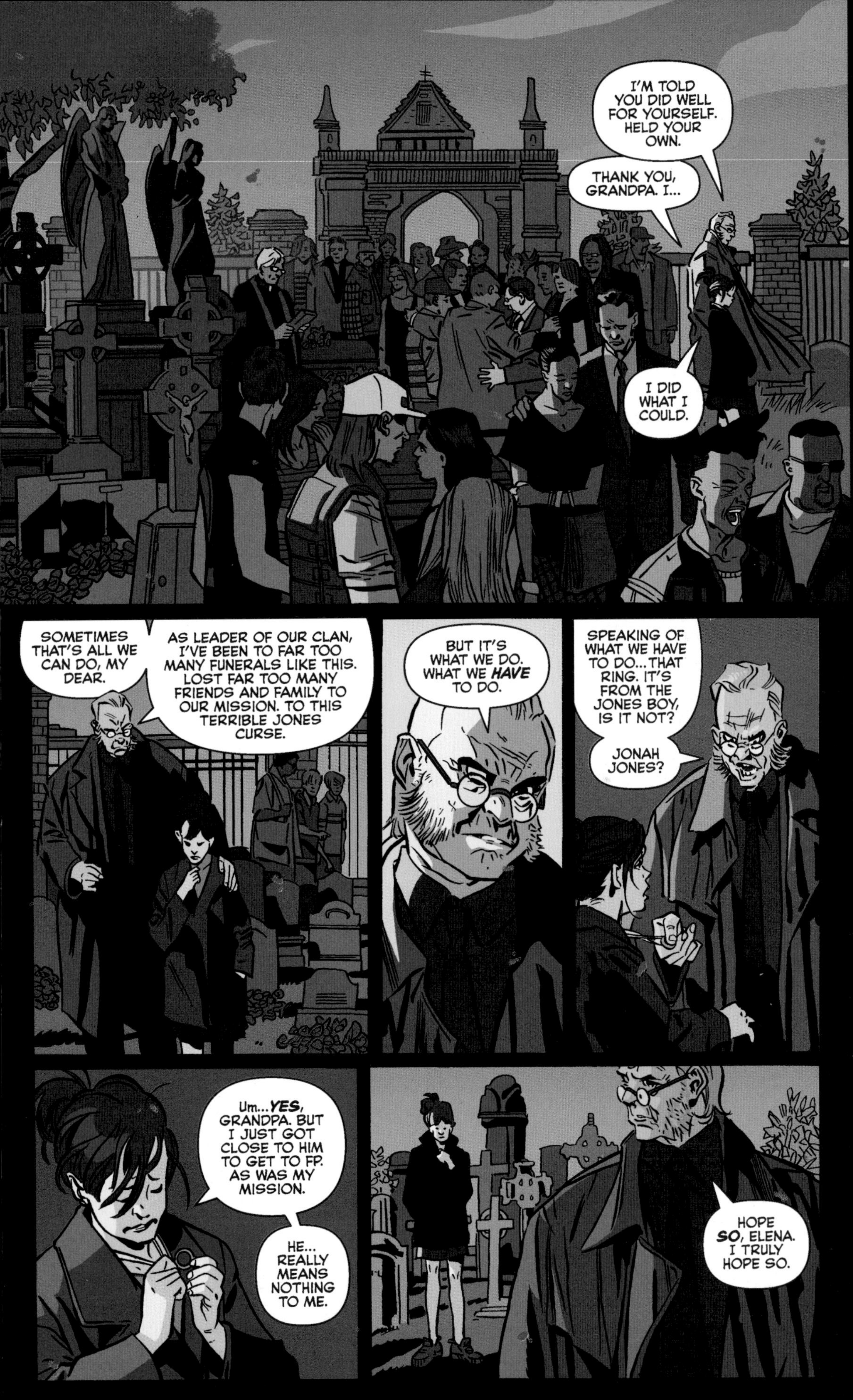
I'M TOLD YOU DID WELL FOR YOURSELF. HELD YOUR OWN.
THANK YOU, GRANDPA. I...
I DID WHAT I COULD.
SOMETIMES THAT'S ALL WE CAN DO, MY DEAR.
AS LEADER OF OUR CLAN, I'VE BEEN TO FAR TOO MANY FUNERALS LIKE THIS. LOST FAR TOO MANY FRIENDS AND FAMILY TO OUR MISSION. TO THIS TERRIBLE JONES CURSE.
BUT IT'S WHAT WE DO. WHAT WE *HAVE* TO DO.
SPEAKING OF WHAT WE HAVE TO DO...THAT RING. IT'S FROM THE JONES BOY, IS IT NOT?
JONAH JONES?
Um...*YES*, GRANDPA. BUT I JUST GOT CLOSE TO HIM TO GET TO FP. AS WAS MY MISSION.
HE... REALLY MEANS NOTHING TO ME.
HOPE *SO*, ELENA. I TRULY HOPE SO.

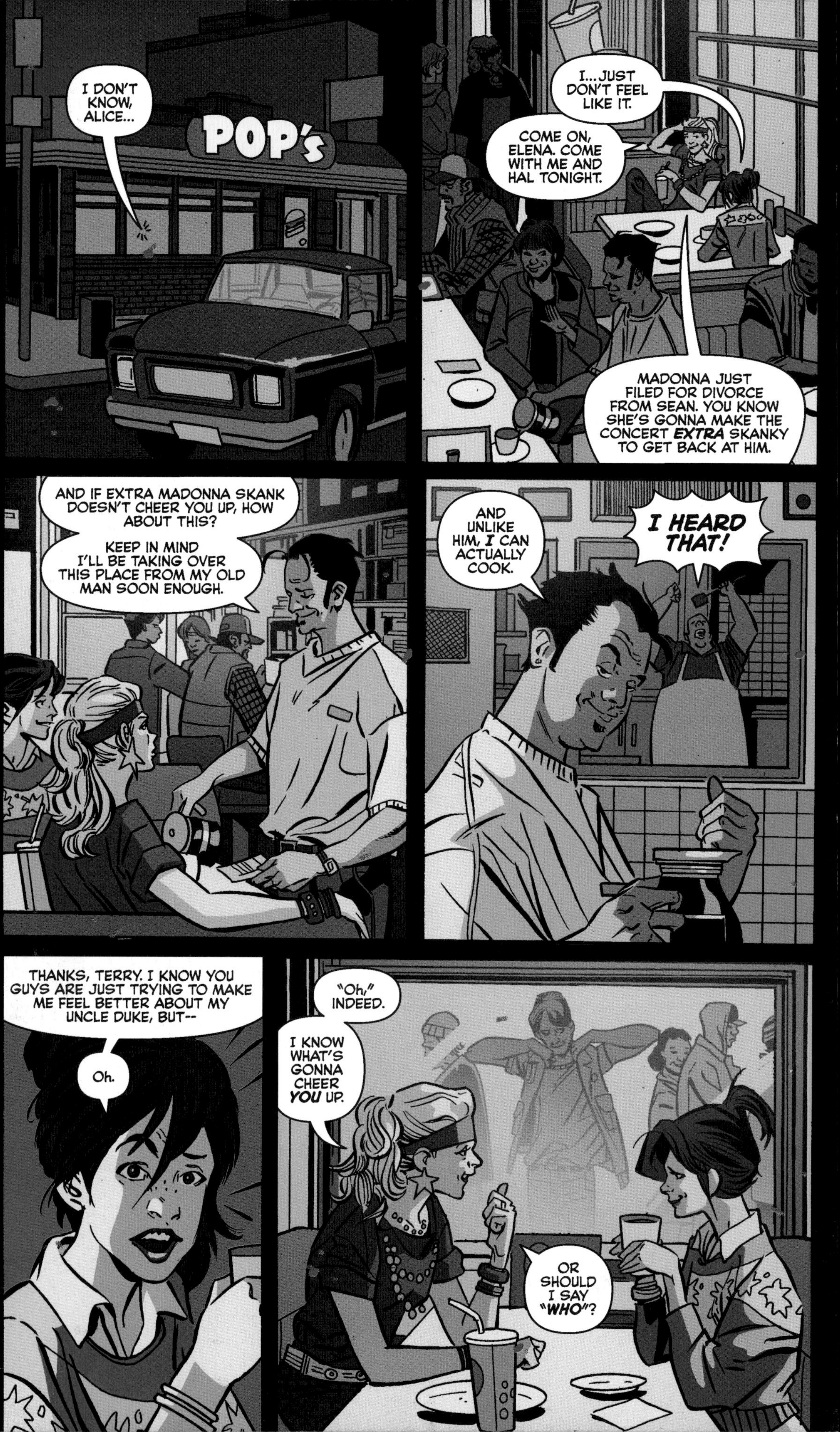
I DON'T KNOW, ALICE...
POP's
I...JUST DON'T FEEL LIKE IT.
COME ON, ELENA. COME WITH ME AND HAL TONIGHT.
MADONNA JUST FILED FOR DIVORCE FROM SEAN. YOU KNOW SHE'S GONNA MAKE THE CONCERT **EXTRA** SKANKY TO GET BACK AT HIM.
AND IF EXTRA MADONNA SKANK DOESN'T CHEER YOU UP, HOW ABOUT THIS?
KEEP IN MIND I'LL BE TAKING OVER THIS PLACE FROM MY OLD MAN SOON ENOUGH.
AND UNLIKE HIM, ***I*** CAN ACTUALLY COOK.
I HEARD THAT!
THANKS, TERRY. I KNOW YOU GUYS ARE JUST TRYING TO MAKE ME FEEL BETTER ABOUT MY UNCLE DUKE, BUT--
Oh.
"Oh," INDEED.
I KNOW WHAT'S GONNA CHEER ***YOU*** UP.
OR SHOULD I SAY "***WHO***"?

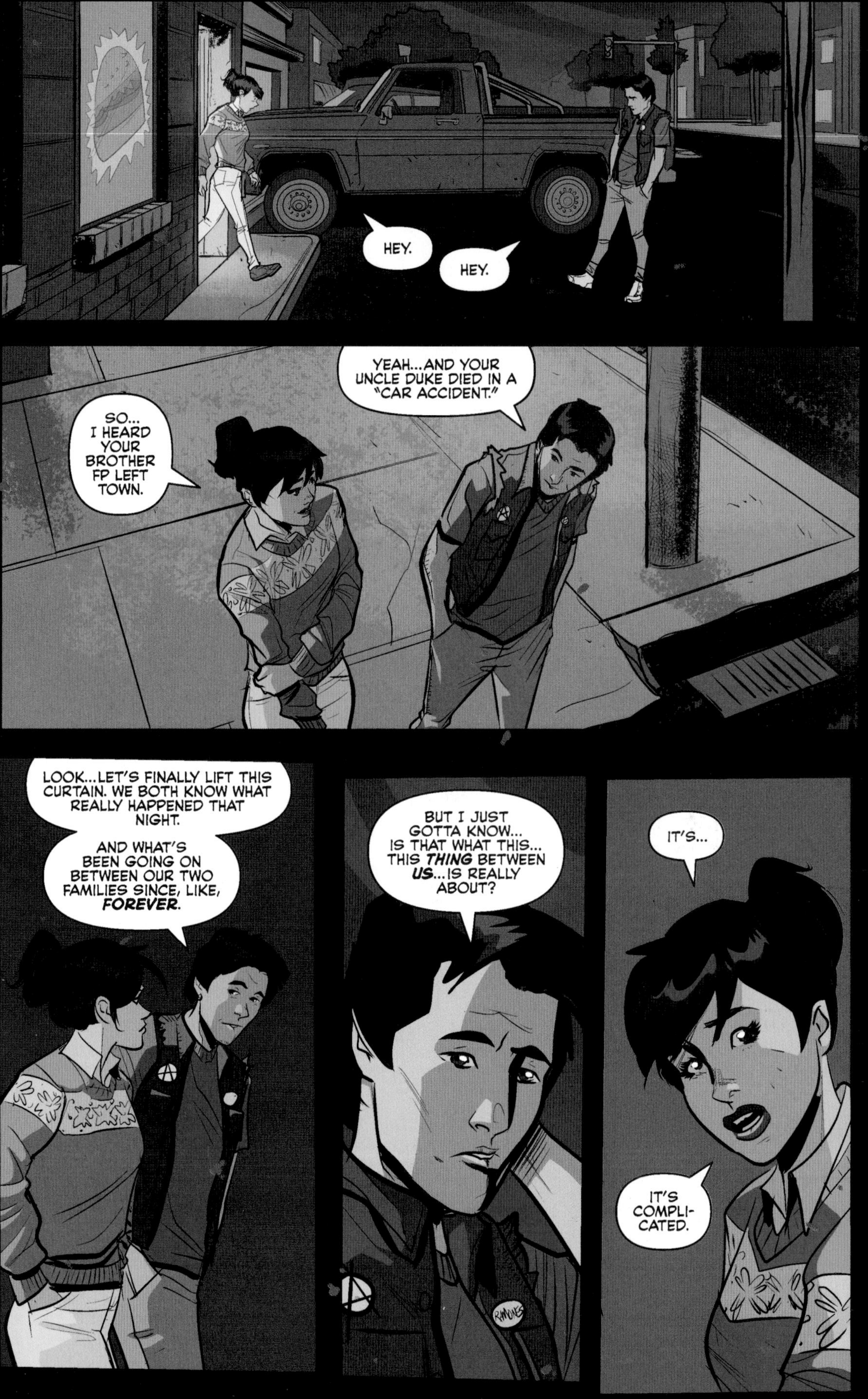
HEY.
HEY.
SO... I HEARD YOUR BROTHER FP LEFT TOWN.
YEAH...AND YOUR UNCLE DUKE DIED IN A "CAR ACCIDENT."
LOOK...LET'S FINALLY LIFT THIS CURTAIN. WE BOTH KNOW WHAT REALLY HAPPENED THAT NIGHT.
AND WHAT'S BEEN GOING ON BETWEEN OUR TWO FAMILIES SINCE, LIKE, ***FOREVER***.
BUT I JUST GOTTA KNOW... IS THAT WHAT THIS... THIS ***THING*** BETWEEN ***US***...IS REALLY ABOUT?
IT'S...
IT'S COMPLI-CATED.
RAMONES

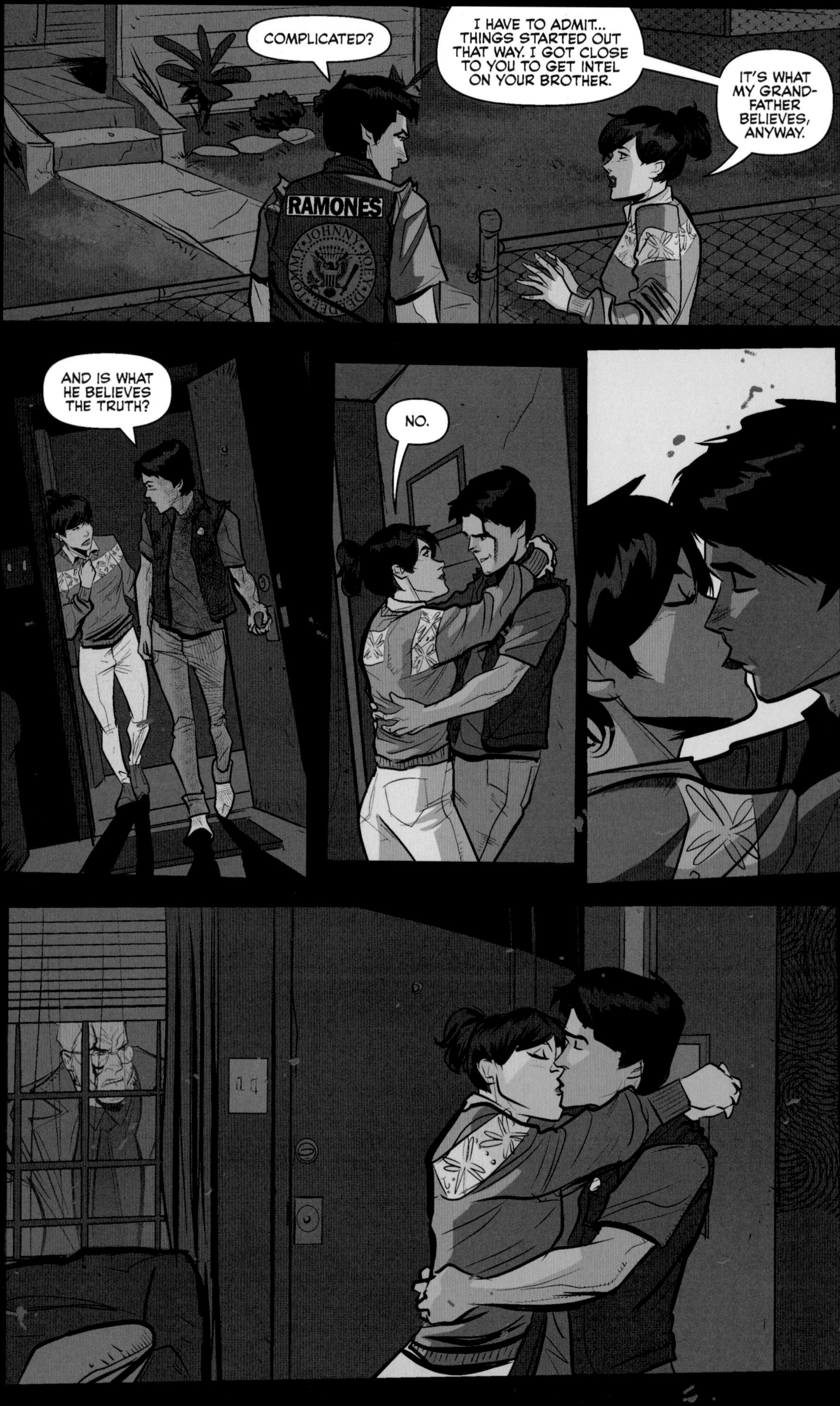
COMPLICATED?
I HAVE TO ADMIT... THINGS STARTED OUT THAT WAY. I GOT CLOSE TO YOU TO GET INTEL ON YOUR BROTHER.
IT'S WHAT MY GRAND-FATHER BELIEVES, ANYWAY.
RAMONES
AND IS WHAT HE BELIEVES THE TRUTH?
NO.

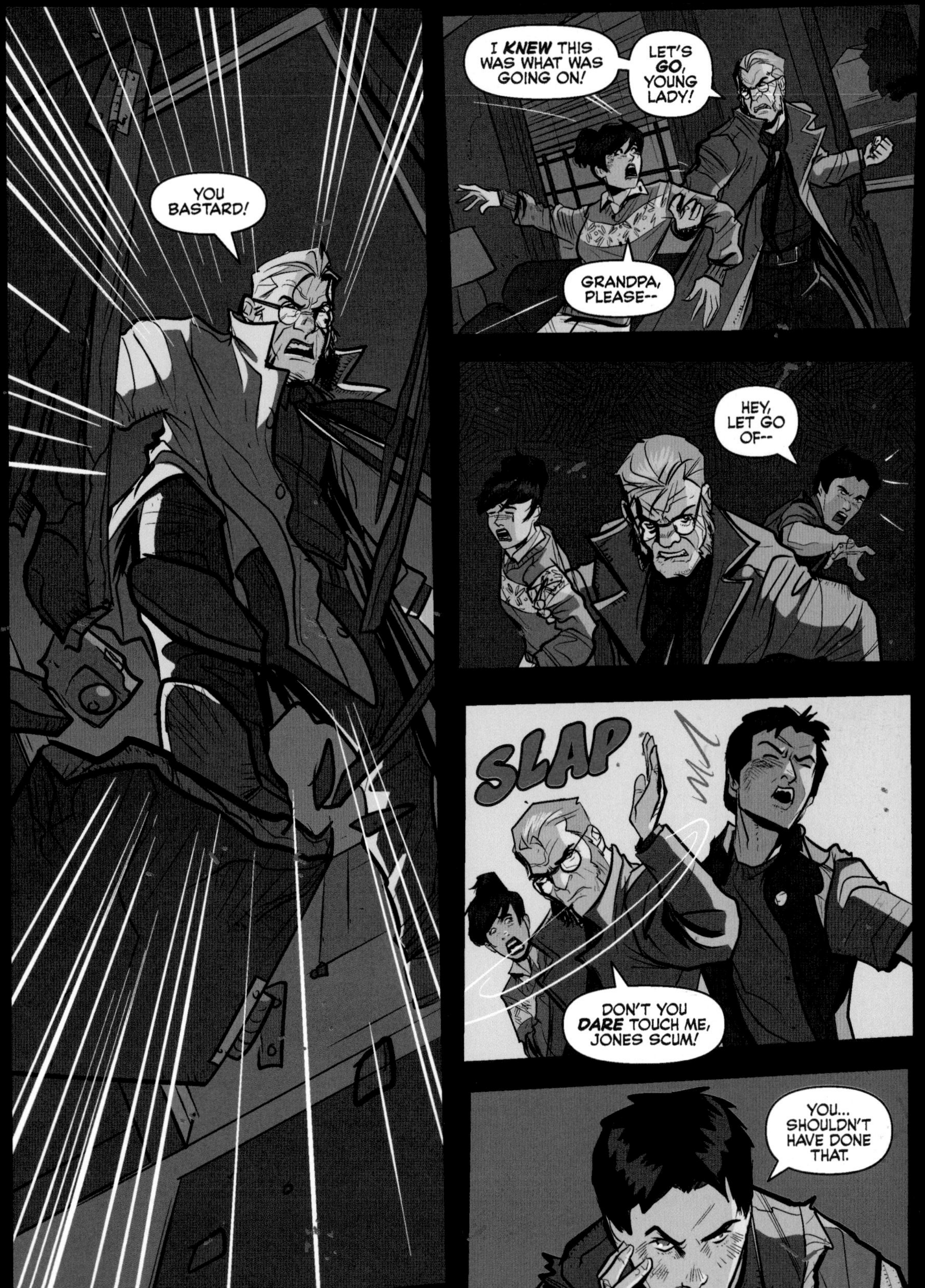
YOU BASTARD!
I KNEW THIS WAS WHAT WAS GOING ON!
LET'S GO, YOUNG LADY!
GRANDPA, PLEASE--
HEY, LET GO OF--
SLAP
DON'T YOU DARE TOUCH ME, JONES SCUM!
YOU... SHOULDN'T HAVE DONE THAT.

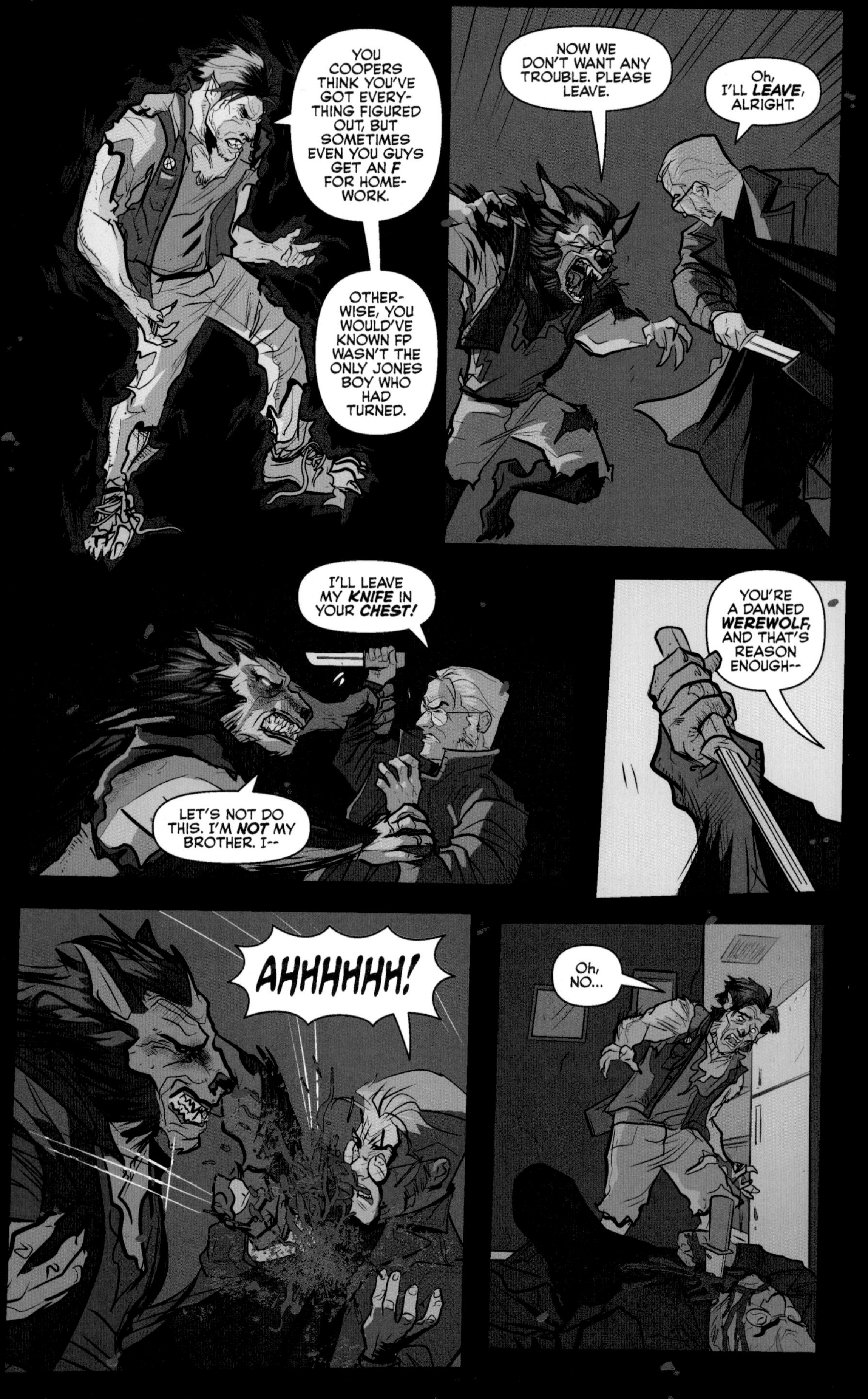
YOU COOPERS THINK YOU'VE GOT EVERY-THING FIGURED OUT, BUT SOMETIMES EVEN YOU GUYS GET AN *F* FOR HOME-WORK.
OTHER-WISE, YOU WOULD'VE KNOWN FP WASN'T THE ONLY JONES BOY WHO HAD TURNED.
NOW WE DON'T WANT ANY TROUBLE. PLEASE LEAVE.
Oh, I'LL ***LEAVE***, ALRIGHT.
I'LL LEAVE MY ***KNIFE*** IN YOUR ***CHEST!***
LET'S NOT DO THIS. I'M ***NOT*** MY BROTHER. I--
YOU'RE A DAMNED ***WEREWOLF***, AND THAT'S REASON ENOUGH--
AHHHHHH!
Oh, NO...

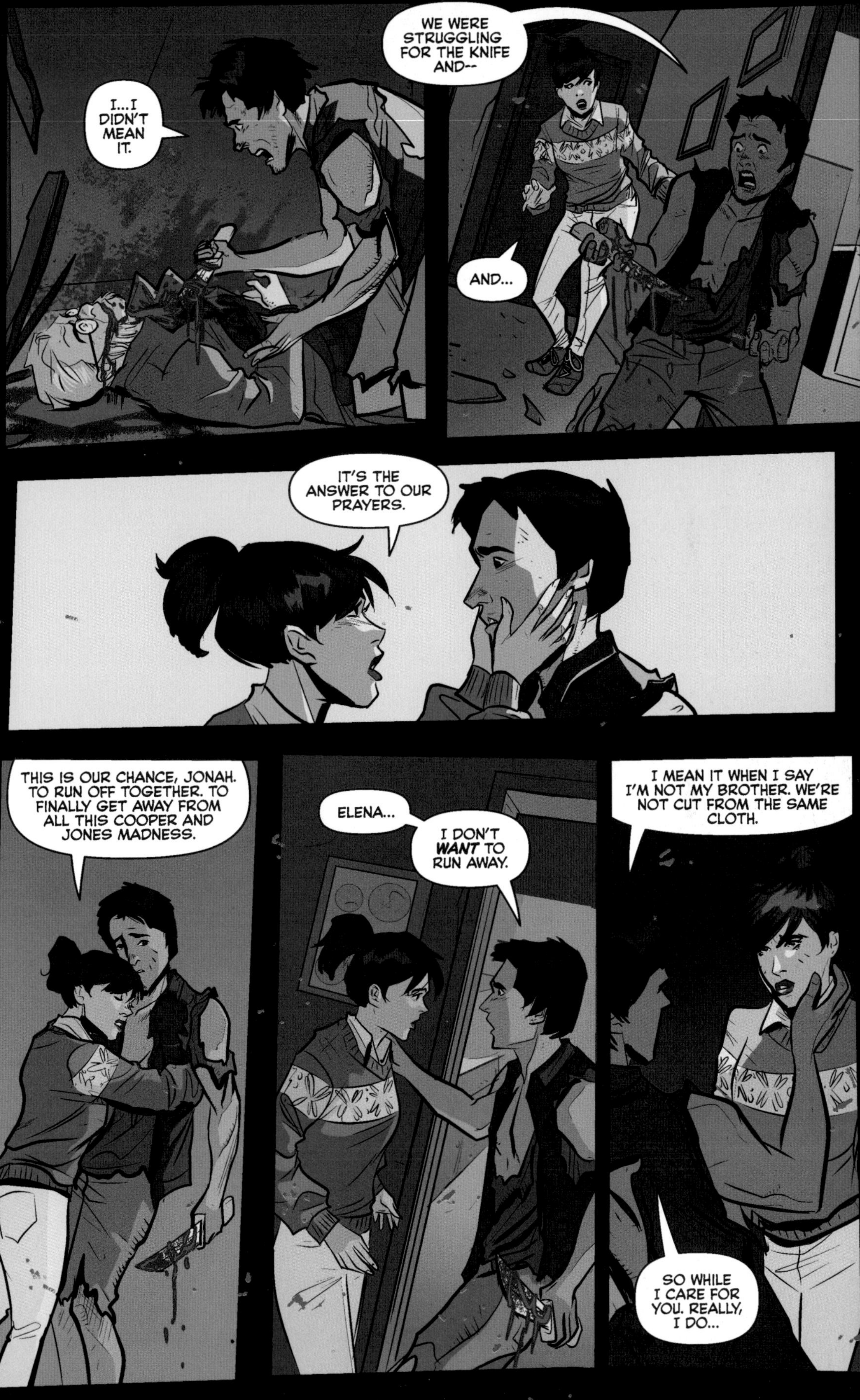
I...I DIDN'T MEAN IT.
WE WERE STRUGGLING FOR THE KNIFE AND--
AND...
IT'S THE ANSWER TO OUR PRAYERS.
THIS IS OUR CHANCE, JONAH. TO RUN OFF TOGETHER. TO FINALLY GET AWAY FROM ALL THIS COOPER AND JONES MADNESS.
ELENA...
I DON'T *WANT* TO RUN AWAY.
I MEAN IT WHEN I SAY I'M NOT MY BROTHER. WE'RE NOT CUT FROM THE SAME CLOTH.
SO WHILE I CARE FOR YOU. REALLY, I DO...

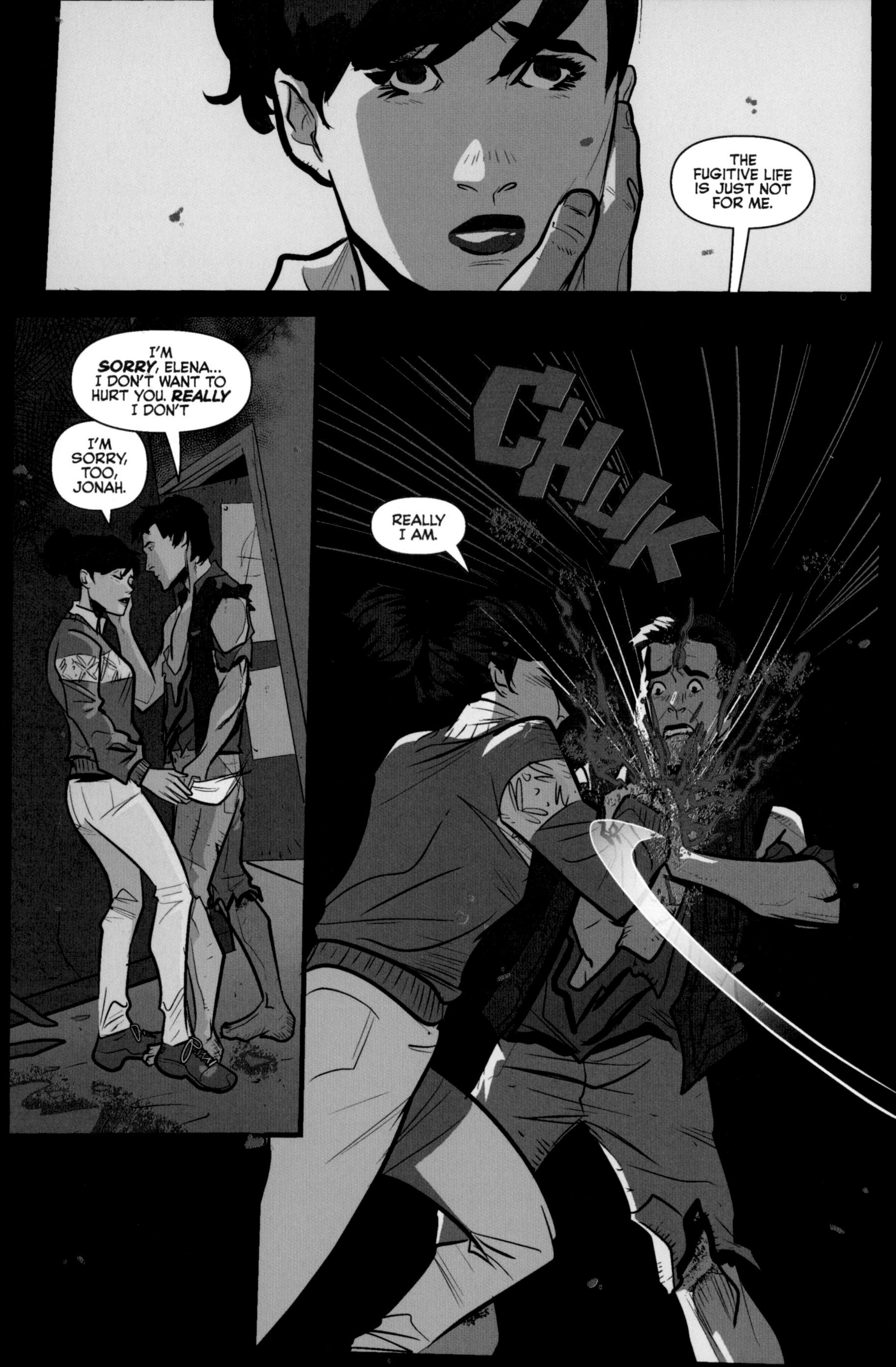
THE FUGITIVE LIFE IS JUST NOT FOR ME.
I'M *SORRY*, ELENA... I DON'T WANT TO HURT YOU. *REALLY* I DON'T
I'M SORRY, TOO, JONAH.
REALLY I AM.
CHUK

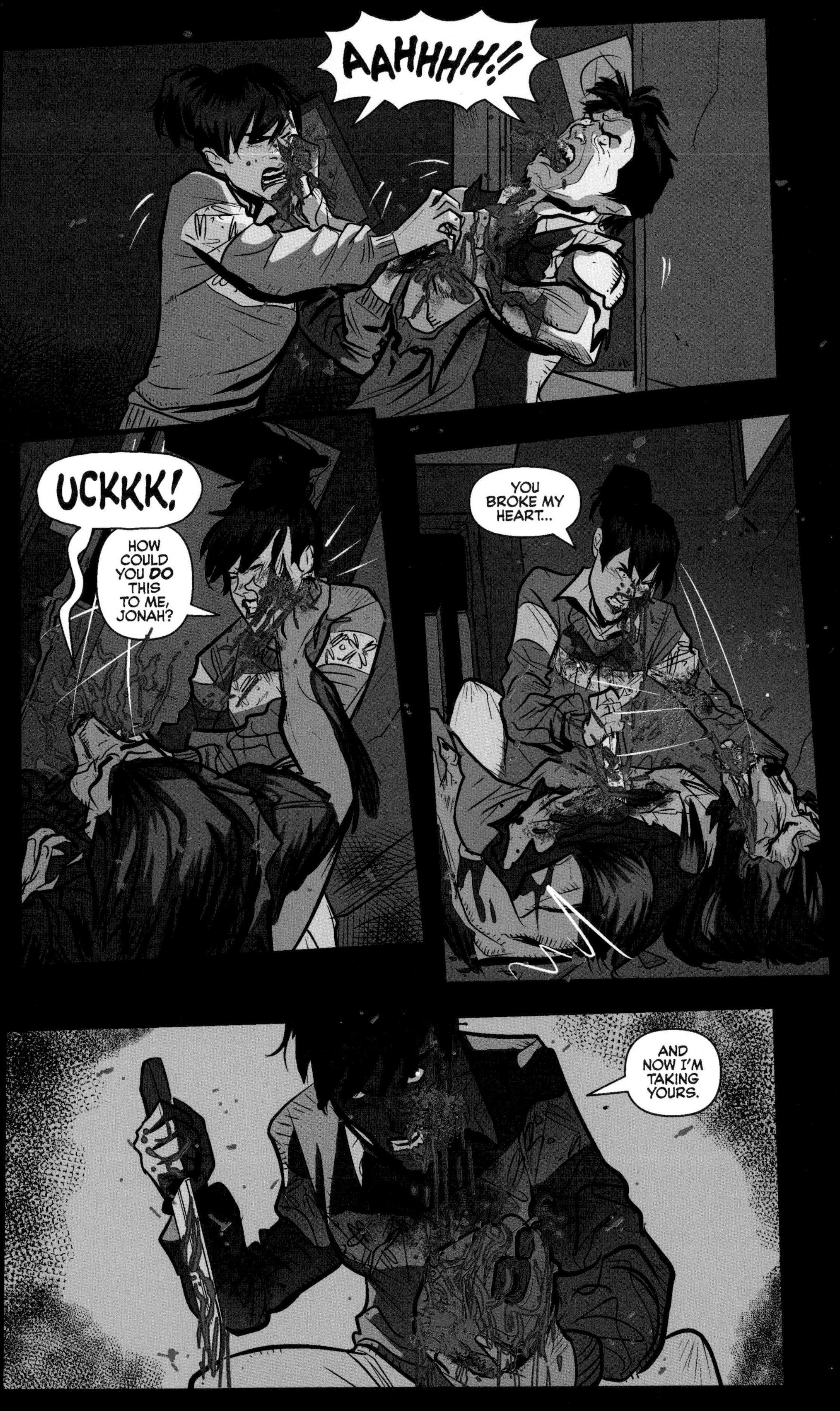
AAHHHH!!
UCKKK!
HOW COULD YOU **DO** THIS TO ME, JONAH?
YOU BROKE MY HEART...
AND NOW I'M TAKING YOURS.

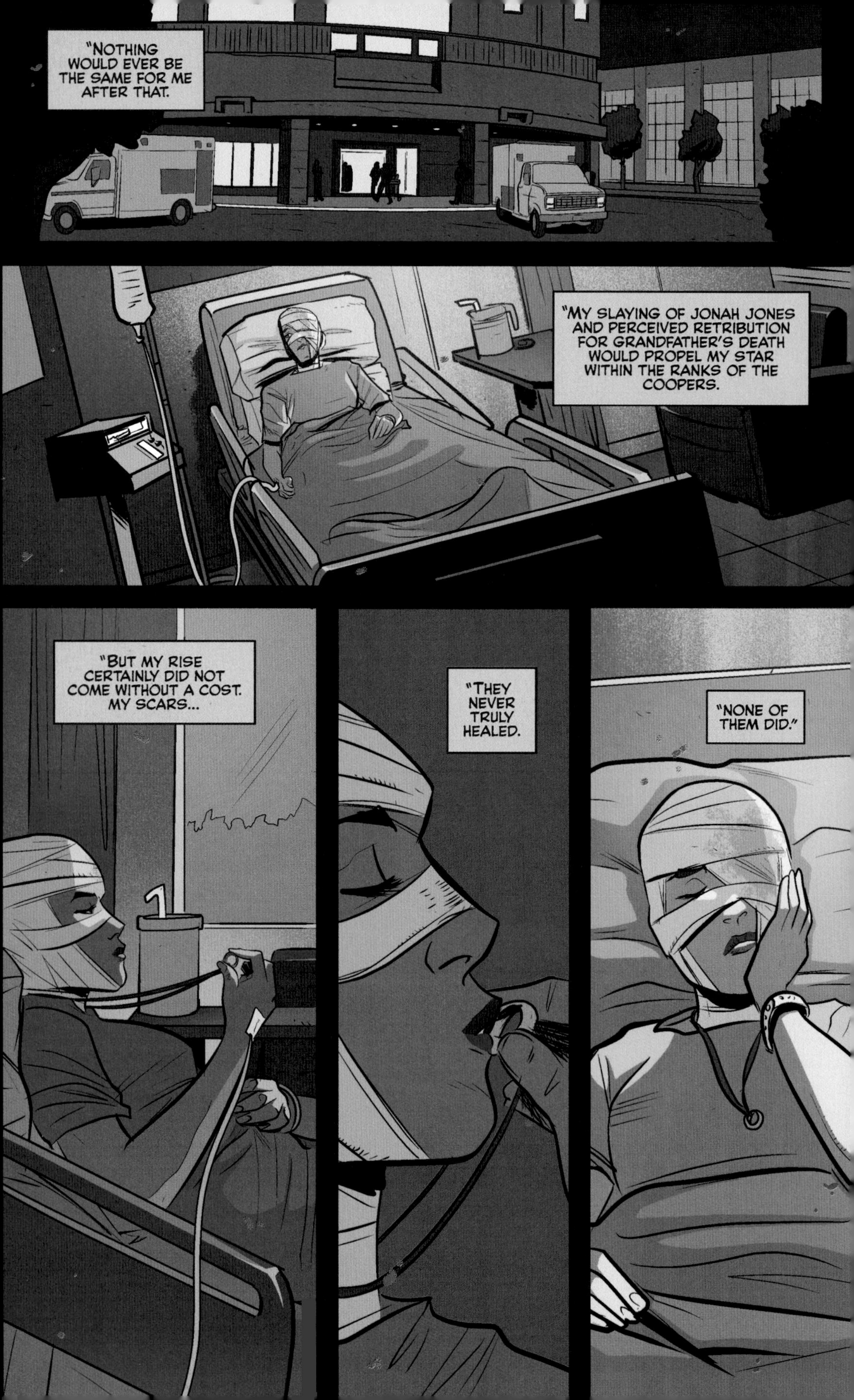
"NOTHING WOULD EVER BE THE SAME FOR ME AFTER THAT.
"MY SLAYING OF JONAH JONES AND PERCEIVED RETRIBUTION FOR GRANDFATHER'S DEATH WOULD PROPEL MY STAR WITHIN THE RANKS OF THE COOPERS.
"BUT MY RISE CERTAINLY DID NOT COME WITHOUT A COST. MY SCARS...
"THEY NEVER TRULY HEALED.
"NONE OF THEM DID."

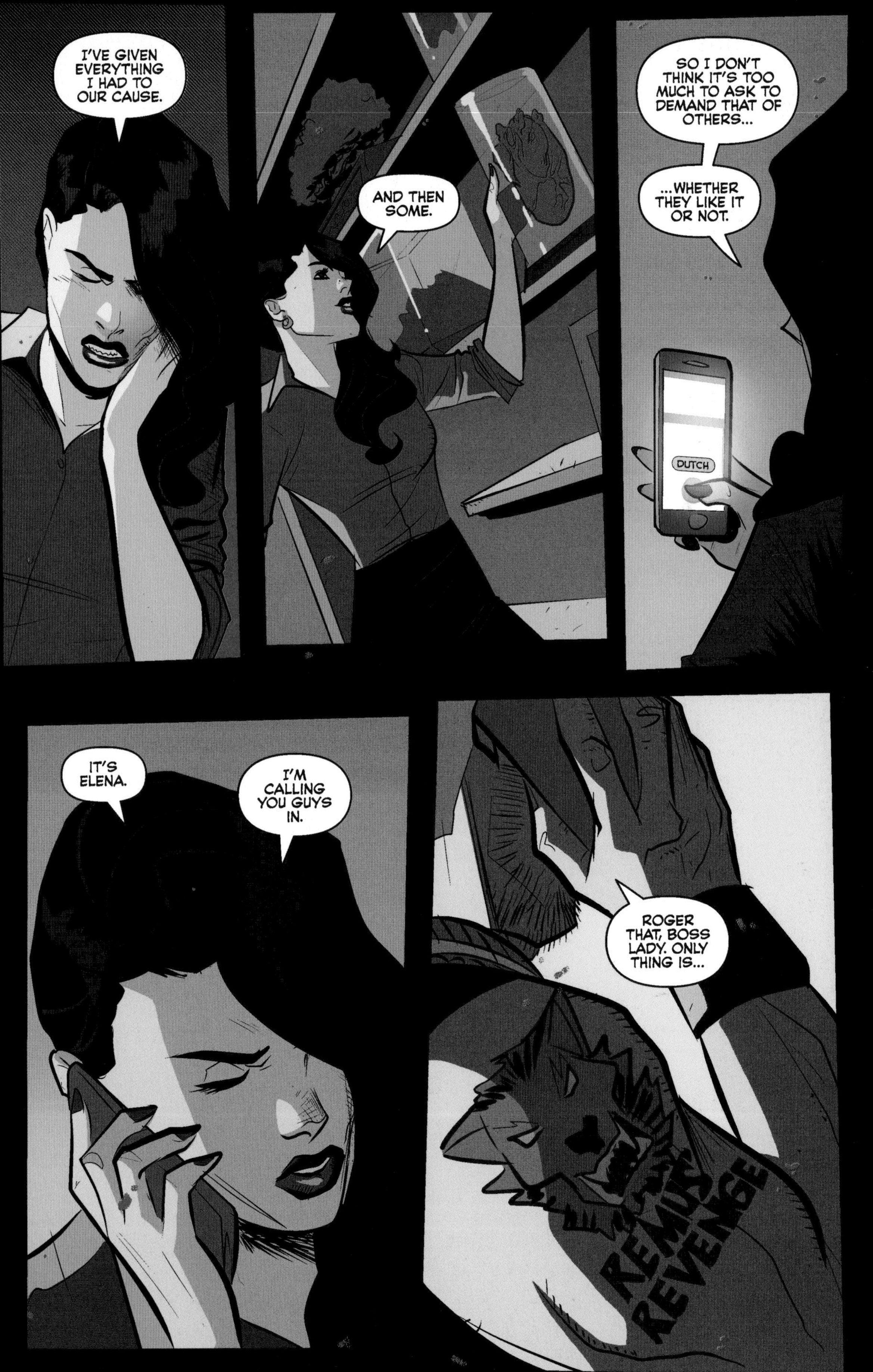
I'VE GIVEN EVERYTHING I HAD TO OUR CAUSE.
AND THEN SOME.
SO I DON'T THINK IT'S TOO MUCH TO ASK TO DEMAND THAT OF OTHERS...
...WHETHER THEY LIKE IT OR NOT.
DUTCH
IT'S ELENA.
I'M CALLING YOU GUYS IN.
ROGER THAT, BOSS LADY. ONLY THING IS...
REMUS REVENGE

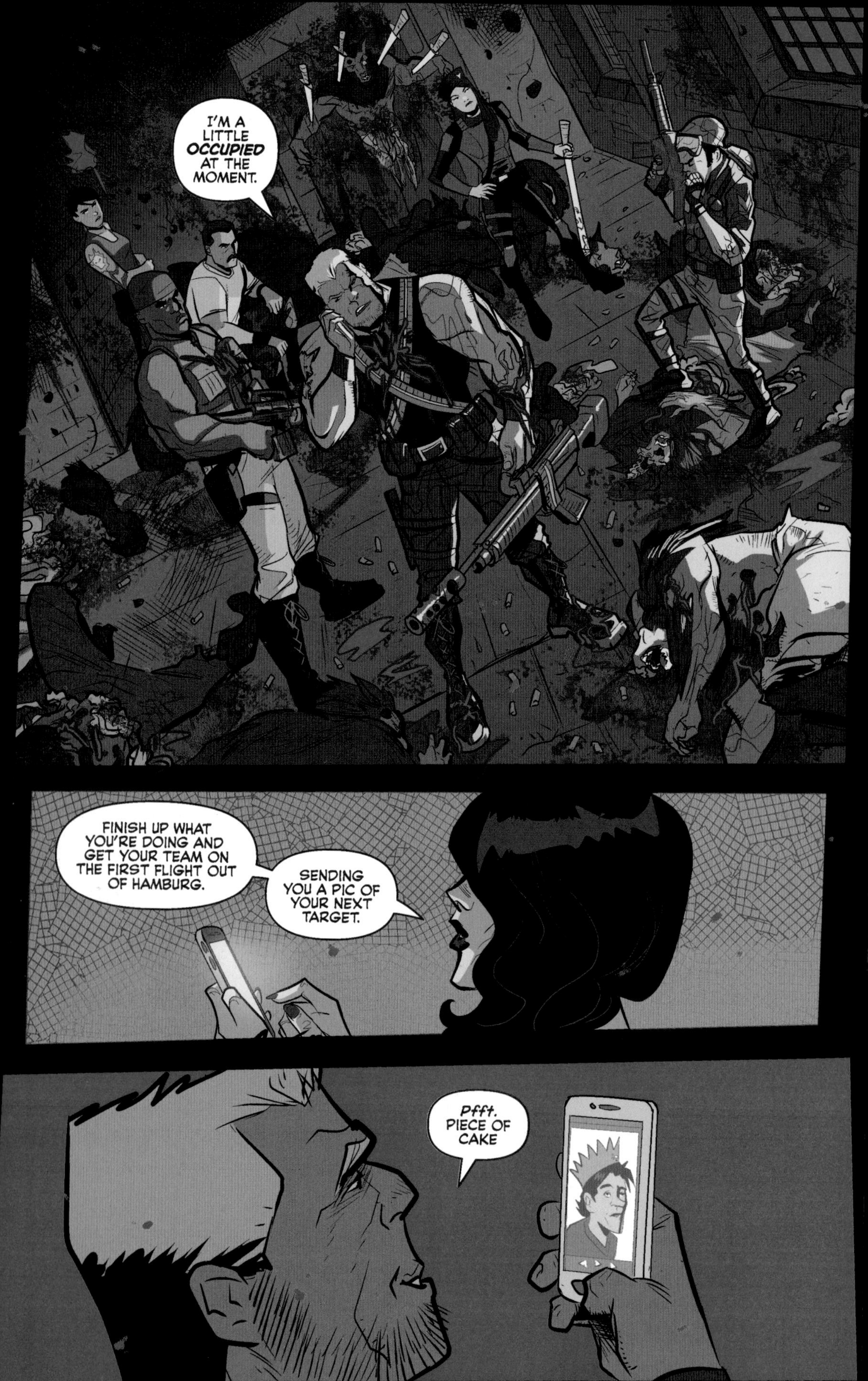
I'M A LITTLE *OCCUPIED* AT THE MOMENT.
FINISH UP WHAT YOU'RE DOING AND GET YOUR TEAM ON THE FIRST FLIGHT OUT OF HAMBURG.
SENDING YOU A PIC OF YOUR NEXT TARGET.
Pfft. PIECE OF CAKE

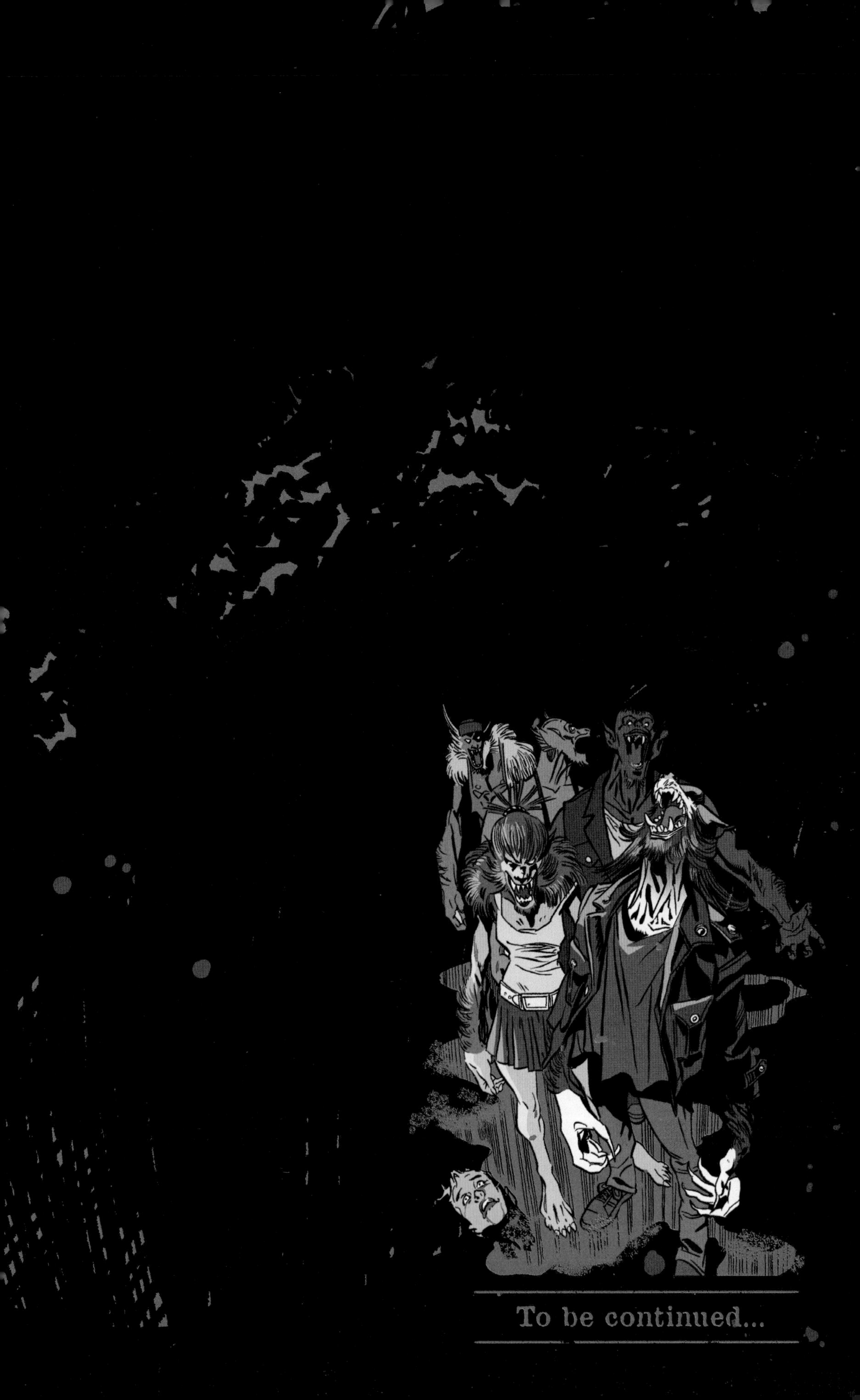
To be continued...

ISSUE FIVE

COVER ART **Adam Gorham**

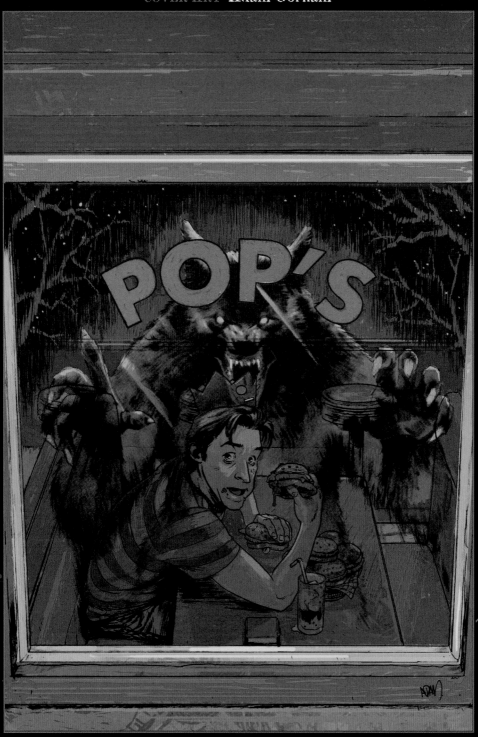

STORY **Frank Tieri**   ART **Pat & Tim Kennedy** (p. 1-10)   **Joe Eisma** (p. 11-20)
COLORS **Matt Herms** (p. 1-2, 11-16)   **Andre Szymanowicz** (p. 3-8)
Kelsey Shannon (p. 9-10, 17-20)   INKS **Bob Smith** (p. 1-8)   **Jim Amash** (p. 9-10)
LETTERING **Jack Morelli**

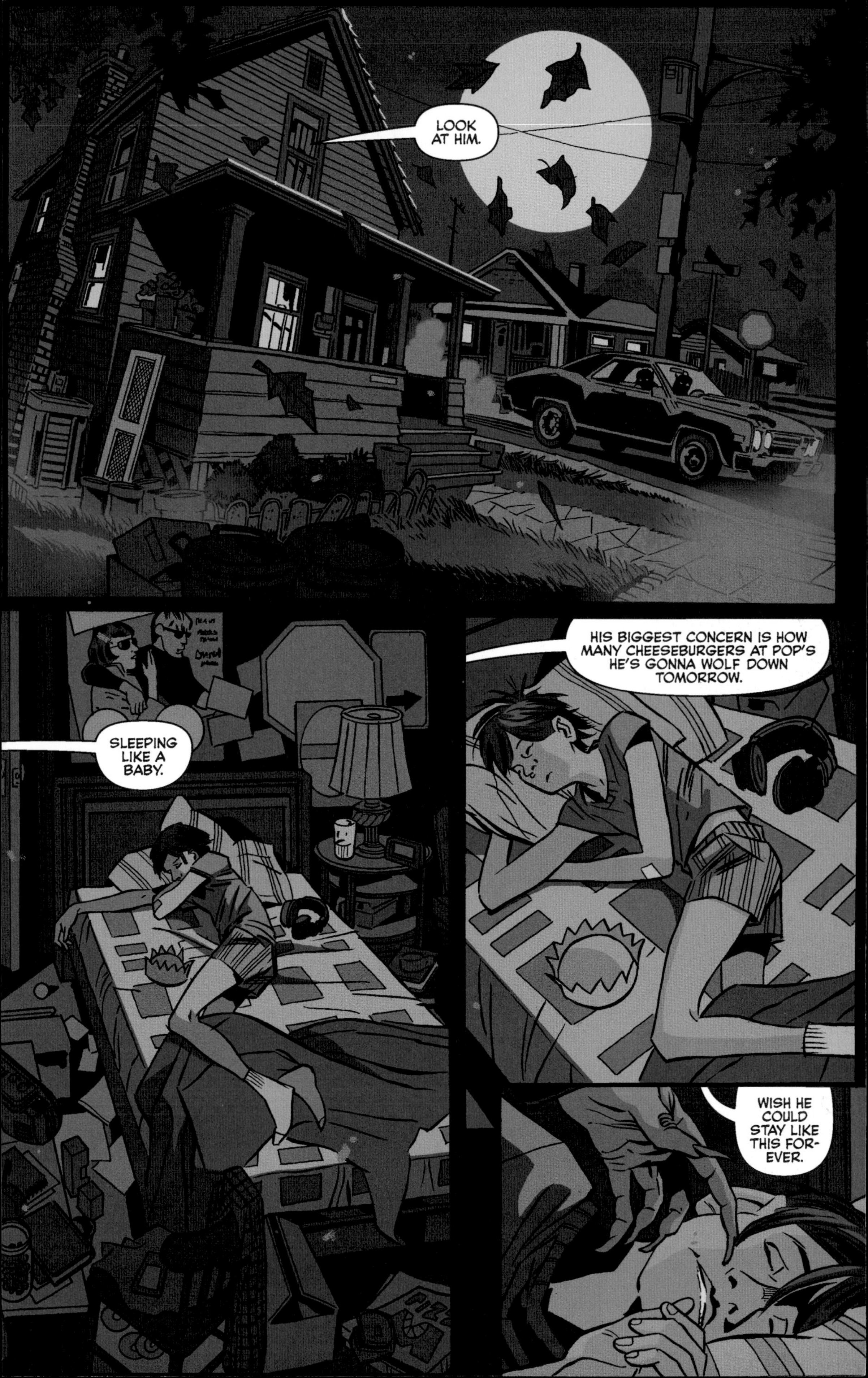
LOOK AT HIM.
SLEEPING LIKE A BABY.
HIS BIGGEST CONCERN IS HOW MANY CHEESEBURGERS AT POP'S HE'S GONNA WOLF DOWN TOMORROW.
WISH HE COULD STAY LIKE THIS FOR-EVER.

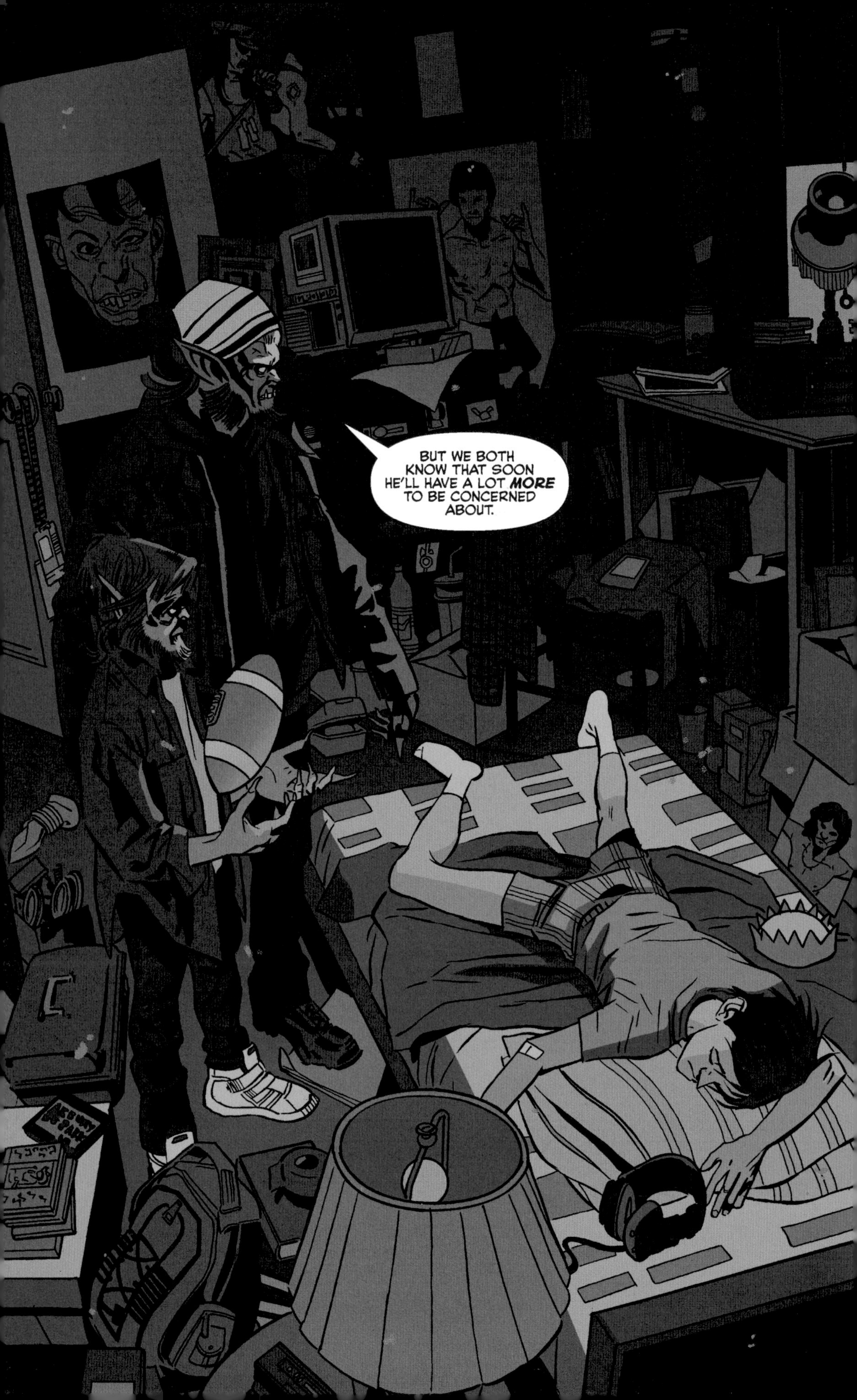
BUT WE BOTH KNOW THAT SOON HE'LL HAVE A LOT *MORE* TO BE CONCERNED ABOUT.

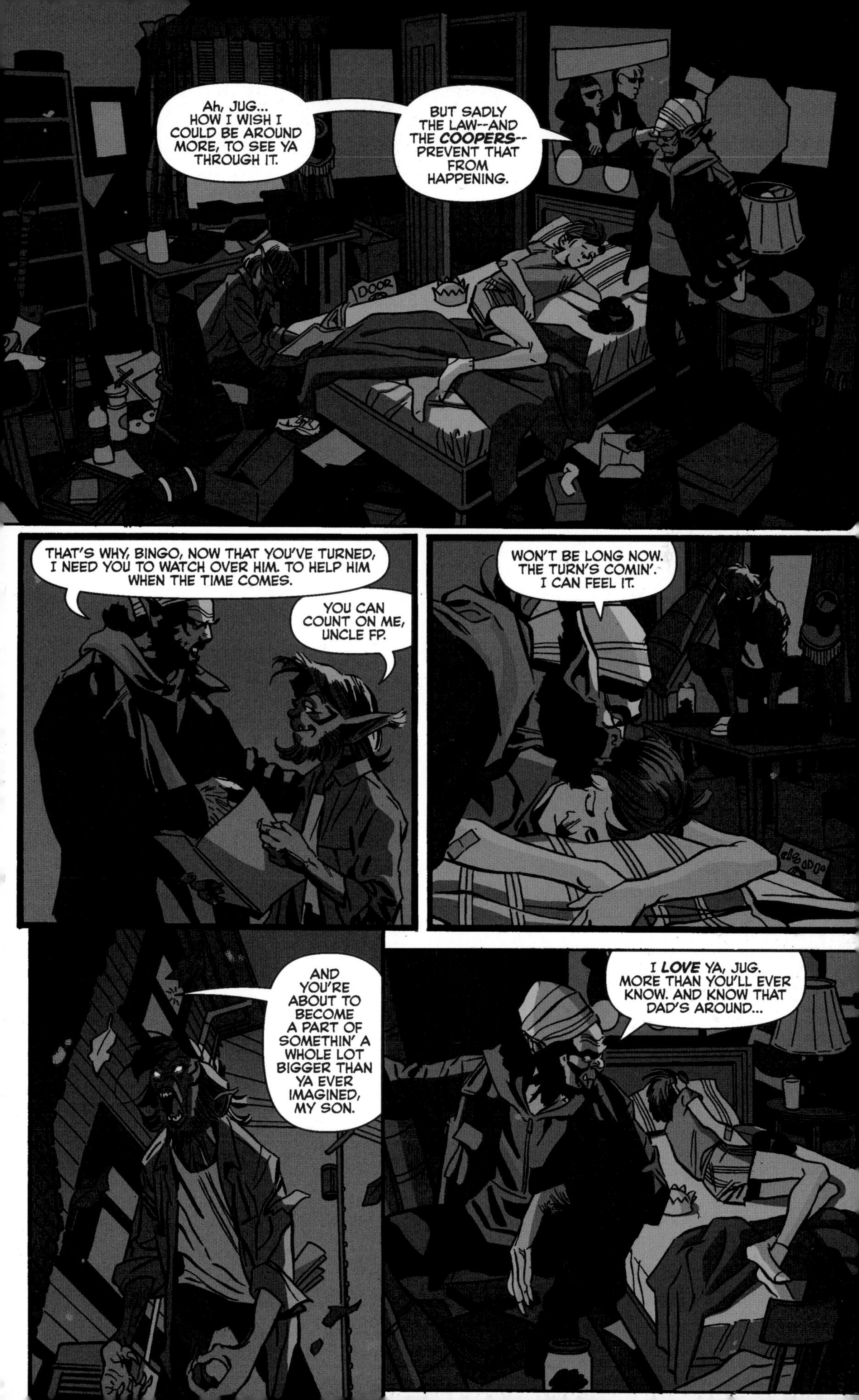
Ah, JUG... HOW I WISH I COULD BE AROUND MORE, TO SEE YA THROUGH IT.
BUT SADLY THE LAW--AND THE COOPERS--PREVENT THAT FROM HAPPENING.
DOOR
THAT'S WHY, BINGO, NOW THAT YOU'VE TURNED, I NEED YOU TO WATCH OVER HIM. TO HELP HIM WHEN THE TIME COMES.
YOU CAN COUNT ON ME, UNCLE FP.
WON'T BE LONG NOW. THE TURN'S COMIN'. I CAN FEEL IT.
AND YOU'RE ABOUT TO BECOME A PART OF SOMETHIN' A WHOLE LOT BIGGER THAN YA EVER IMAGINED, MY SON.
I LOVE YA, JUG. MORE THAN YOU'LL EVER KNOW. AND KNOW THAT DAD'S AROUND...

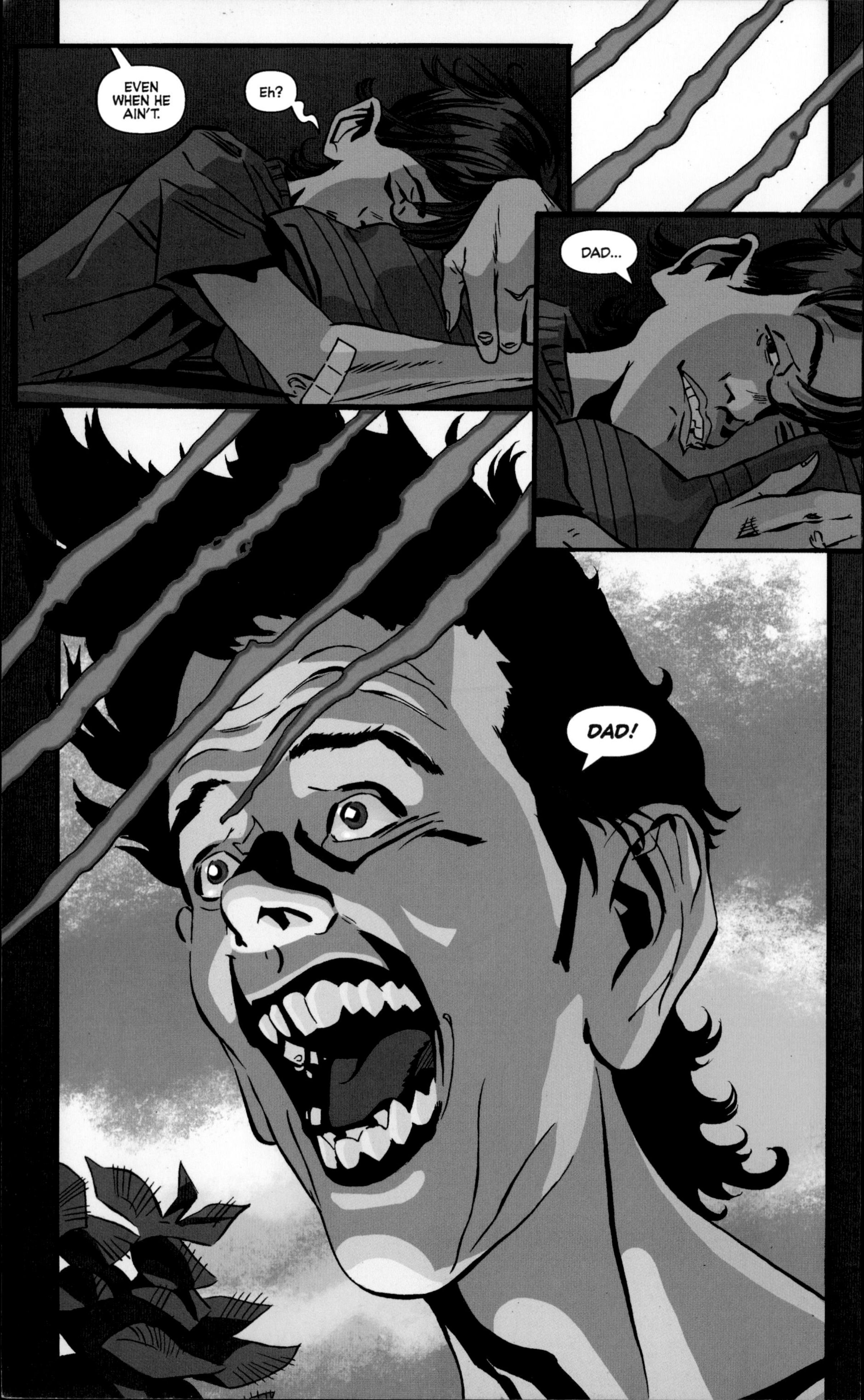
EVEN WHEN HE AIN'T.
Eh?
DAD...
DAD!

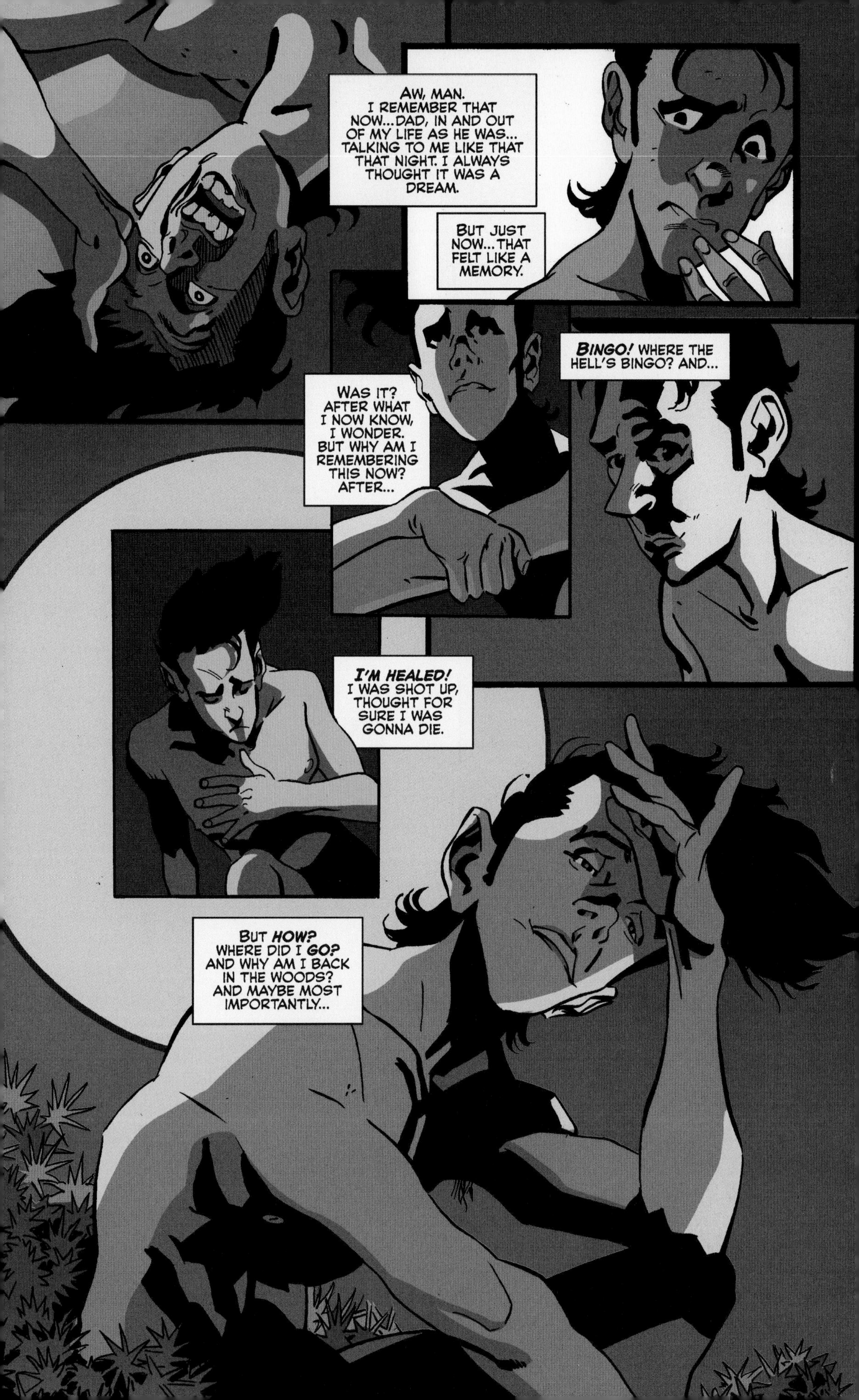
AW, MAN. I REMEMBER THAT NOW...DAD, IN AND OUT OF MY LIFE AS HE WAS... TALKING TO ME LIKE THAT THAT NIGHT. I ALWAYS THOUGHT IT WAS A DREAM.
BUT JUST NOW...THAT FELT LIKE A MEMORY.
WAS IT? AFTER WHAT I NOW KNOW, I WONDER. BUT WHY AM I REMEMBERING THIS NOW? AFTER...
BINGO! WHERE THE HELL'S BINGO? AND...
I'M HEALED! I WAS SHOT UP, THOUGHT FOR SURE I WAS GONNA DIE.
BUT HOW? WHERE DID I GO? AND WHY AM I BACK IN THE WOODS? AND MAYBE MOST IMPORTANTLY...

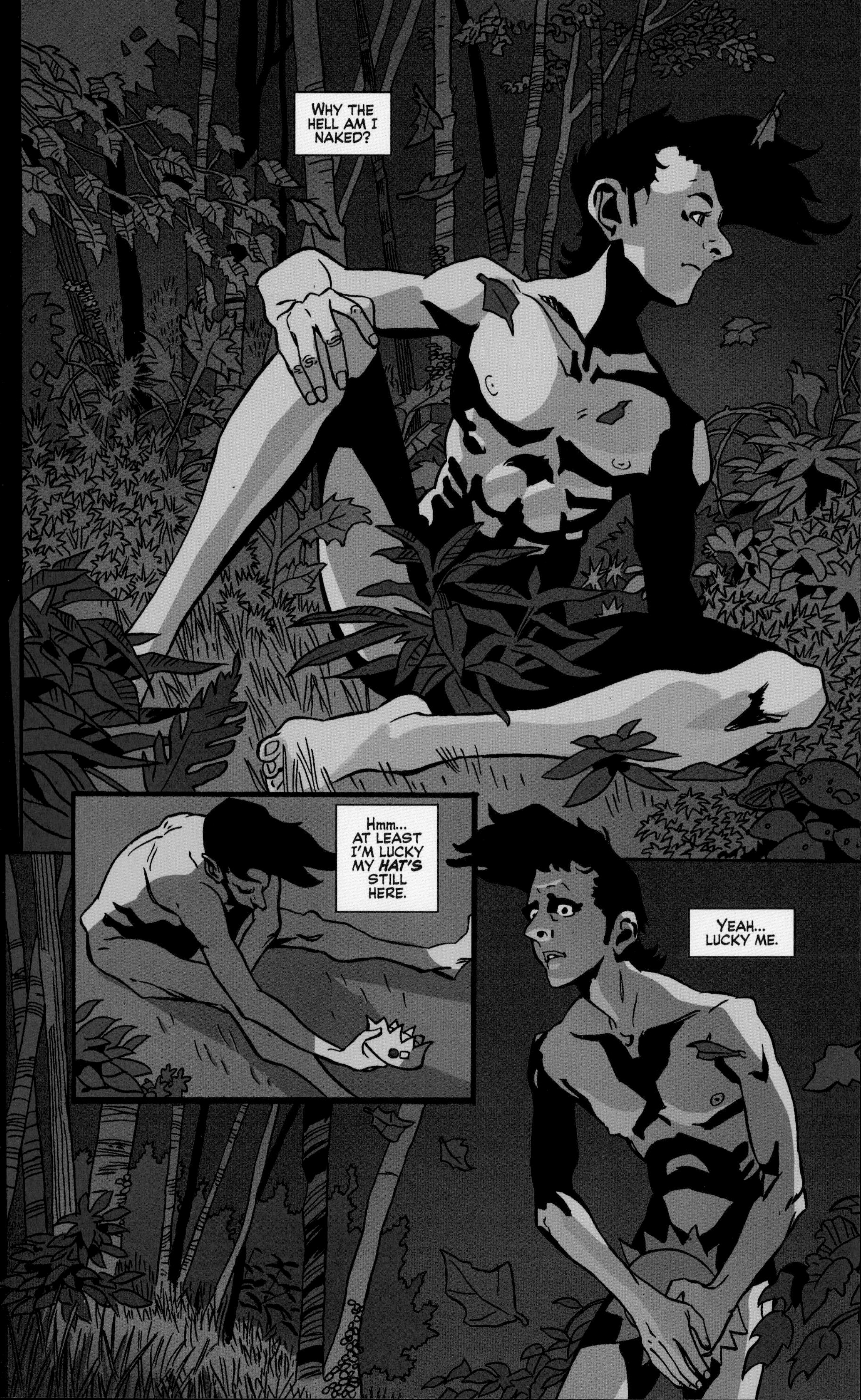
WHY THE HELL AM I NAKED?
Hmm... AT LEAST I'M LUCKY MY HAT'S STILL HERE.
YEAH... LUCKY ME.

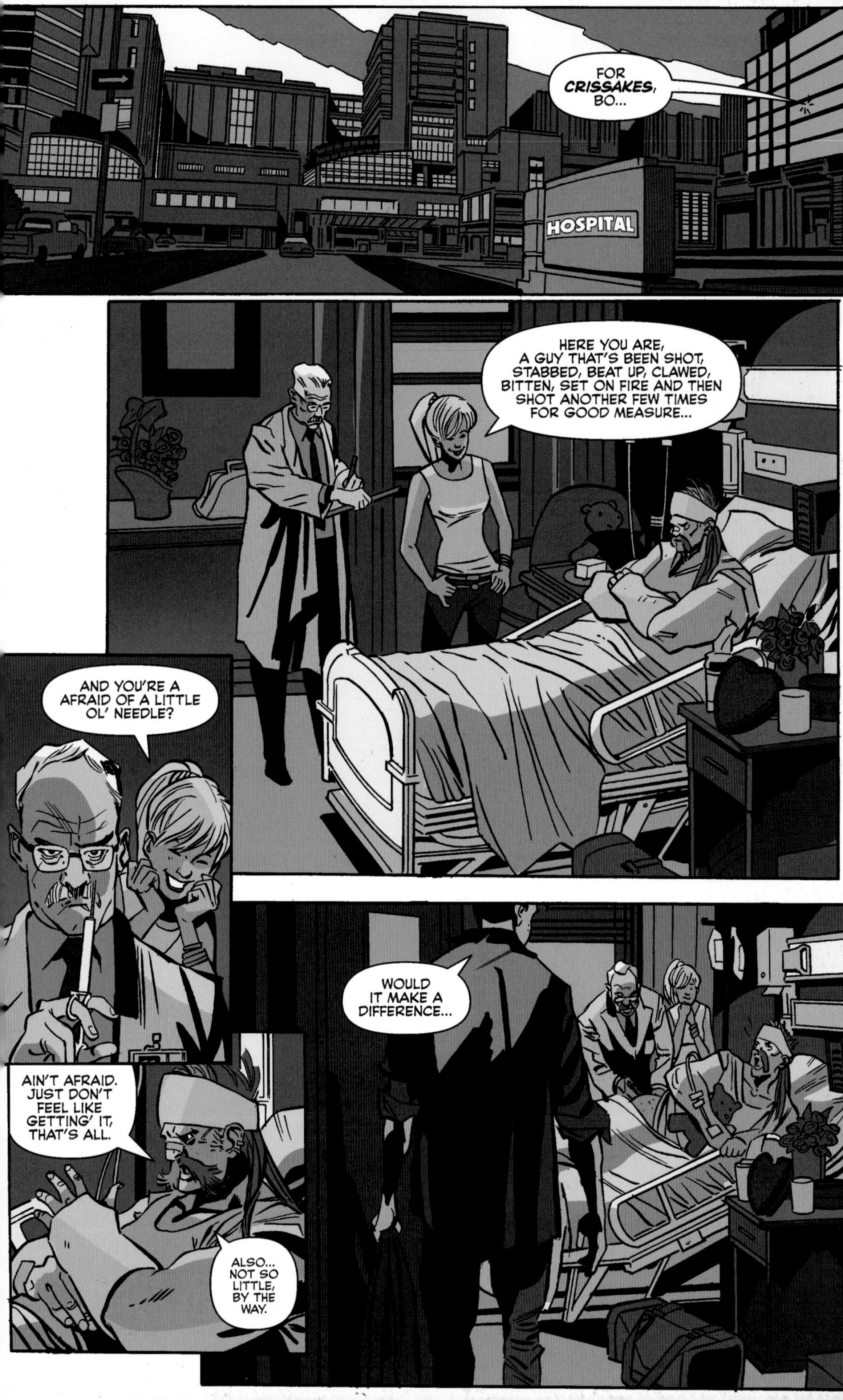
FOR CRISSAKES, BO...
HOSPITAL
HERE YOU ARE, A GUY THAT'S BEEN SHOT, STABBED, BEAT UP, CLAWED, BITTEN, SET ON FIRE AND THEN SHOT ANOTHER FEW TIMES FOR GOOD MEASURE...
AND YOU'RE A AFRAID OF A LITTLE OL' NEEDLE?
AIN'T AFRAID. JUST DON'T FEEL LIKE GETTING' IT, THAT'S ALL.
ALSO... NOT SO LITTLE, BY THE WAY.
WOULD IT MAKE A DIFFERENCE...

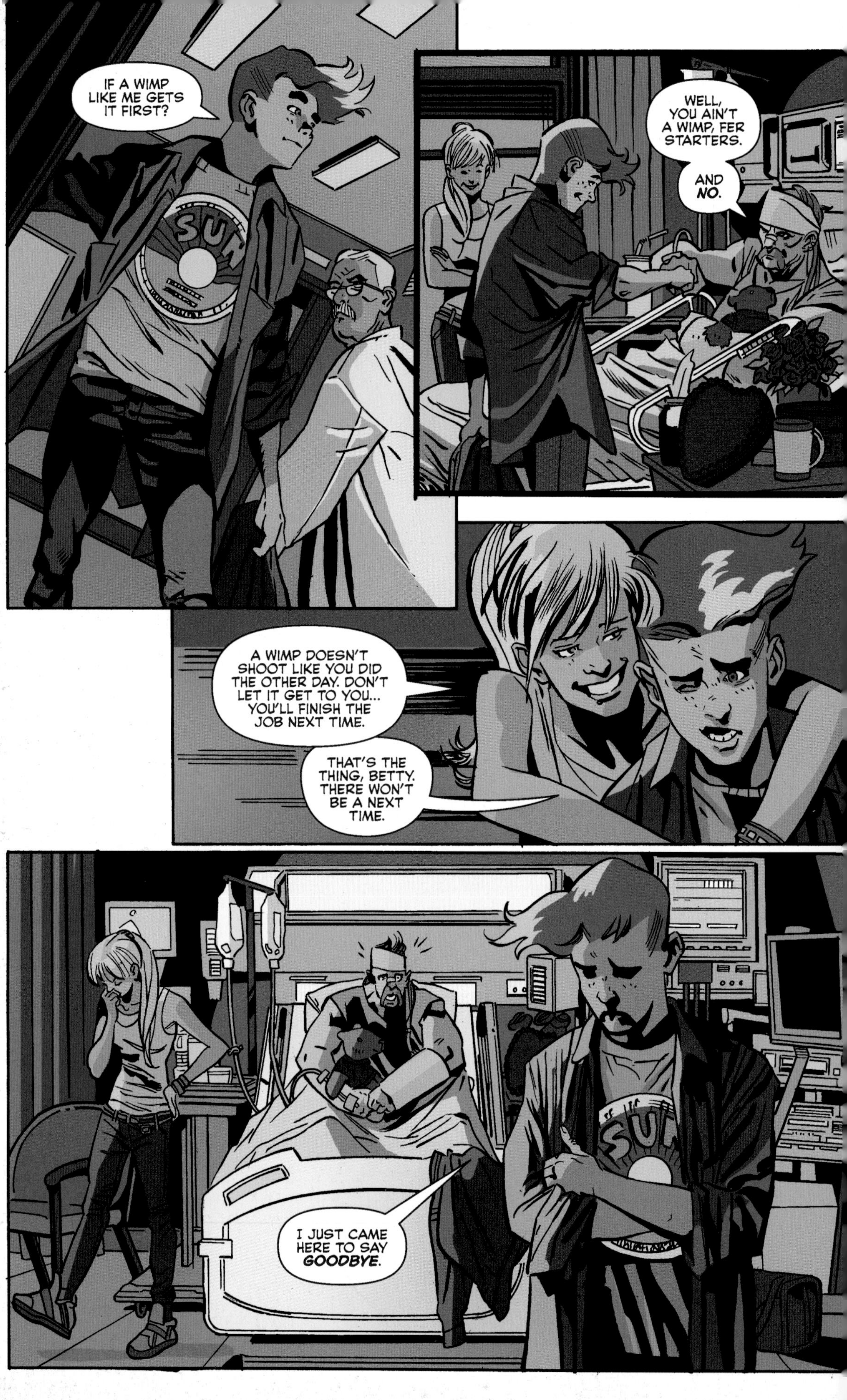
IF A WIMP LIKE ME GETS IT FIRST?
WELL, YOU AIN'T A WIMP, FER STARTERS.
AND NO.
A WIMP DOESN'T SHOOT LIKE YOU DID THE OTHER DAY. DON'T LET IT GET TO YOU... YOU'LL FINISH THE JOB NEXT TIME.
THAT'S THE THING, BETTY. THERE WON'T BE A NEXT TIME.
I JUST CAME HERE TO SAY GOODBYE.

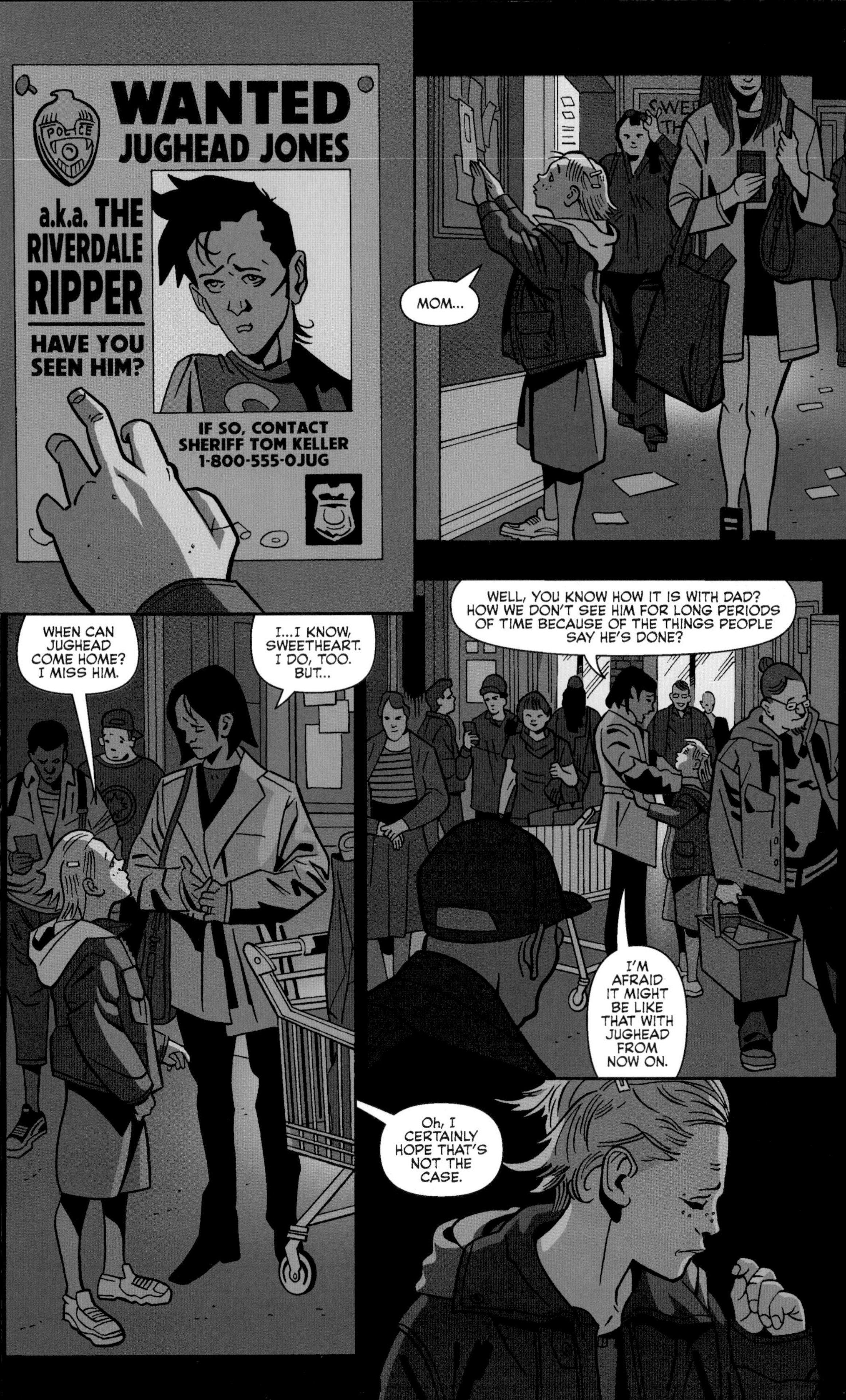
WANTED
JUGHEAD JONES
a.k.a. THE RIVERDALE RIPPER
HAVE YOU SEEN HIM?
IF SO, CONTACT SHERIFF TOM KELLER 1-800-555-0JUG
MOM...
WHEN CAN JUGHEAD COME HOME? I MISS HIM.
I...I KNOW, SWEETHEART. I DO, TOO. BUT...
WELL, YOU KNOW HOW IT IS WITH DAD? HOW WE DON'T SEE HIM FOR LONG PERIODS OF TIME BECAUSE OF THE THINGS PEOPLE SAY HE'S DONE?
I'M AFRAID IT MIGHT BE LIKE THAT WITH JUGHEAD FROM NOW ON.
Oh, I CERTAINLY HOPE THAT'S NOT THE CASE.

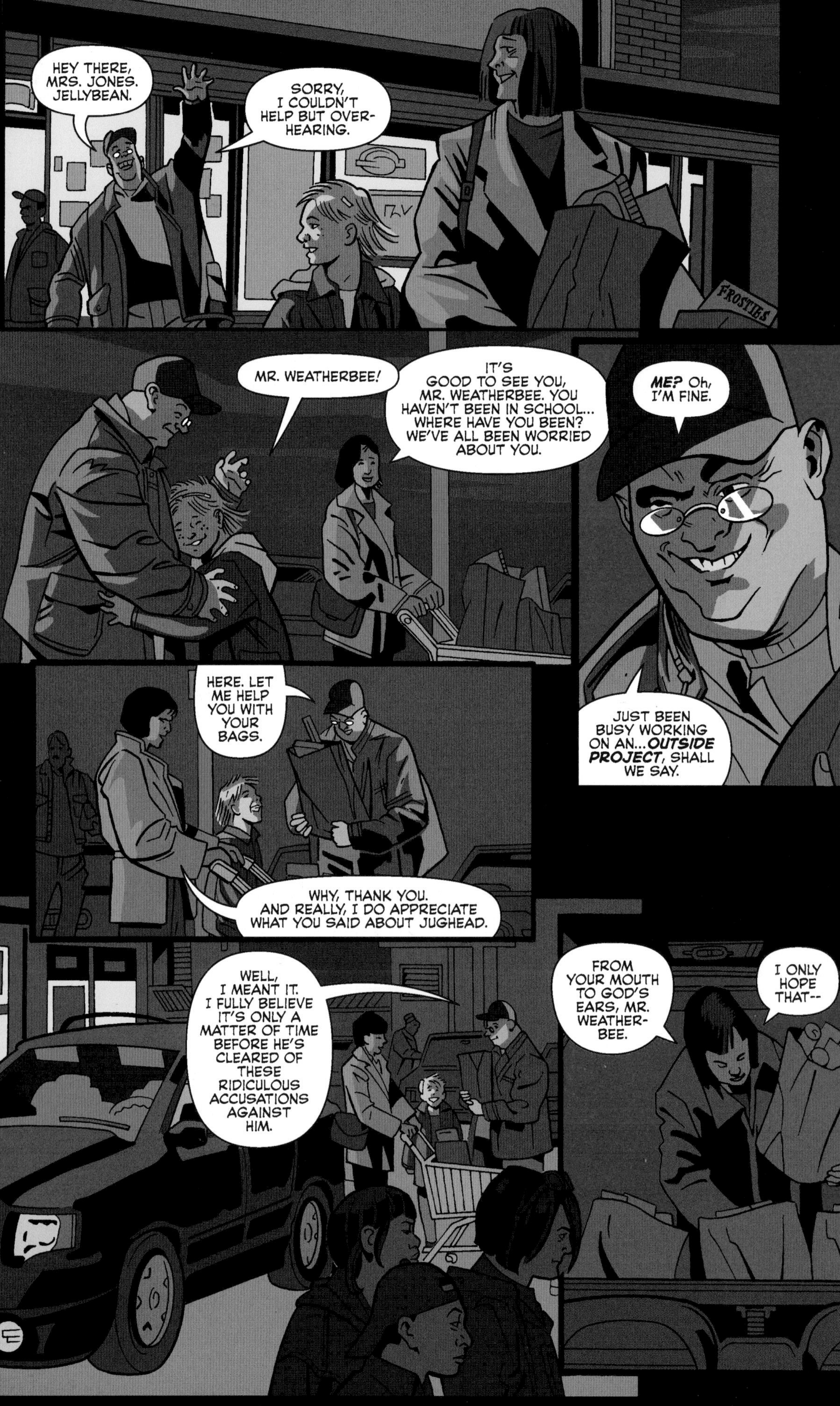
HEY THERE, MRS. JONES. JELLYBEAN.
SORRY, I COULDN'T HELP BUT OVER-HEARING.
FROSTIES
MR. WEATHERBEE!
IT'S GOOD TO SEE YOU, MR. WEATHERBEE. YOU HAVEN'T BEEN IN SCHOOL... WHERE HAVE YOU BEEN? WE'VE ALL BEEN WORRIED ABOUT YOU.
ME? Oh, I'M FINE.
JUST BEEN BUSY WORKING ON AN...OUTSIDE PROJECT, SHALL WE SAY.
HERE. LET ME HELP YOU WITH YOUR BAGS.
WHY, THANK YOU. AND REALLY, I DO APPRECIATE WHAT YOU SAID ABOUT JUGHEAD.
WELL, I MEANT IT. I FULLY BELIEVE IT'S ONLY A MATTER OF TIME BEFORE HE'S CLEARED OF THESE RIDICULOUS ACCUSATIONS AGAINST HIM.
FROM YOUR MOUTH TO GOD'S EARS, MR. WEATHER-BEE.
I ONLY HOPE THAT--

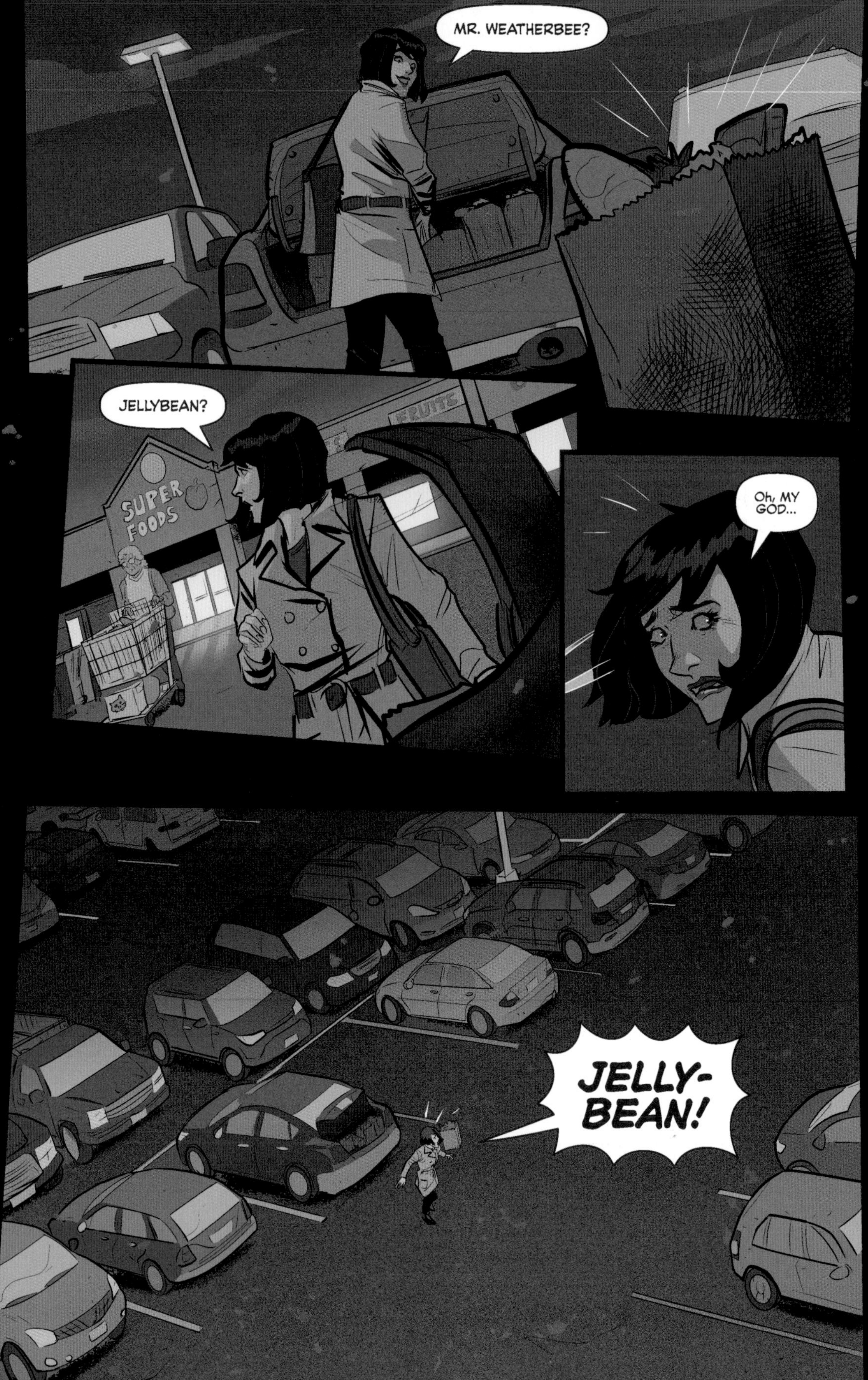
MR. WEATHERBEE?
JELLYBEAN?
SUPER FOODS
FRUITS
Oh, MY GOD...
JELLY-BEAN!

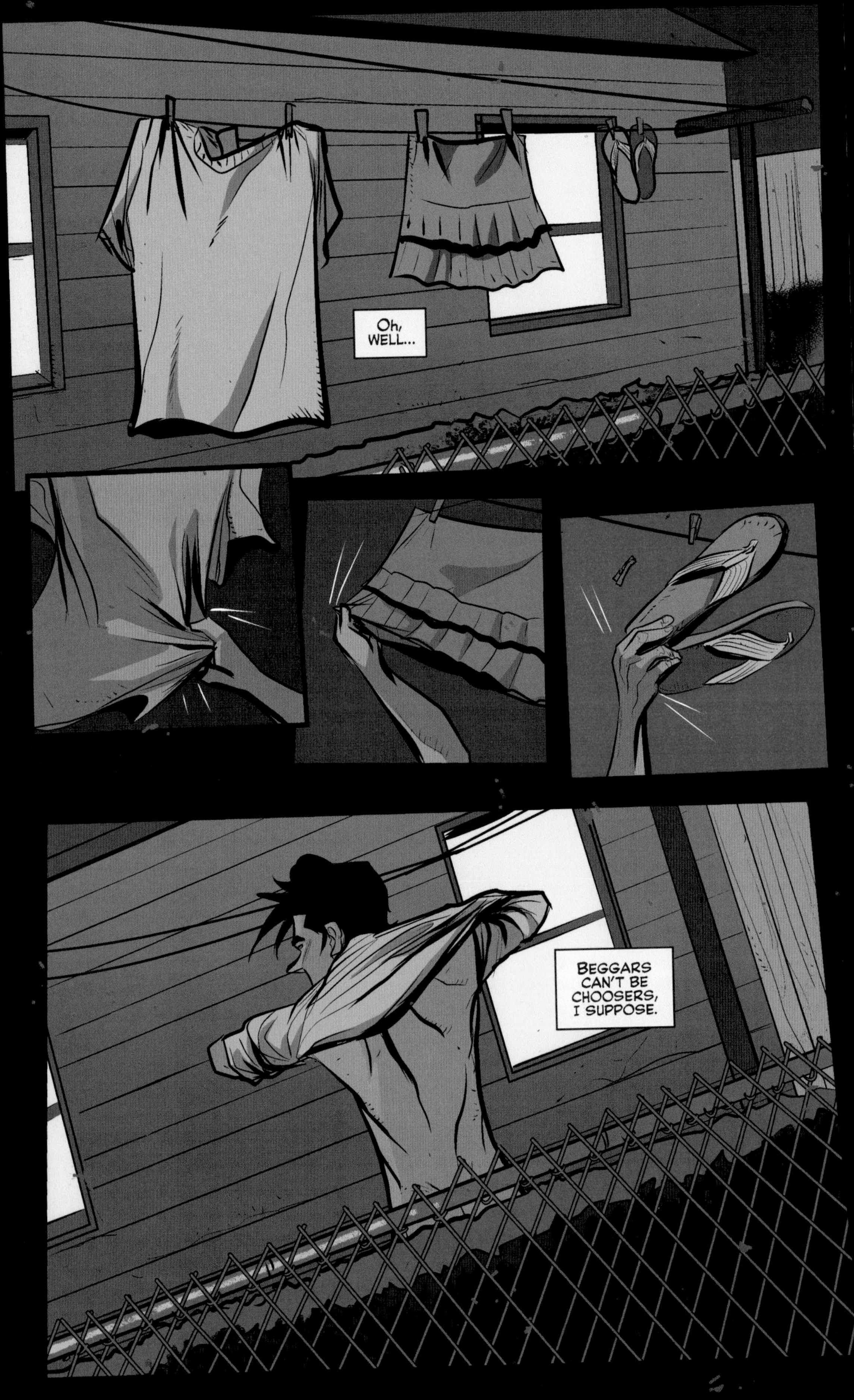
Oh, WELL...
BEGGARS CAN'T BE CHOOSERS, I SUPPOSE.

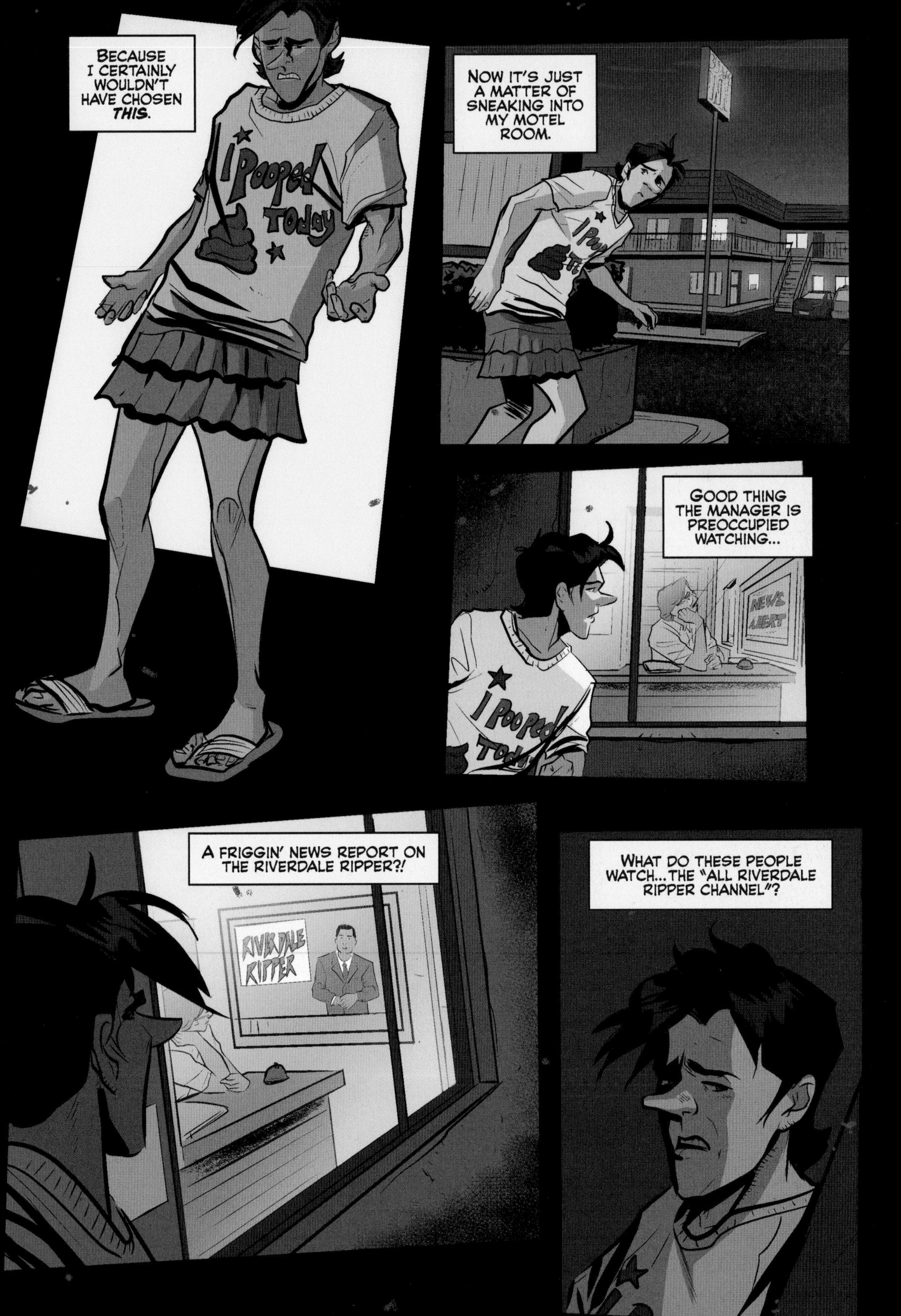

BECAUSE I CERTAINLY WOULDN'T HAVE CHOSEN *THIS*.
I Pooped Today
NOW IT'S JUST A MATTER OF SNEAKING INTO MY MOTEL ROOM.
GOOD THING THE MANAGER IS PREOCCUPIED WATCHING...
NEWS ALERT
A FRIGGIN' NEWS REPORT ON THE RIVERDALE RIPPER?!
RIVERDALE RIPPER
WHAT DO THESE PEOPLE WATCH... THE "ALL RIVERDALE RIPPER CHANNEL"?

IT'S OKAY. HE DOESN'T SEE YOU AND RIGHT NOW THAT'S ALL THAT MATTERS.

NOW IT'S JUST A MATTER OF SCOOPING UP HOT DOG AND MY STUFF AND...

AND...

sniff! sniff!

THAT *SCENT*. IT'S FAMILIAR.

SOMEONE I *KNOW*...

Oh, MY GOD...

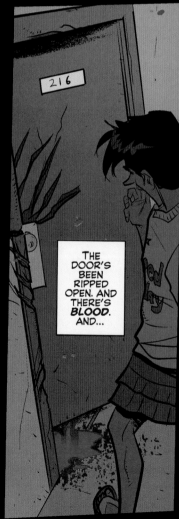

216

THE DOOR'S BEEN RIPPED OPEN. AND THERE'S *BLOOD*. AND...

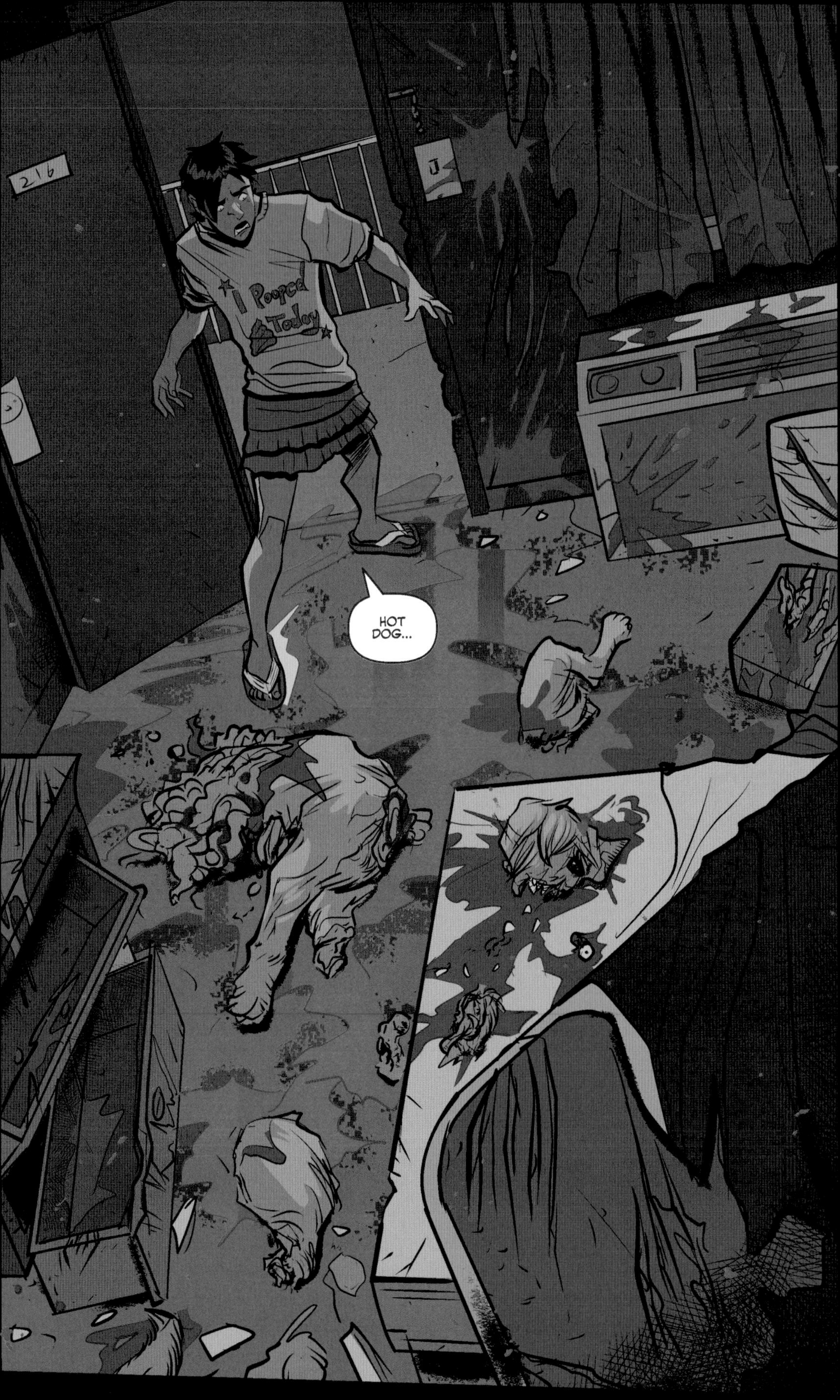
216
I Pooped Today
HOT DOG...

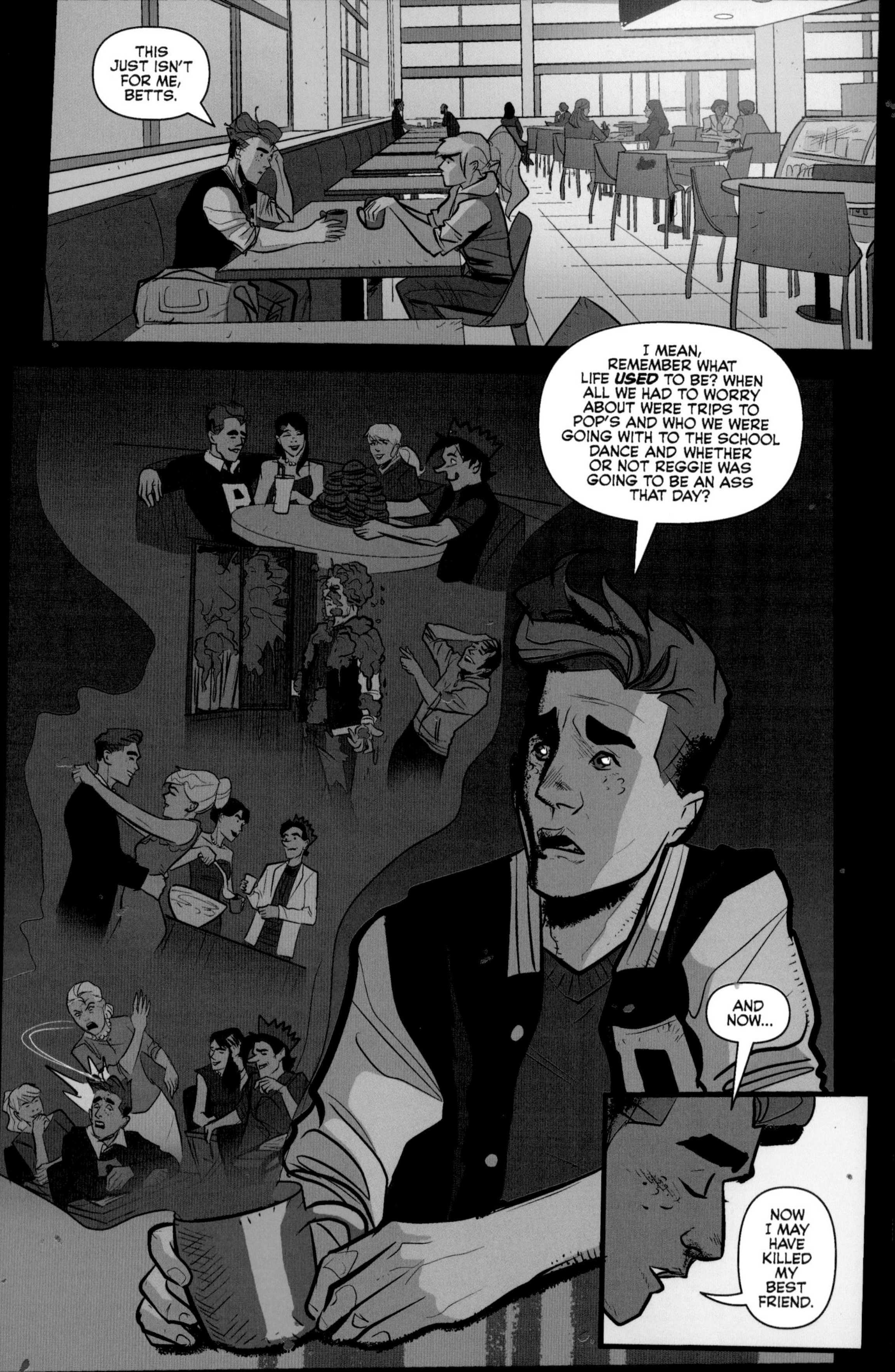
THIS JUST ISN'T FOR ME, BETTS.
I MEAN, REMEMBER WHAT LIFE *USED* TO BE? WHEN ALL WE HAD TO WORRY ABOUT WERE TRIPS TO POP'S AND WHO WE WERE GOING WITH TO THE SCHOOL DANCE AND WHETHER OR NOT REGGIE WAS GOING TO BE AN ASS THAT DAY?
AND NOW...
NOW I MAY HAVE KILLED MY BEST FRIEND.

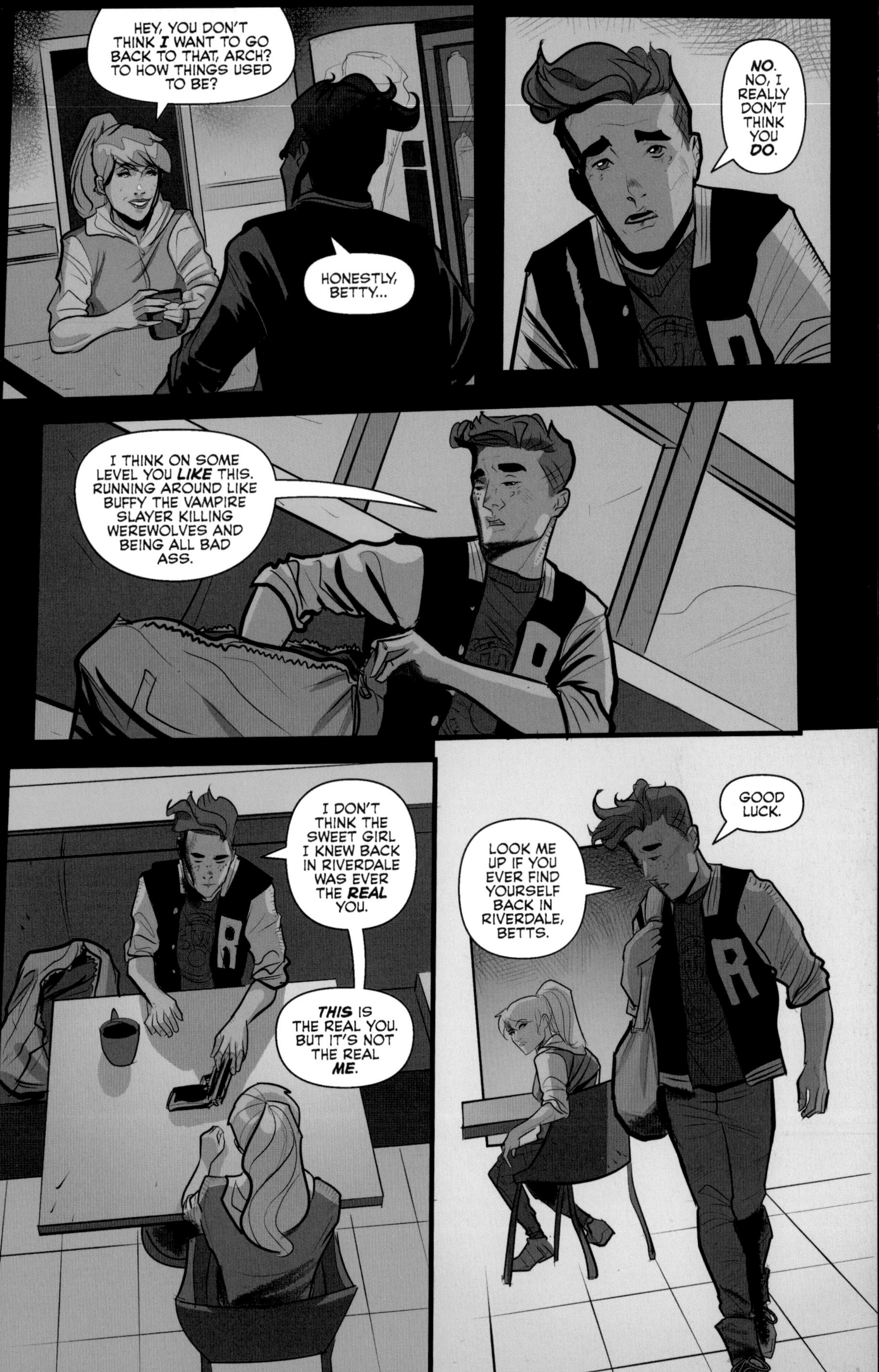
HEY, YOU DON'T THINK *I* WANT TO GO BACK TO THAT, ARCH? TO HOW THINGS USED TO BE?
HONESTLY, BETTY...
NO. NO, I REALLY DON'T THINK YOU *DO*.
I THINK ON SOME LEVEL YOU *LIKE* THIS. RUNNING AROUND LIKE BUFFY THE VAMPIRE SLAYER KILLING WEREWOLVES AND BEING ALL BAD ASS.
I DON'T THINK THE SWEET GIRL I KNEW BACK IN RIVERDALE WAS EVER THE *REAL* YOU.
THIS IS THE REAL YOU. BUT IT'S NOT THE REAL *ME*.
LOOK ME UP IF YOU EVER FIND YOURSELF BACK IN RIVERDALE, BETTS.
GOOD LUCK.

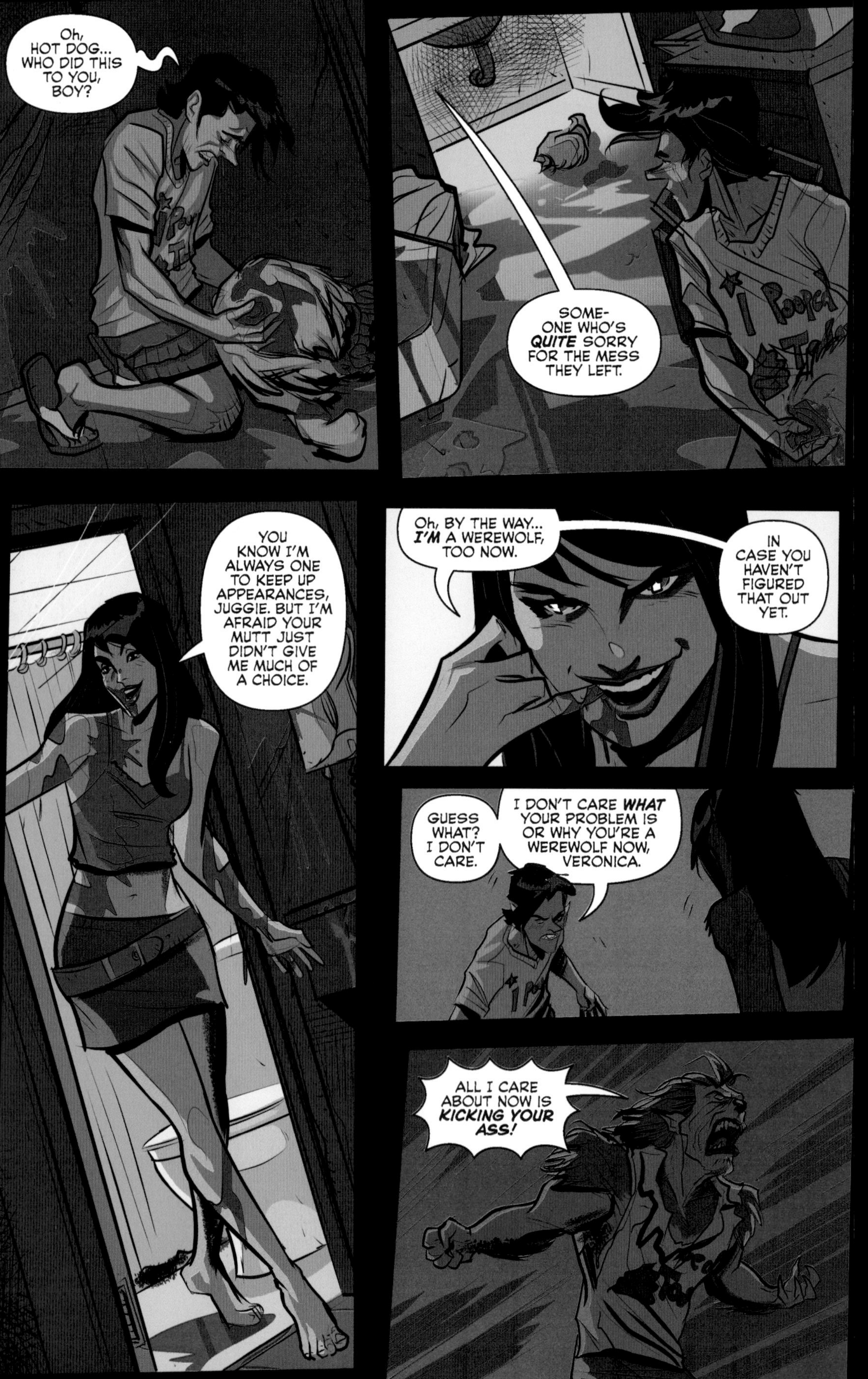
Oh, HOT DOG... WHO DID THIS TO YOU, BOY?
SOME-ONE WHO'S **QUITE** SORRY FOR THE MESS THEY LEFT.
YOU KNOW I'M ALWAYS ONE TO KEEP UP APPEARANCES, JUGGIE. BUT I'M AFRAID YOUR MUTT JUST DIDN'T GIVE ME MUCH OF A CHOICE.
Oh, BY THE WAY... ***I'M*** A WEREWOLF, TOO NOW.
IN CASE YOU HAVEN'T FIGURED THAT OUT YET.
GUESS WHAT? I DON'T CARE.
I DON'T CARE ***WHAT*** YOUR PROBLEM IS OR WHY YOU'RE A WEREWOLF NOW, VERONICA.
ALL I CARE ABOUT NOW IS ***KICKING YOUR ASS!***

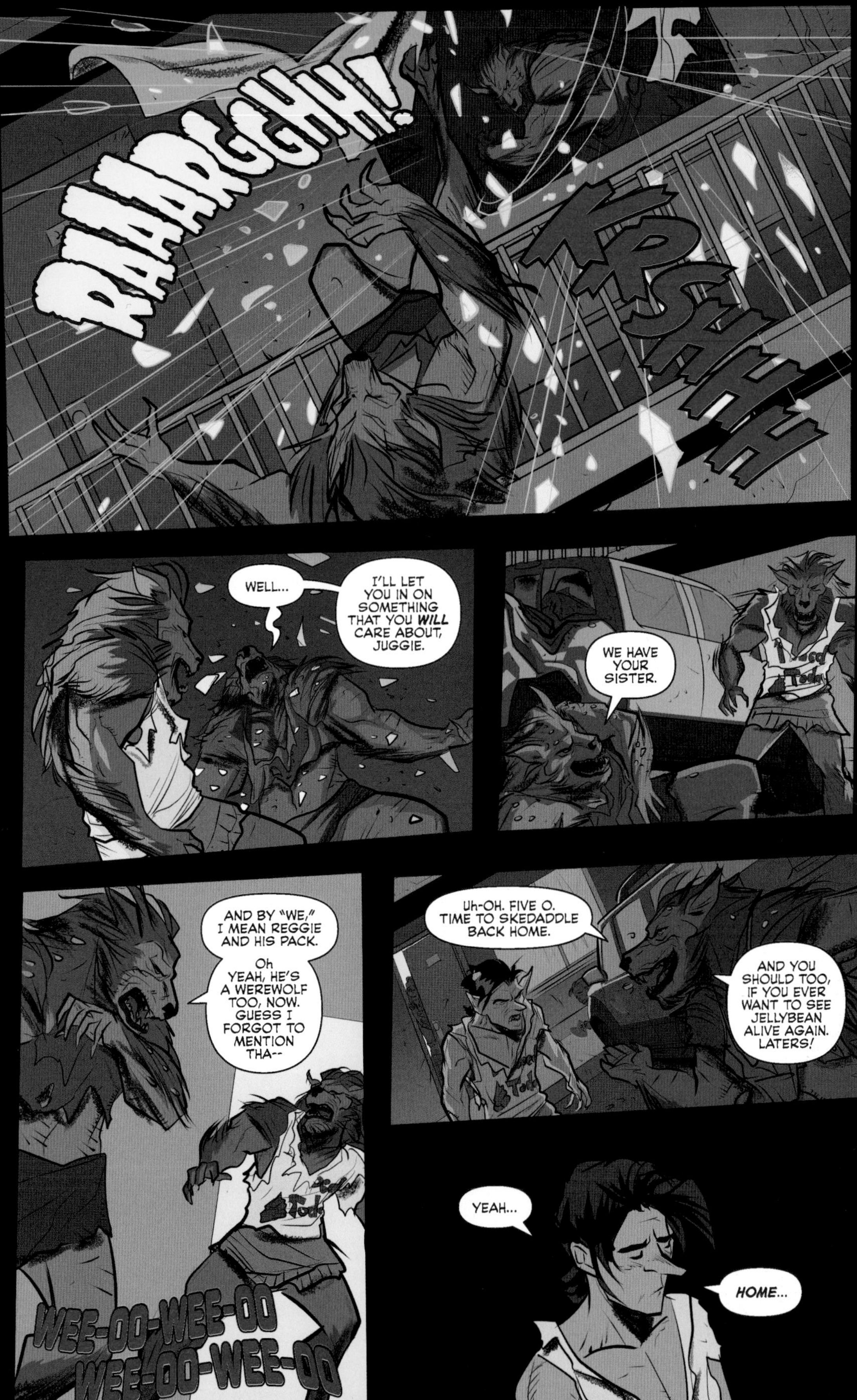
RAAARGGH!
KRSHHHH
WELL...
I'LL LET YOU IN ON SOMETHING THAT YOU *WILL* CARE ABOUT, JUGGIE.
WE HAVE YOUR SISTER.
AND BY "WE," I MEAN REGGIE AND HIS PACK.
Oh YEAH, HE'S A WEREWOLF TOO, NOW. GUESS I FORGOT TO MENTION THA--
WEE-OO-WEE-OO
WEE-OO-WEE-OO
Uh-OH. FIVE O. TIME TO SKEDADDLE BACK HOME.
AND YOU SHOULD TOO, IF YOU EVER WANT TO SEE JELLYBEAN ALIVE AGAIN. LATERS!
YEAH...
HOME...

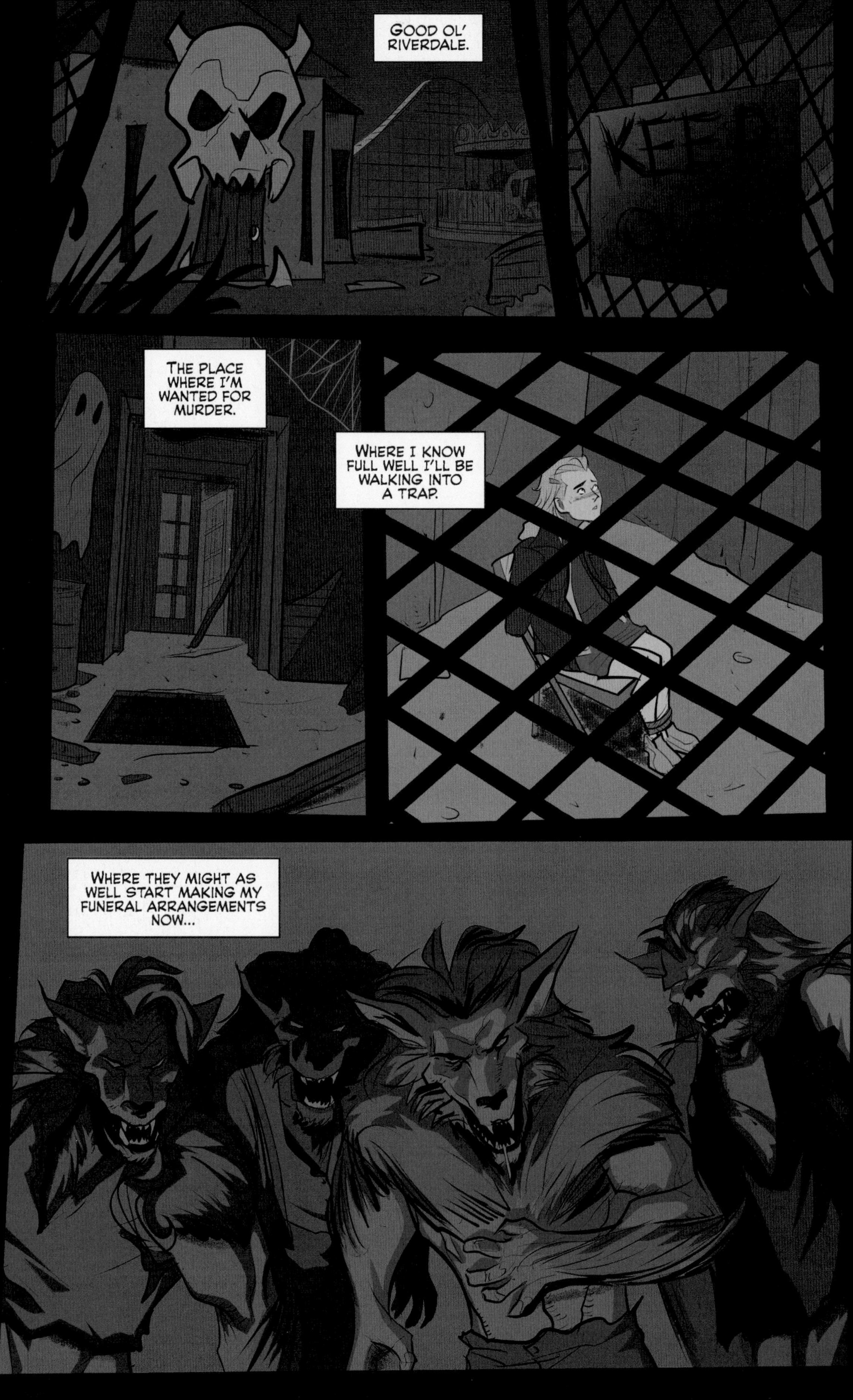
GOOD OL' RIVERDALE.
THE PLACE WHERE I'M WANTED FOR MURDER.
WHERE I KNOW FULL WELL I'LL BE WALKING INTO A TRAP.
WHERE THEY MIGHT AS WELL START MAKING MY FUNERAL ARRANGEMENTS NOW...

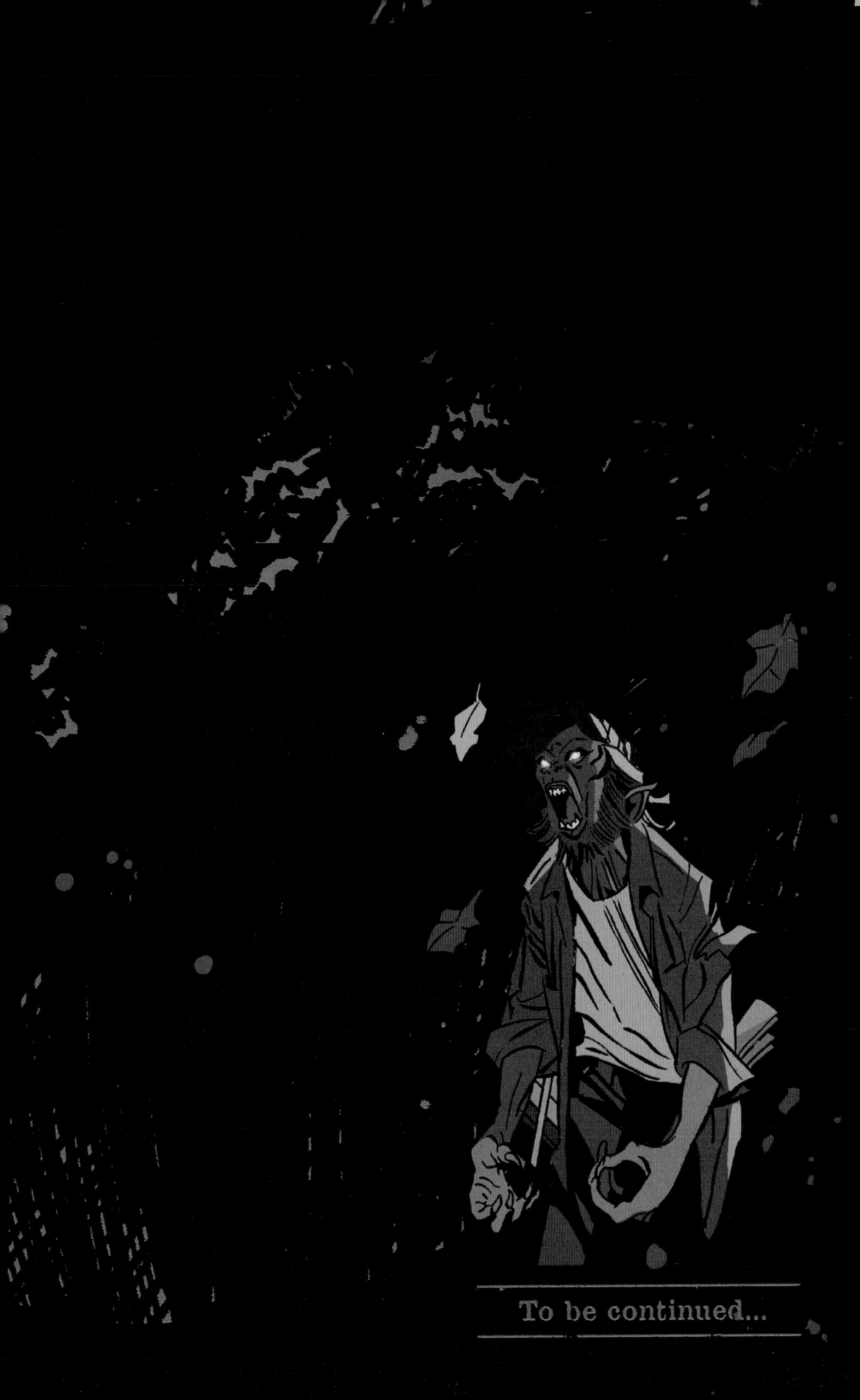
To be continued...

ISSUE SIX

COVER ART **Adam Gorham**

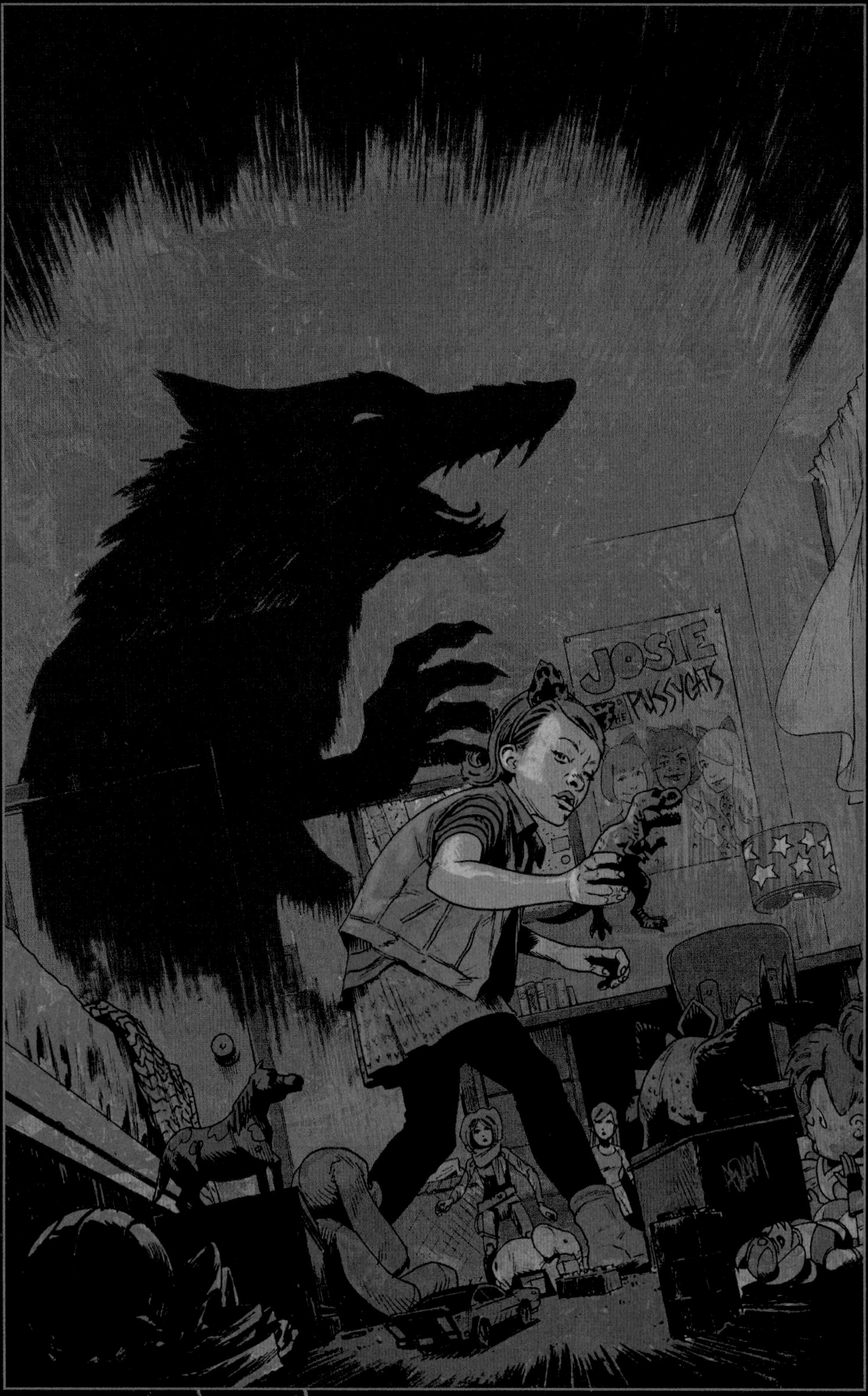
JOSIE
PUSSYCATS

STORY **Frank Tieri** ART **Pat & Tim Kennedy** (p. 1-10) **Joe Eisma** (p. 11-20)
COLORS **Matt Herms** INKS **Bob Smith** (p. 1-10) LETTERING **Jack Morelli**

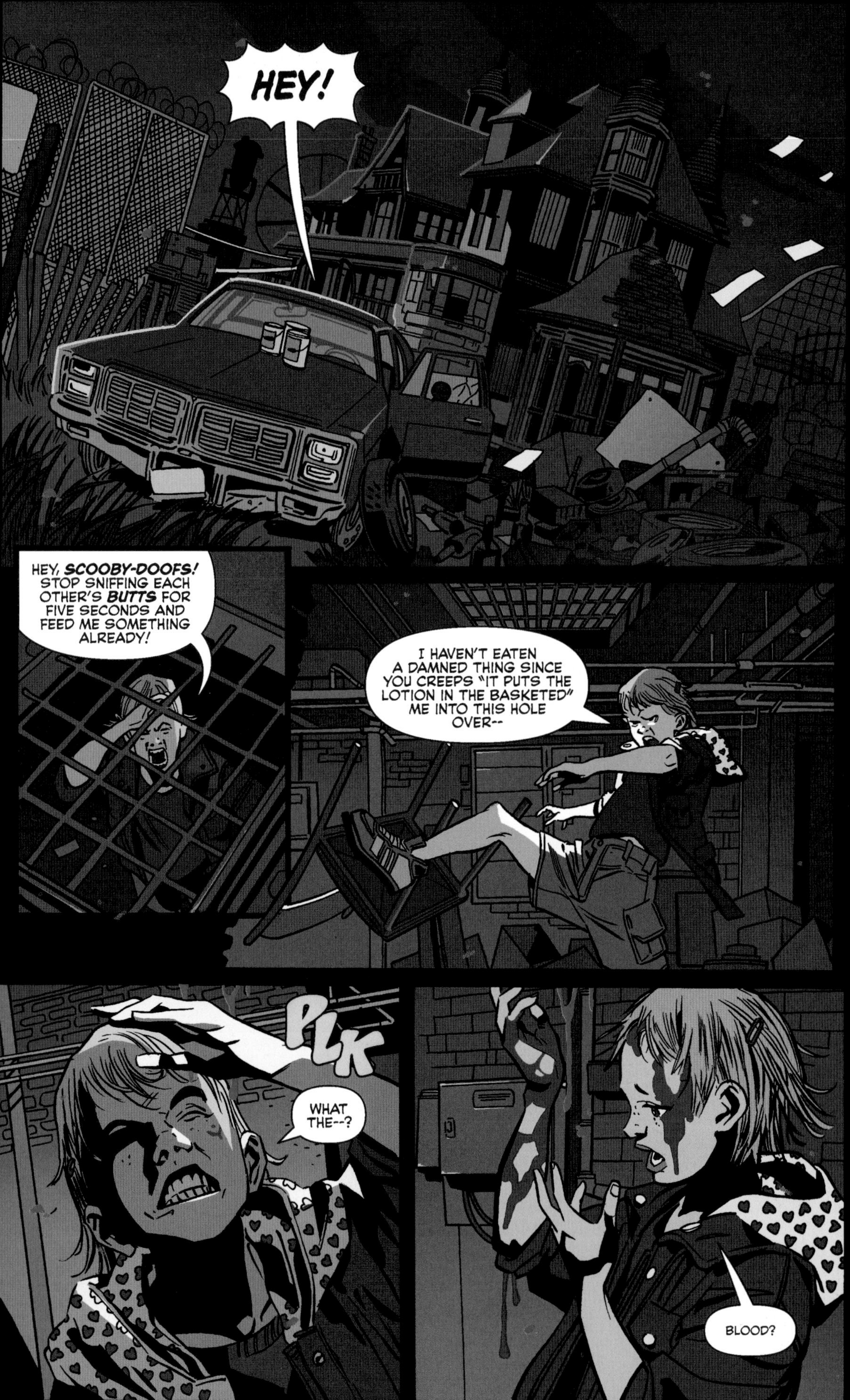
HEY!
HEY, SCOOBY-DOOFS! STOP SNIFFING EACH OTHER'S BUTTS FOR FIVE SECONDS AND FEED ME SOMETHING ALREADY!
I HAVEN'T EATEN A DAMNED THING SINCE YOU CREEPS "IT PUTS THE LOTION IN THE BASKETED" ME INTO THIS HOLE OVER--
PLK
WHAT THE--?
BLOOD?

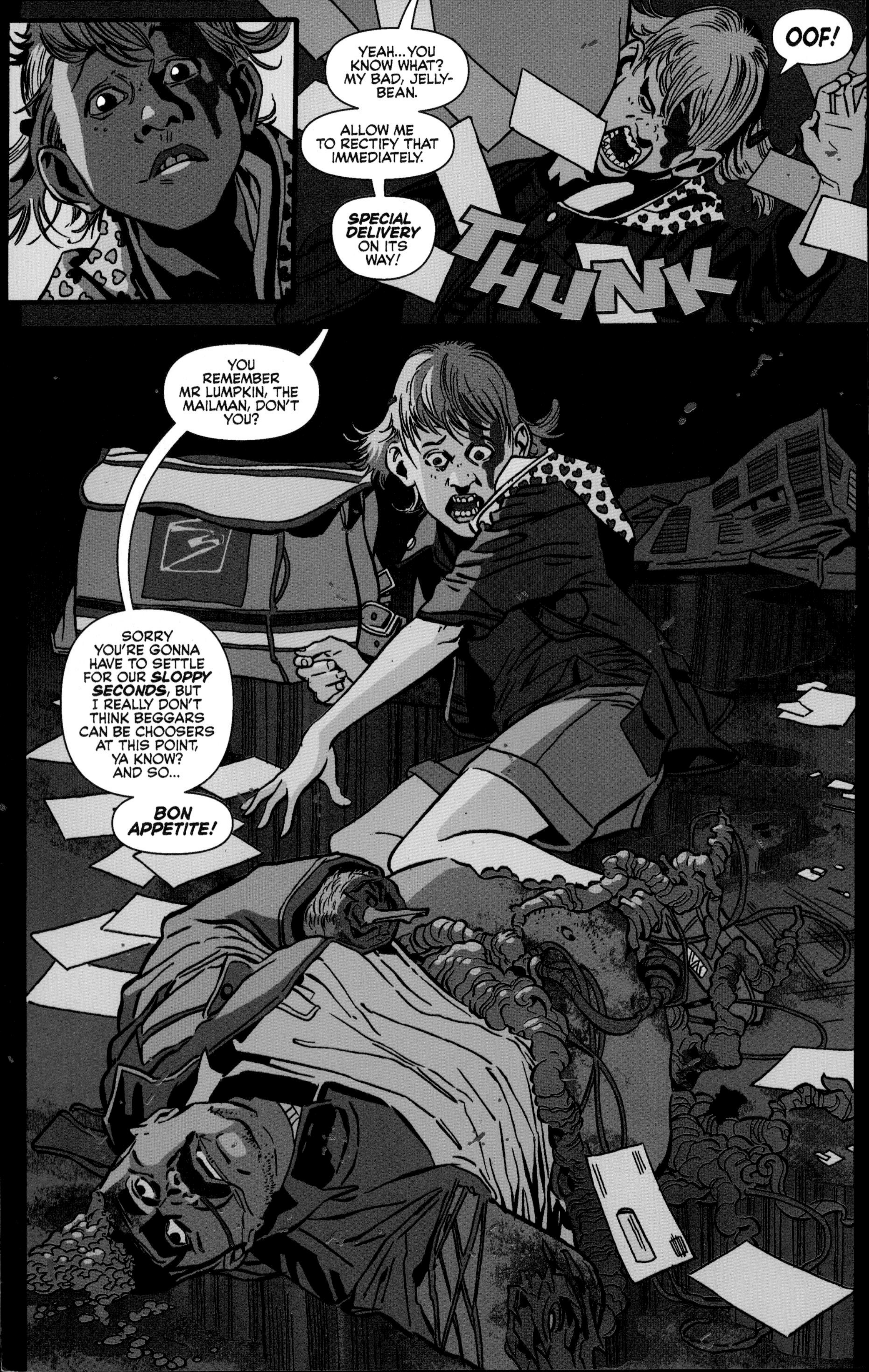
YEAH... YOU KNOW WHAT? MY BAD, JELLY-BEAN.
ALLOW ME TO RECTIFY THAT IMMEDIATELY.
SPECIAL DELIVERY ON ITS WAY!
OOF!
THUNK
YOU REMEMBER MR LUMPKIN, THE MAILMAN, DON'T YOU?
SORRY YOU'RE GONNA HAVE TO SETTLE FOR OUR SLOPPY SECONDS, BUT I REALLY DON'T THINK BEGGARS CAN BE CHOOSERS AT THIS POINT, YA KNOW? AND SO...
BON APPETITE!

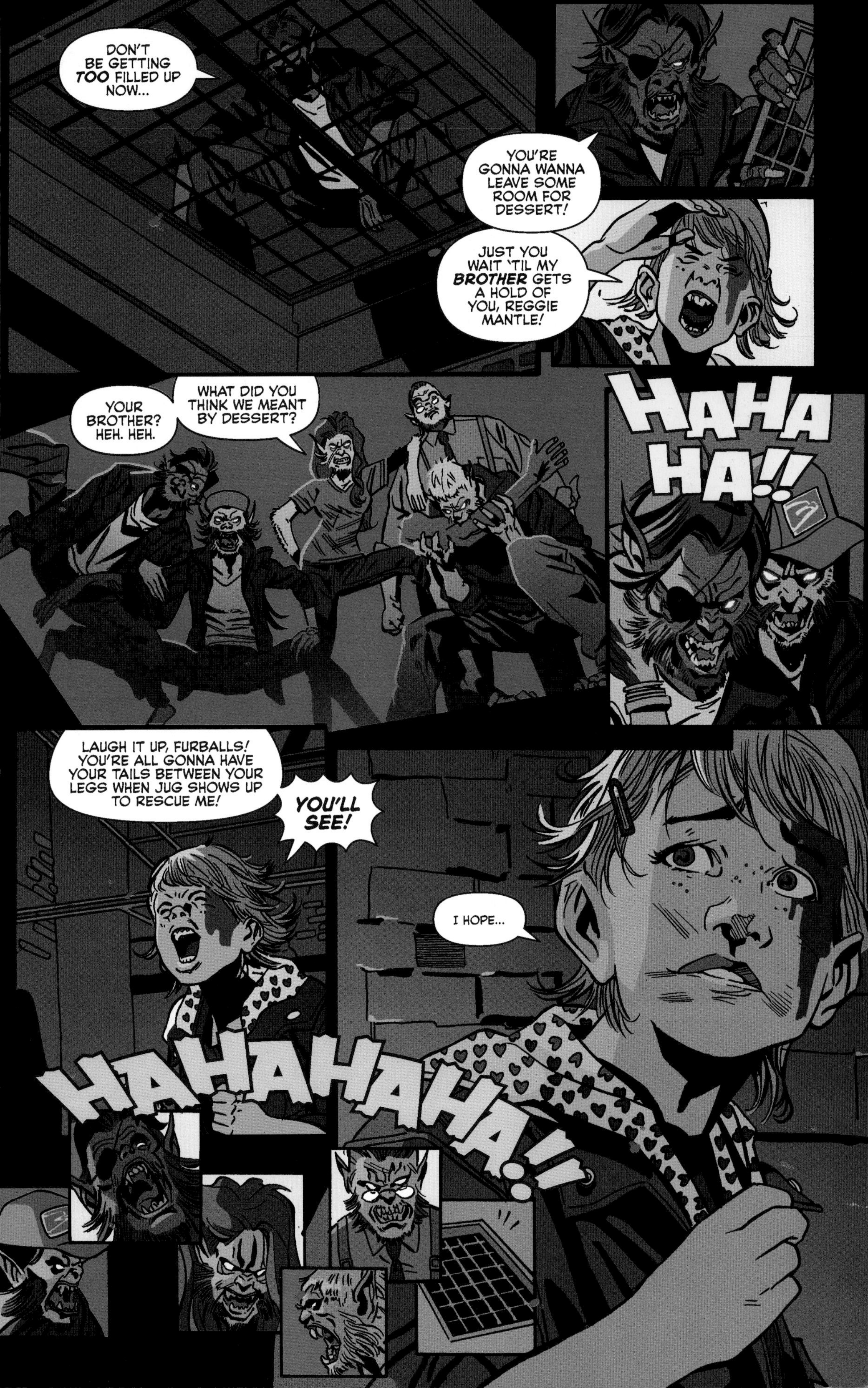
DON'T BE GETTING TOO FILLED UP NOW...
YOU'RE GONNA WANNA LEAVE SOME ROOM FOR DESSERT!
JUST YOU WAIT 'TIL MY BROTHER GETS A HOLD OF YOU, REGGIE MANTLE!
YOUR BROTHER? HEH. HEH.
WHAT DID YOU THINK WE MEANT BY DESSERT?
HAHAHA!!
LAUGH IT UP, FURBALLS! YOU'RE ALL GONNA HAVE YOUR TAILS BETWEEN YOUR LEGS WHEN JUG SHOWS UP TO RESCUE ME!
YOU'LL SEE!
I HOPE...
HAHAHAHAHA!!!

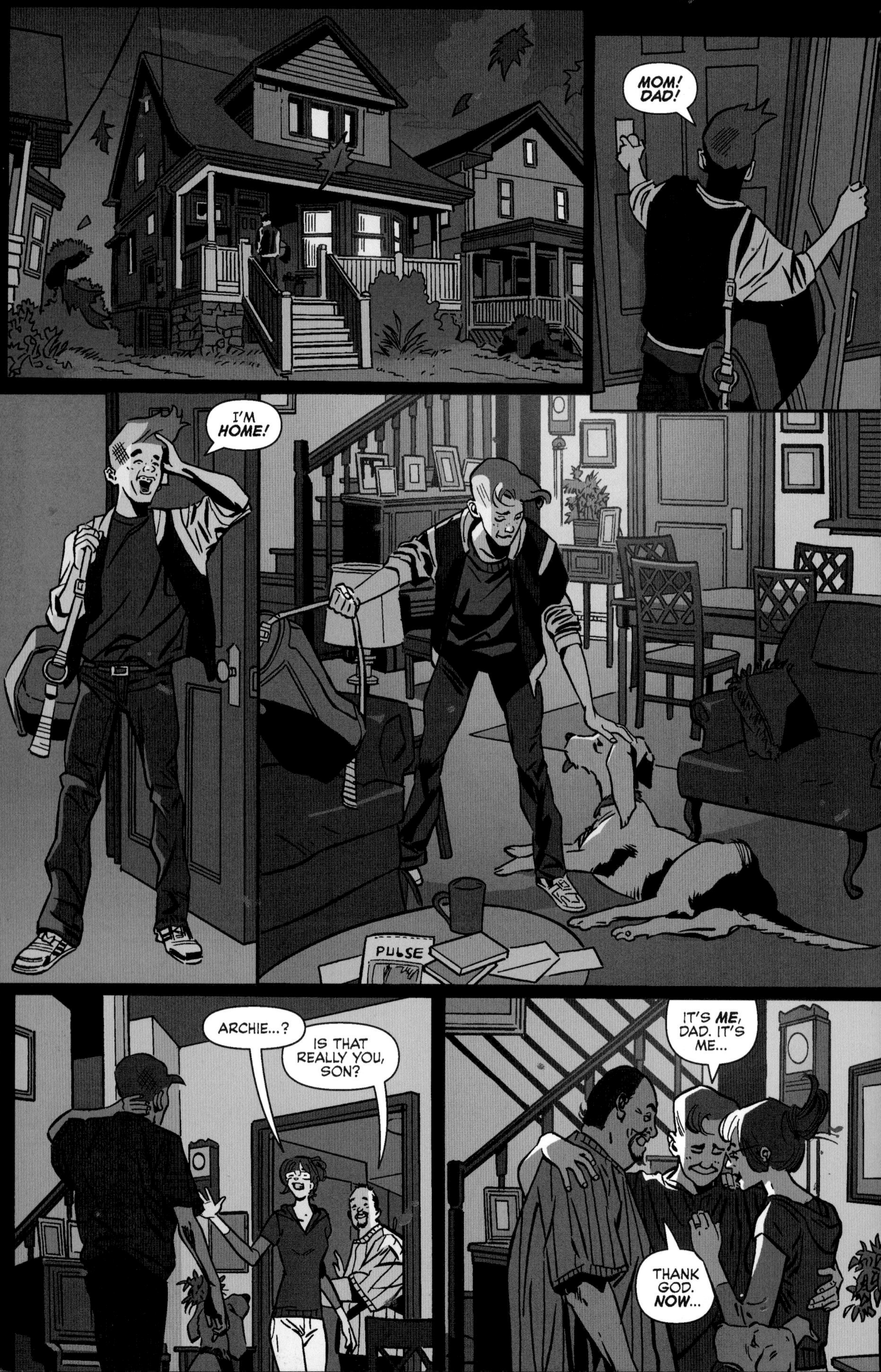
MOM! DAD!
I'M HOME!
PULSE
ARCHIE...?
IS THAT REALLY YOU, SON?
IT'S ME, DAD. IT'S ME...
THANK GOD. NOW...

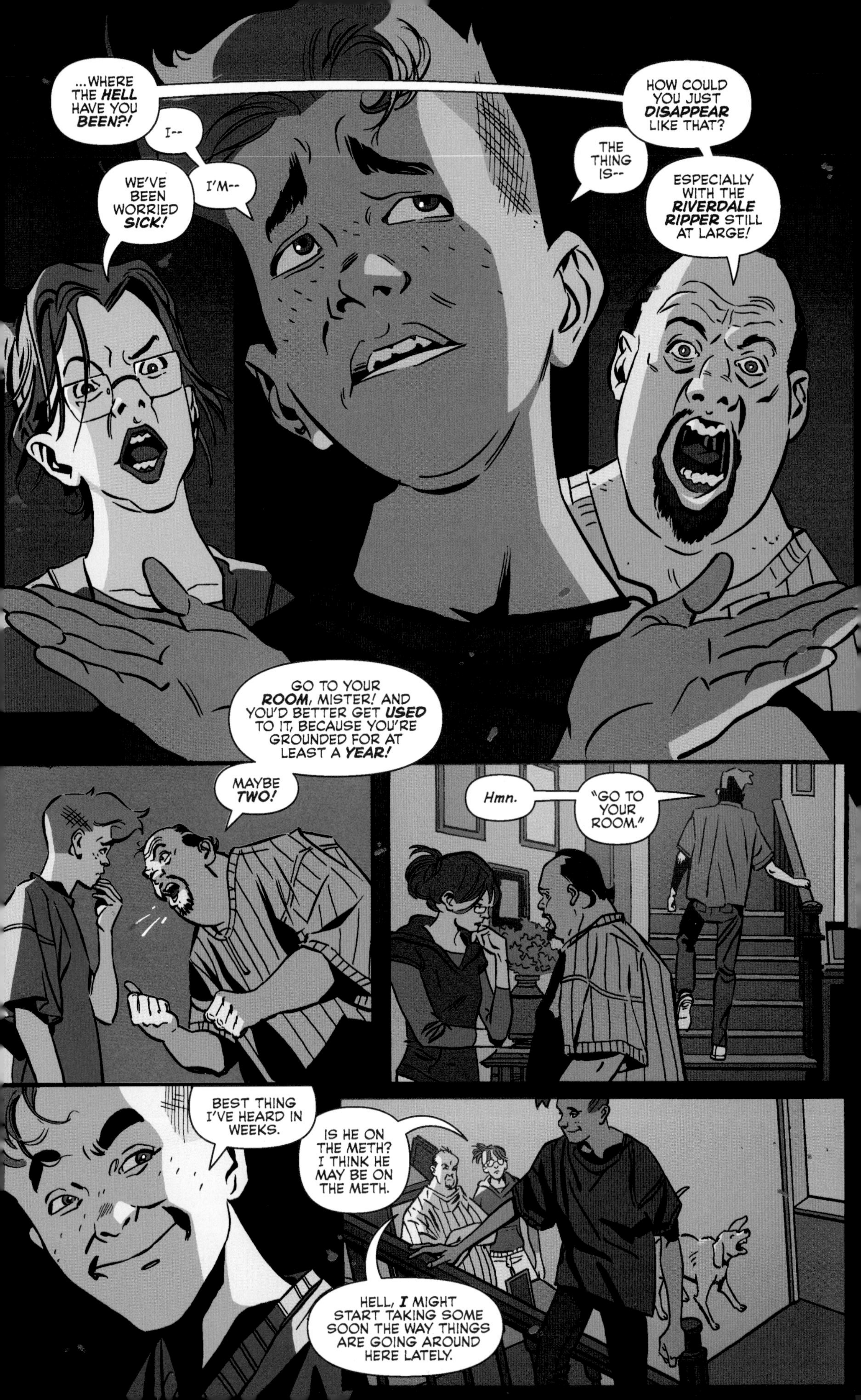
...WHERE THE HELL HAVE YOU BEEN?!
HOW COULD YOU JUST DISAPPEAR LIKE THAT?
I--
I'M--
WE'VE BEEN WORRIED SICK!
THE THING IS--
ESPECIALLY WITH THE RIVERDALE RIPPER STILL AT LARGE!
GO TO YOUR ROOM, MISTER! AND YOU'D BETTER GET USED TO IT, BECAUSE YOU'RE GROUNDED FOR AT LEAST A YEAR!
MAYBE TWO!
Hmn.
"GO TO YOUR ROOM."
BEST THING I'VE HEARD IN WEEKS.
IS HE ON THE METH? I THINK HE MAY BE ON THE METH.
HELL, I MIGHT START TAKING SOME SOON THE WAY THINGS ARE GOING AROUND HERE LATELY.

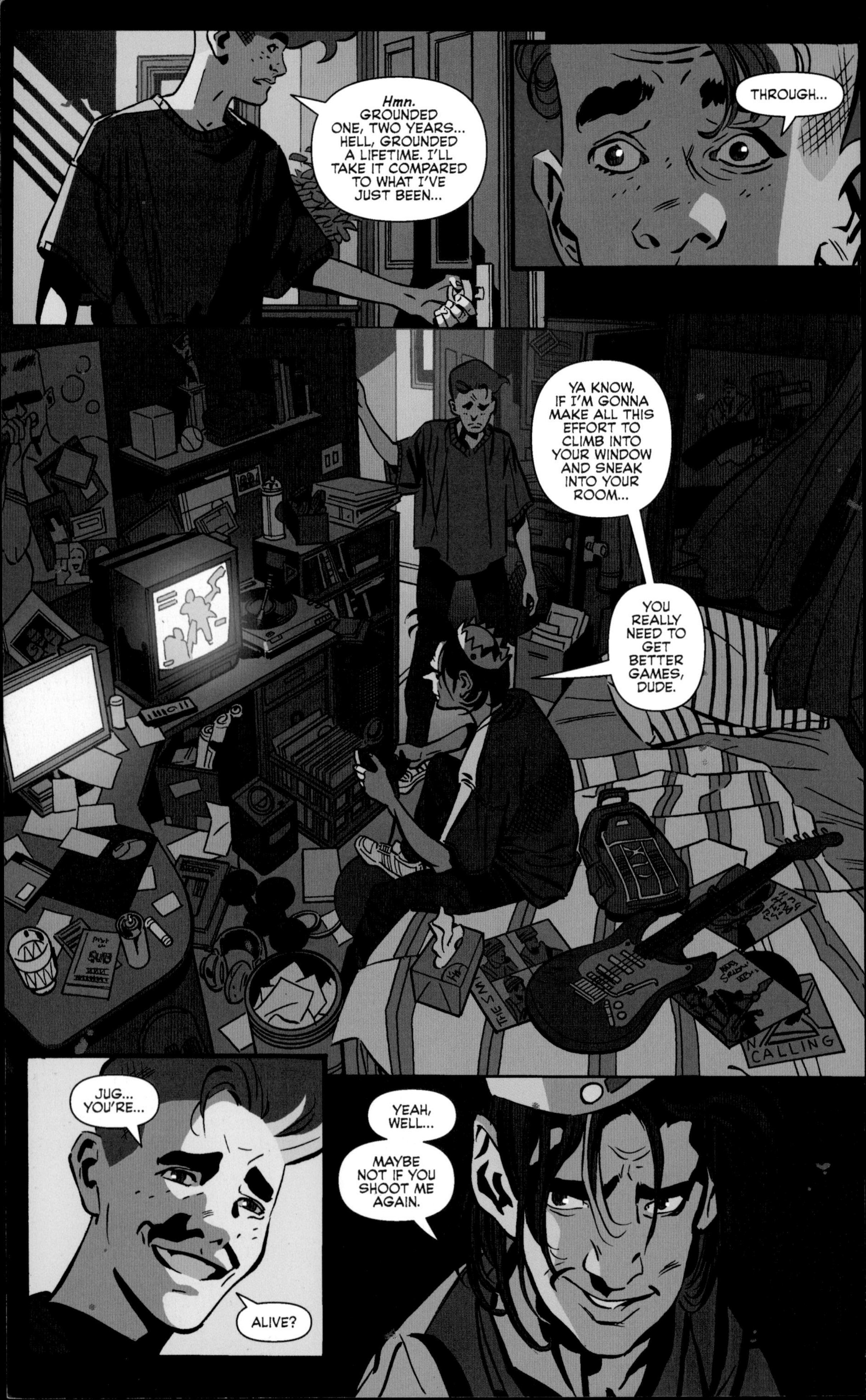

Hmn. GROUNDED ONE, TWO YEARS... HELL, GROUNDED A LIFETIME. I'LL TAKE IT COMPARED TO WHAT I'VE JUST BEEN...
THROUGH...
YA KNOW, IF I'M GONNA MAKE ALL THIS EFFORT TO CLIMB INTO YOUR WINDOW AND SNEAK INTO YOUR ROOM...
YOU REALLY NEED TO GET BETTER GAMES, DUDE.
CALLING
JUG... YOU'RE...
ALIVE?
YEAH, WELL...
MAYBE NOT IF YOU SHOOT ME AGAIN.

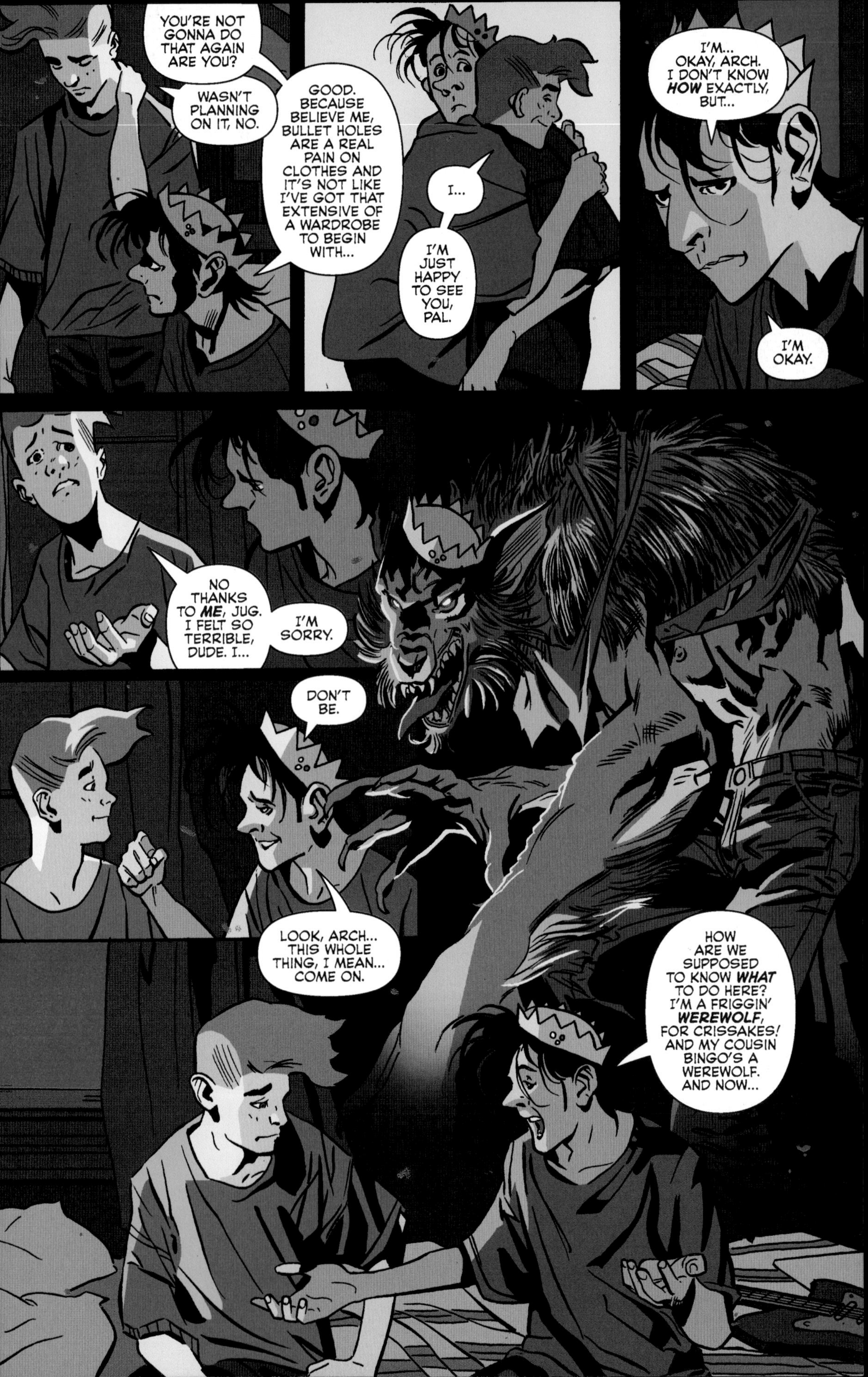
YOU'RE NOT GONNA DO THAT AGAIN ARE YOU?
WASN'T PLANNING ON IT, NO.
GOOD. BECAUSE BELIEVE ME, BULLET HOLES ARE A REAL PAIN ON CLOTHES AND IT'S NOT LIKE I'VE GOT THAT EXTENSIVE OF A WARDROBE TO BEGIN WITH...
I...
I'M JUST HAPPY TO SEE YOU, PAL.
I'M... OKAY, ARCH. I DON'T KNOW HOW EXACTLY, BUT...
I'M OKAY.
NO THANKS TO ME, JUG. I FELT SO TERRIBLE, DUDE. I...
I'M SORRY.
DON'T BE.
LOOK, ARCH... THIS WHOLE THING, I MEAN... COME ON.
HOW ARE WE SUPPOSED TO KNOW WHAT TO DO HERE? I'M A FRIGGIN' WEREWOLF, FOR CRISSAKES! AND MY COUSIN BINGO'S A WEREWOLF. AND NOW...

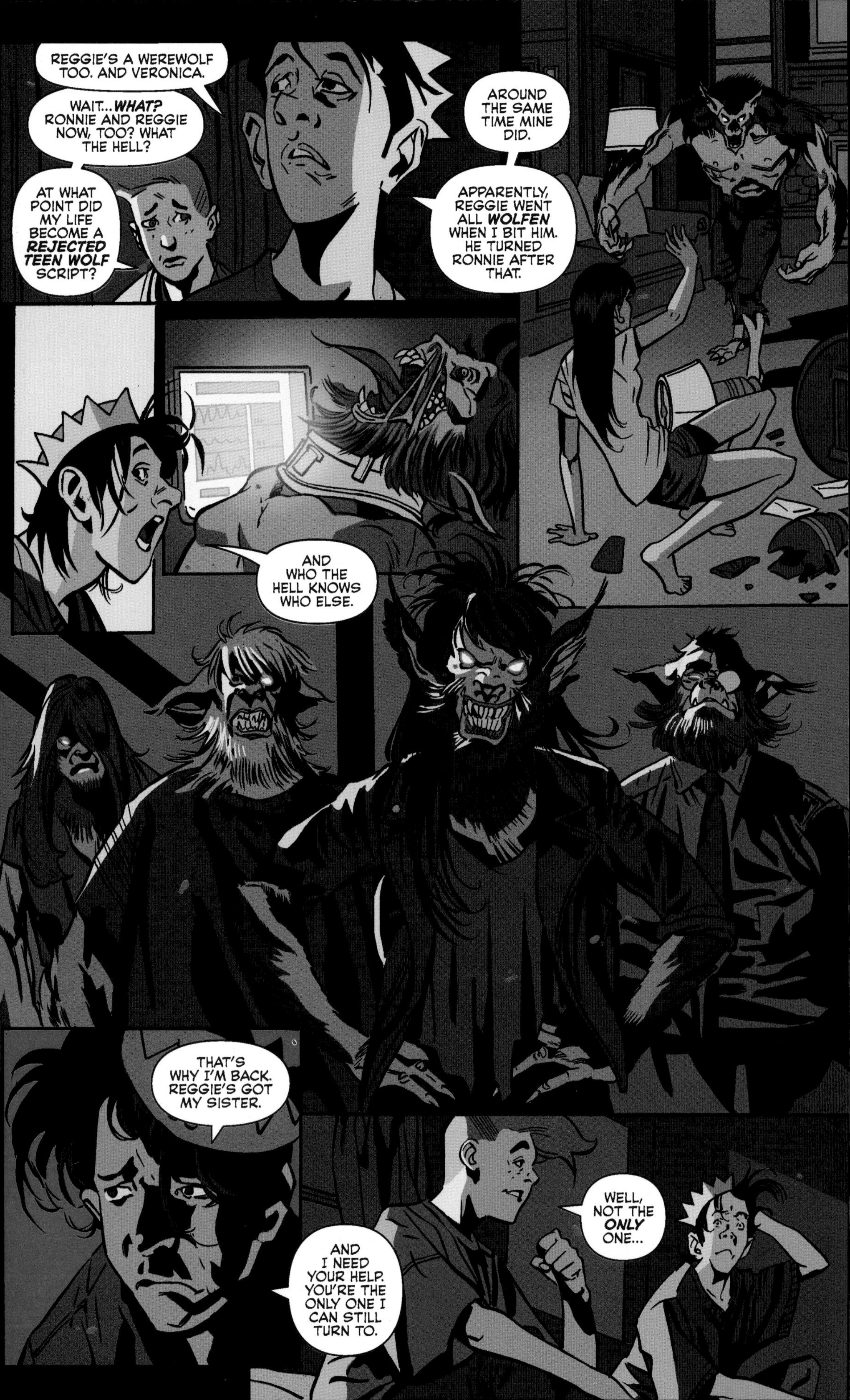
REGGIE'S A WEREWOLF TOO. AND VERONICA.
WAIT... **WHAT?** RONNIE AND REGGIE NOW, TOO? WHAT THE HELL?
AT WHAT POINT DID MY LIFE BECOME A ***REJECTED TEEN WOLF*** SCRIPT?
AROUND THE SAME TIME MINE DID.
APPARENTLY, REGGIE WENT ALL ***WOLFEN*** WHEN I BIT HIM. HE TURNED RONNIE AFTER THAT.
AND WHO THE HELL KNOWS WHO ELSE.
THAT'S WHY I'M BACK. REGGIE'S GOT MY SISTER.
AND I NEED YOUR HELP. YOU'RE THE ONLY ONE I CAN STILL TURN TO.
WELL, NOT THE ***ONLY*** ONE...

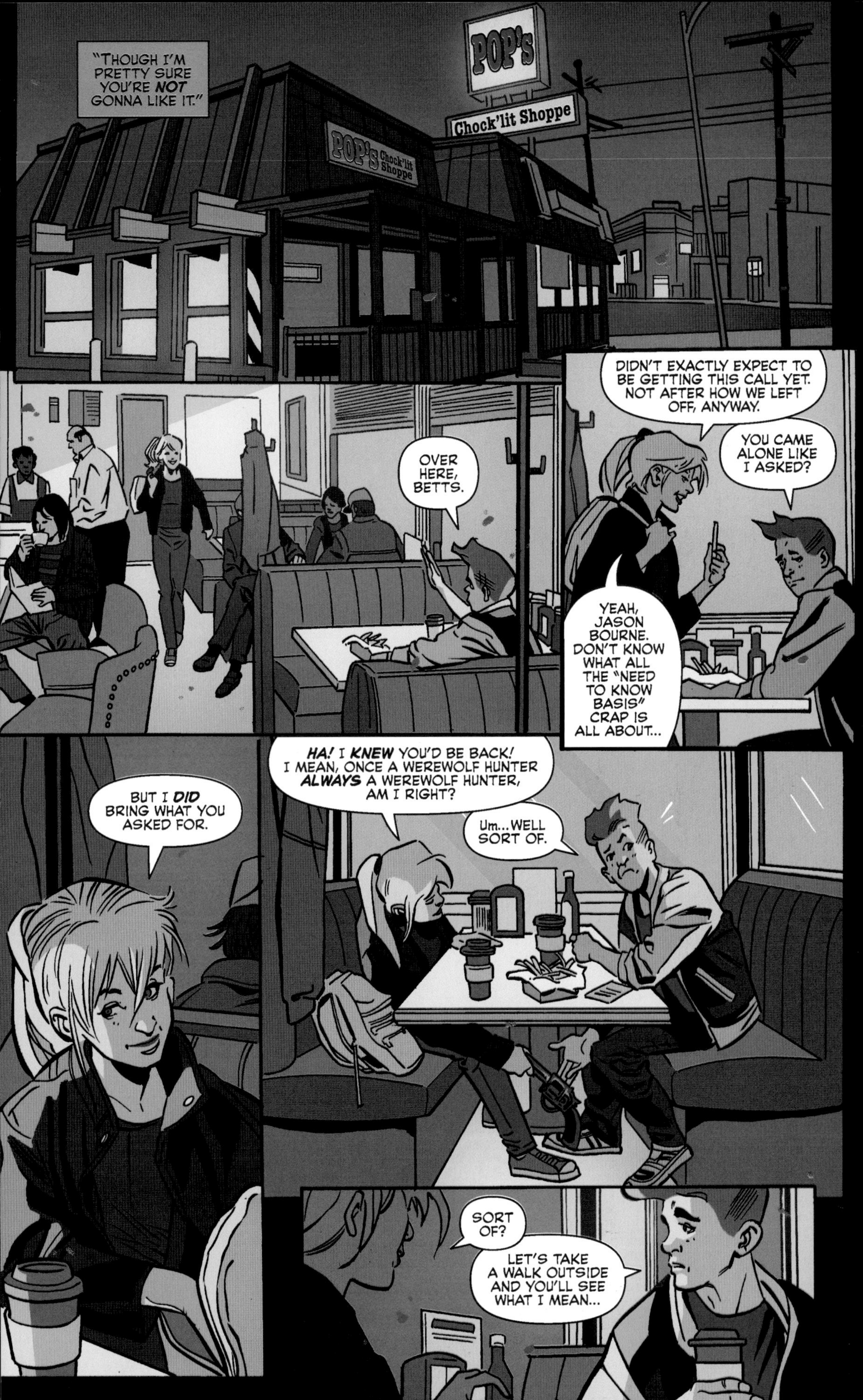
"THOUGH I'M PRETTY SURE YOU'RE NOT GONNA LIKE IT."
POP's
Chock'lit Shoppe
POP's Chock'lit Shoppe
OVER HERE, BETTS.
DIDN'T EXACTLY EXPECT TO BE GETTING THIS CALL YET. NOT AFTER HOW WE LEFT OFF, ANYWAY.
YOU CAME ALONE LIKE I ASKED?
YEAH, JASON BOURNE. DON'T KNOW WHAT ALL THE "NEED TO KNOW BASIS" CRAP IS ALL ABOUT...
BUT I DID BRING WHAT YOU ASKED FOR.
HA! I KNEW YOU'D BE BACK! I MEAN, ONCE A WEREWOLF HUNTER ALWAYS A WEREWOLF HUNTER, AM I RIGHT?
Um...WELL SORT OF.
SORT OF?
LET'S TAKE A WALK OUTSIDE AND YOU'LL SEE WHAT I MEAN...

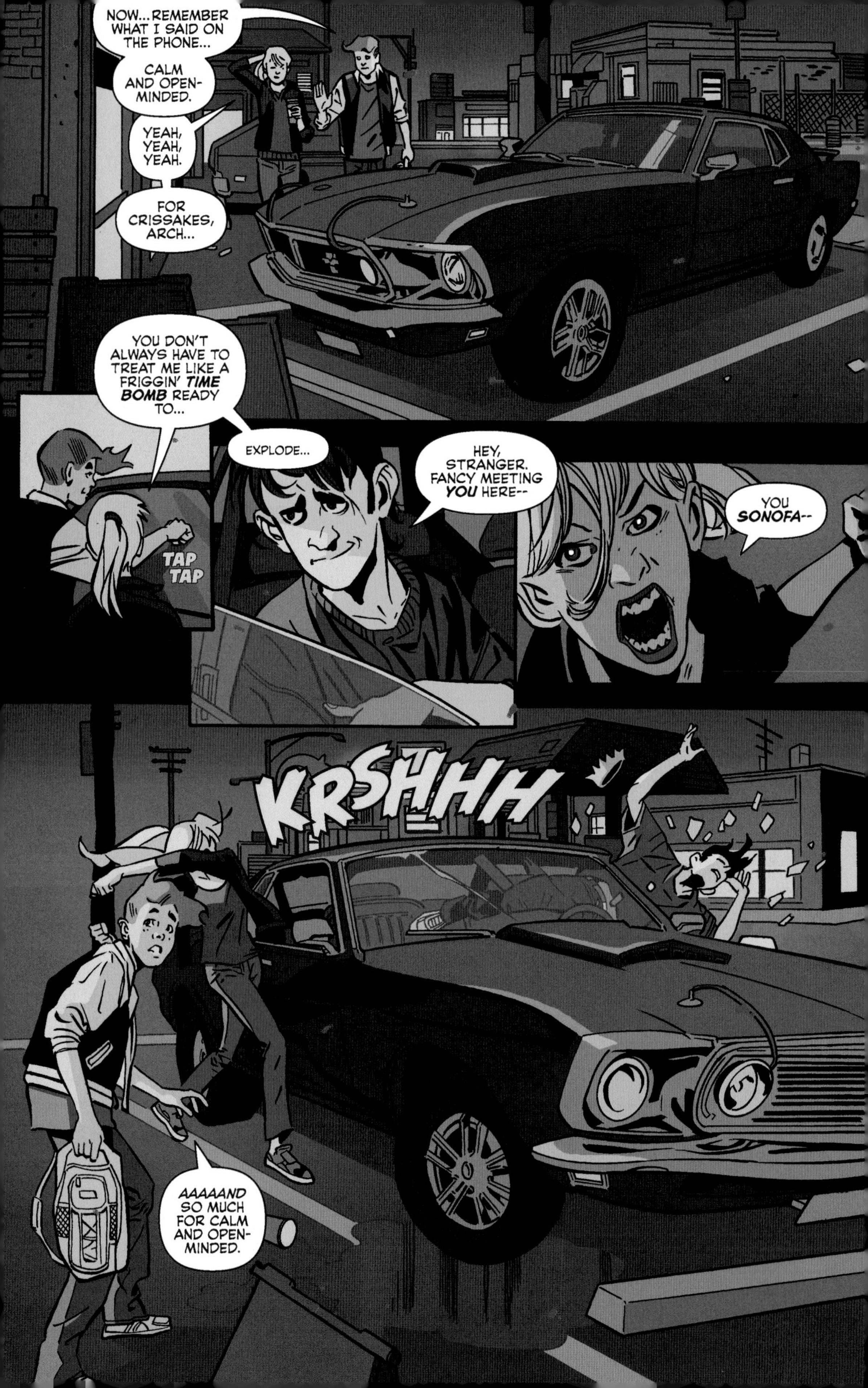

NOW... REMEMBER WHAT I SAID ON THE PHONE...
CALM AND OPEN-MINDED.
YEAH, YEAH, YEAH.
FOR CRISSAKES, ARCH...
YOU DON'T ALWAYS HAVE TO TREAT ME LIKE A FRIGGIN' *TIME BOMB* READY TO...
TAP TAP
EXPLODE...
HEY, STRANGER. FANCY MEETING *YOU* HERE--
YOU *SONOFA*--
KRSHHH
AAAAAND SO MUCH FOR CALM AND OPEN-MINDED.

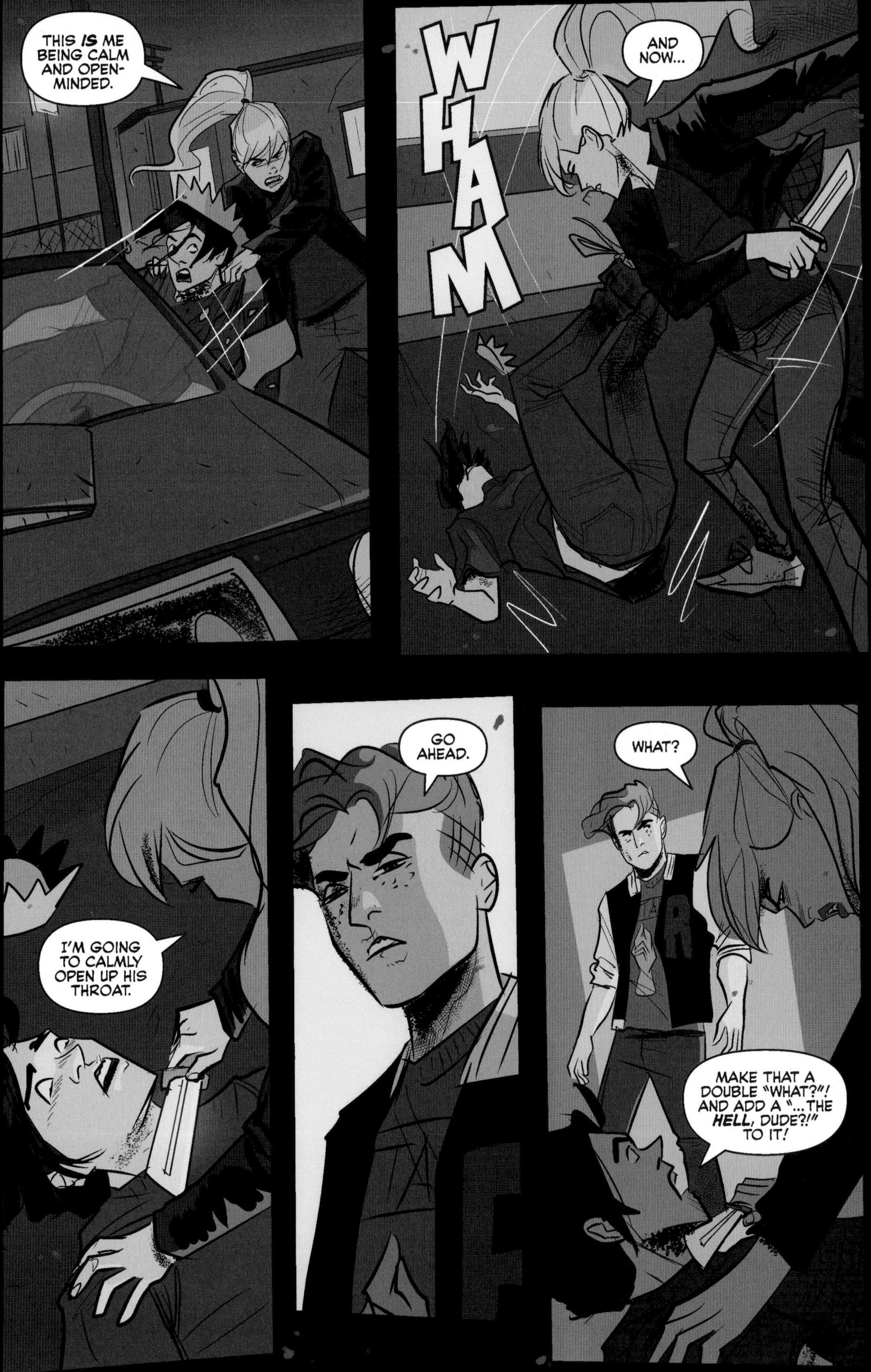
THIS IS ME BEING CALM AND OPEN-MINDED.
WHAM
AND NOW...
I'M GOING TO CALMLY OPEN UP HIS THROAT.
GO AHEAD.
WHAT?
MAKE THAT A DOUBLE "WHAT?"! AND ADD A "...THE HELL, DUDE?!" TO IT!

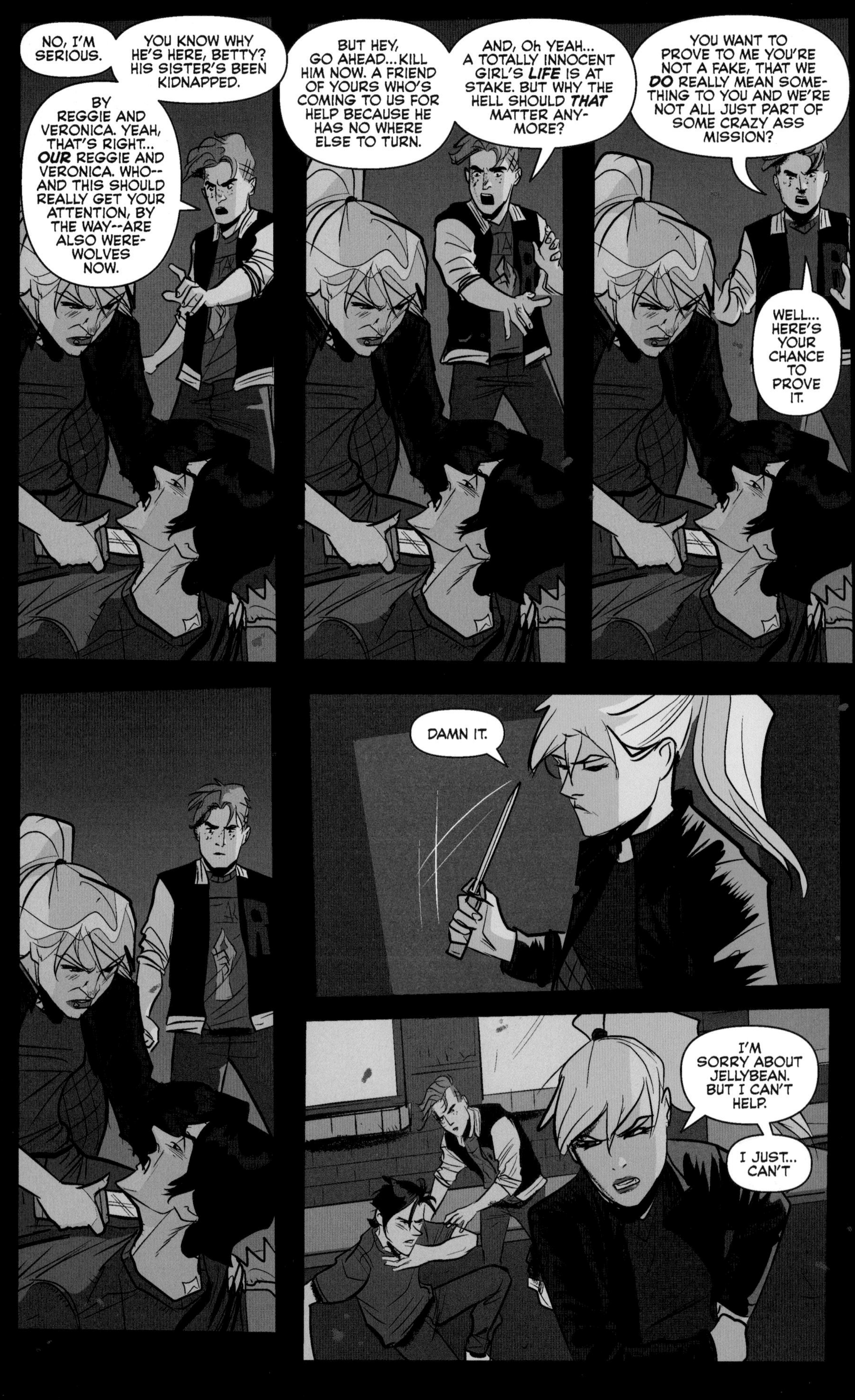
NO, I'M SERIOUS.
YOU KNOW WHY HE'S HERE, BETTY? HIS SISTER'S BEEN KIDNAPPED.
BY REGGIE AND VERONICA. YEAH, THAT'S RIGHT... OUR REGGIE AND VERONICA. WHO-- AND THIS SHOULD REALLY GET YOUR ATTENTION, BY THE WAY--ARE ALSO WERE-WOLVES NOW.
BUT HEY, GO AHEAD...KILL HIM NOW. A FRIEND OF YOURS WHO'S COMING TO US FOR HELP BECAUSE HE HAS NO WHERE ELSE TO TURN.
AND, Oh YEAH... A TOTALLY INNOCENT GIRL'S LIFE IS AT STAKE. BUT WHY THE HELL SHOULD THAT MATTER ANY-MORE?
YOU WANT TO PROVE TO ME YOU'RE NOT A FAKE, THAT WE DO REALLY MEAN SOME-THING TO YOU AND WE'RE NOT ALL JUST PART OF SOME CRAZY ASS MISSION?
WELL... HERE'S YOUR CHANCE TO PROVE IT.
DAMN IT.
I'M SORRY ABOUT JELLYBEAN. BUT I CAN'T HELP.
I JUST... CAN'T

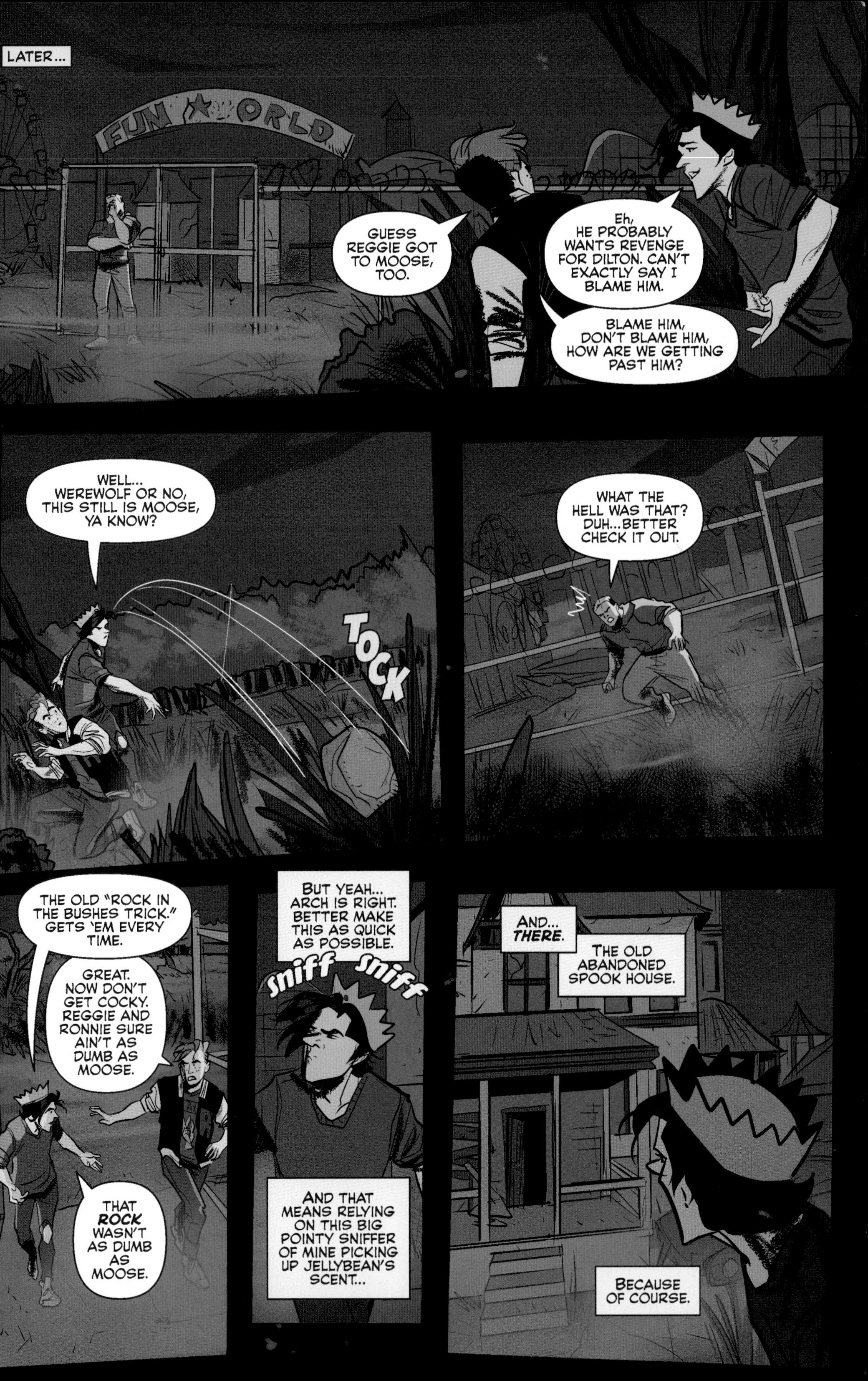
LATER...
FUN ★ ORLD
GUESS REGGIE GOT TO MOOSE, TOO.
Eh, HE PROBABLY WANTS REVENGE FOR DILTON. CAN'T EXACTLY SAY I BLAME HIM.
BLAME HIM, DON'T BLAME HIM, HOW ARE WE GETTING PAST HIM?
WELL... WEREWOLF OR NO, THIS STILL IS MOOSE, YA KNOW?
TOCK
WHAT THE HELL WAS THAT? DUH...BETTER CHECK IT OUT.
THE OLD "ROCK IN THE BUSHES TRICK." GETS 'EM EVERY TIME.
GREAT. NOW DON'T GET COCKY. REGGIE AND RONNIE SURE AIN'T AS DUMB AS MOOSE.
THAT ROCK WASN'T AS DUMB AS MOOSE.
BUT YEAH... ARCH IS RIGHT. BETTER MAKE THIS AS QUICK AS POSSIBLE.
SNIFF SNIFF
AND THAT MEANS RELYING ON THIS BIG POINTY SNIFFER OF MINE PICKING UP JELLYBEAN'S SCENT...
AND... THERE.
THE OLD ABANDONED SPOOK HOUSE.
BECAUSE OF COURSE.

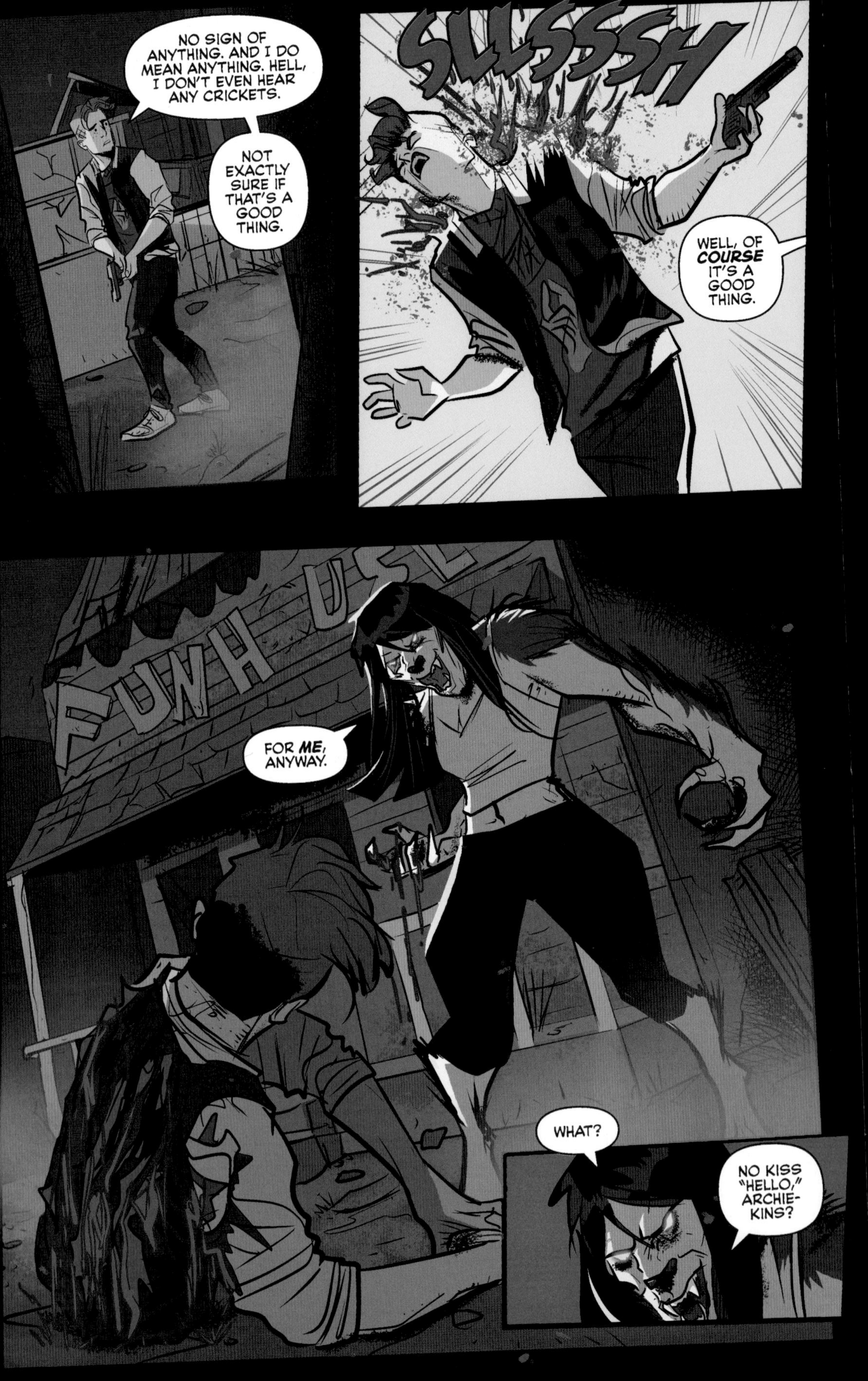
NO SIGN OF ANYTHING. AND I DO MEAN ANYTHING. HELL, I DON'T EVEN HEAR ANY CRICKETS.
NOT EXACTLY SURE IF THAT'S A GOOD THING.
SLLSSSH
WELL, OF COURSE IT'S A GOOD THING.
FOR ME, ANYWAY.
WHAT?
NO KISS "HELLO," ARCHIE-KINS?

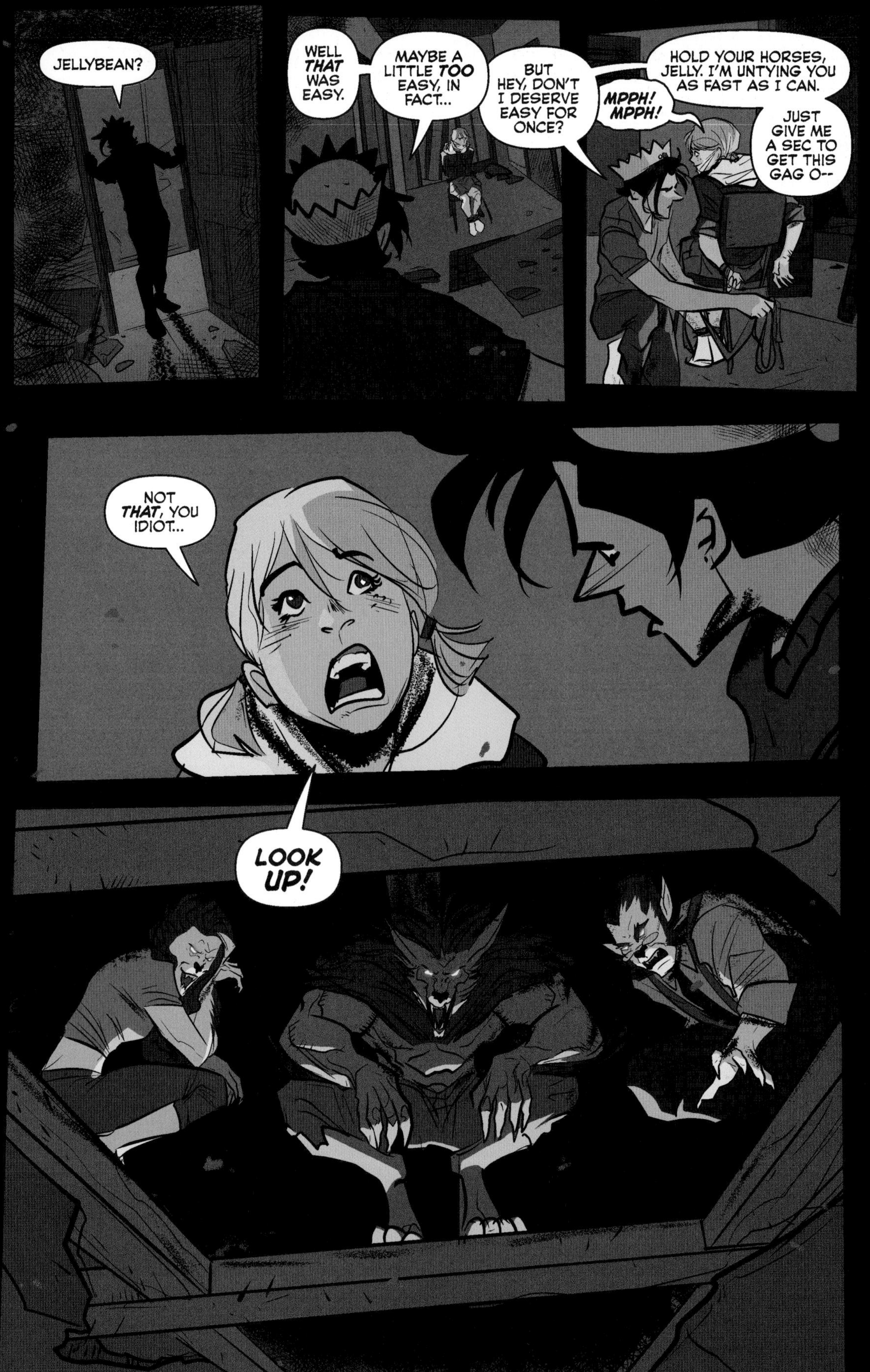
JELLYBEAN?
WELL *THAT* WAS EASY.
MAYBE A LITTLE *TOO* EASY, IN FACT...
BUT HEY, DON'T I DESERVE EASY FOR ONCE?
HOLD YOUR HORSES, JELLY. I'M UNTYING YOU AS FAST AS I CAN.
MPPH! MPPH!
JUST GIVE ME A SEC TO GET THIS GAG O--
NOT *THAT*, YOU IDIOT...
LOOK UP!

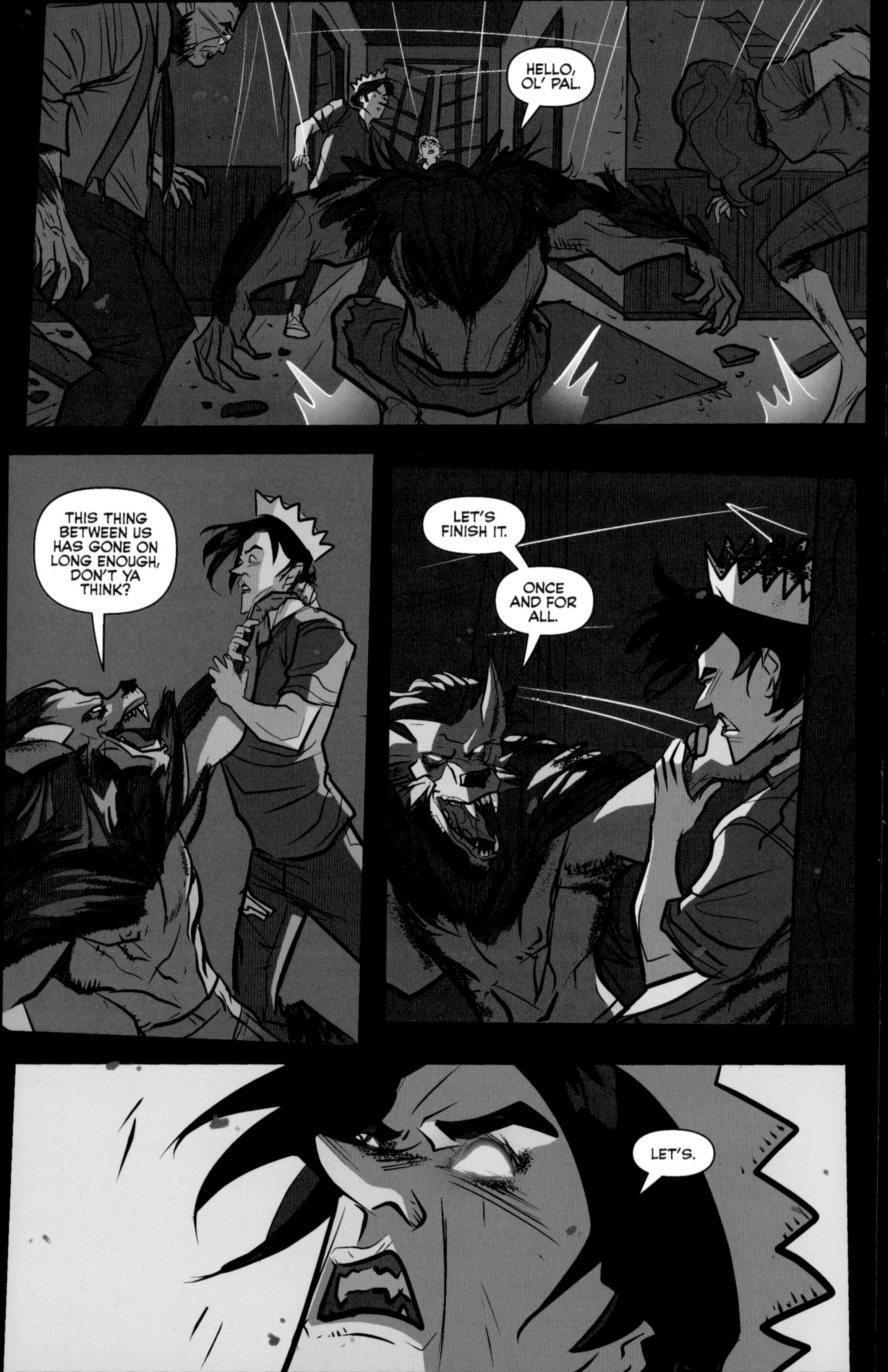
HELLO, OL' PAL.
THIS THING BETWEEN US HAS GONE ON LONG ENOUGH, DON'T YA THINK?
LET'S FINISH IT.
ONCE AND FOR ALL.
LET'S.

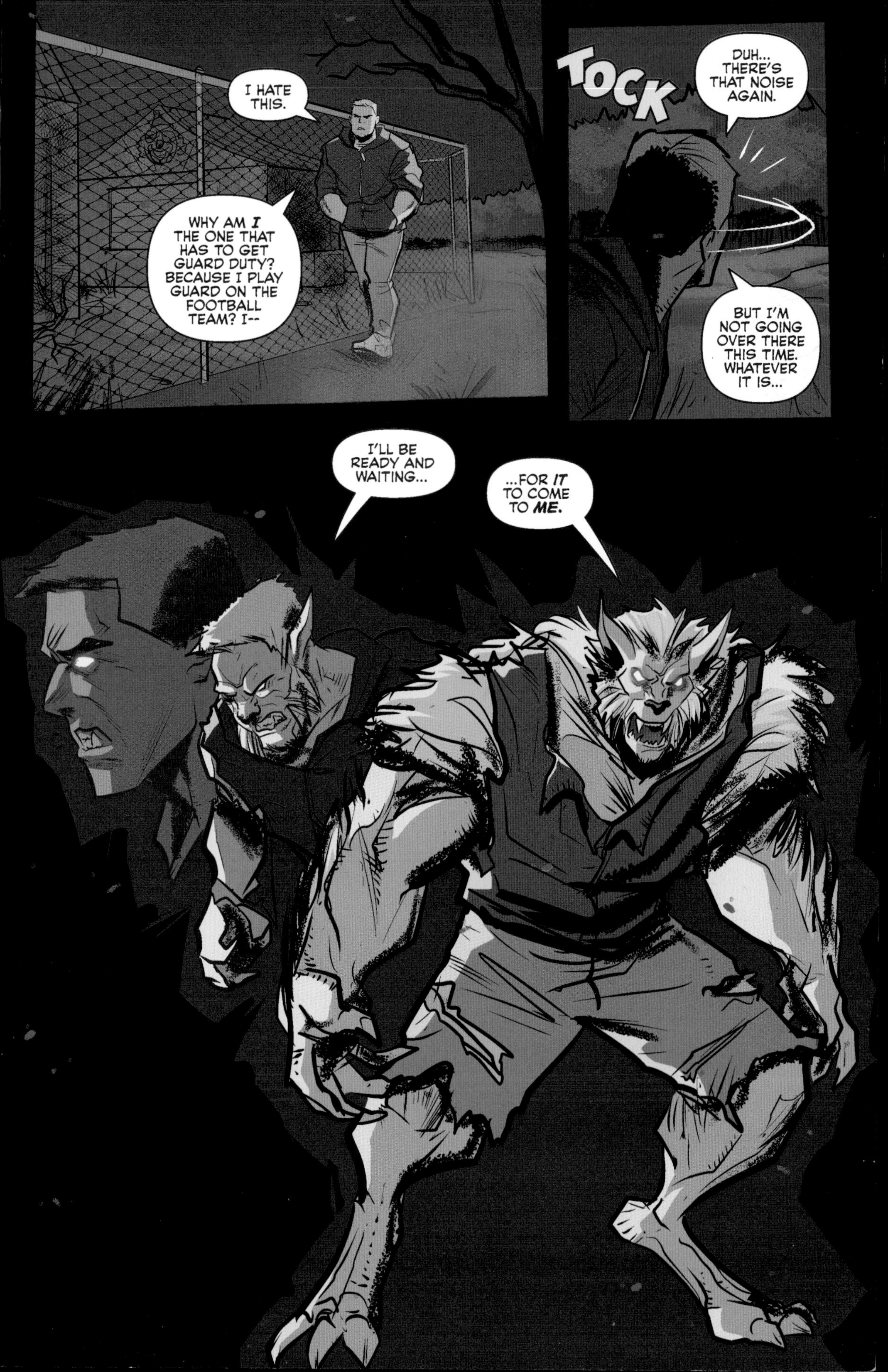
I HATE THIS.
WHY AM *I* THE ONE THAT HAS TO GET GUARD DUTY? BECAUSE I PLAY GUARD ON THE FOOTBALL TEAM? I--
TOCK
DUH... THERE'S THAT NOISE AGAIN.
BUT I'M NOT GOING OVER THERE THIS TIME. WHATEVER IT IS...
I'LL BE READY AND WAITING...
...FOR *IT* TO COME TO ***ME.***

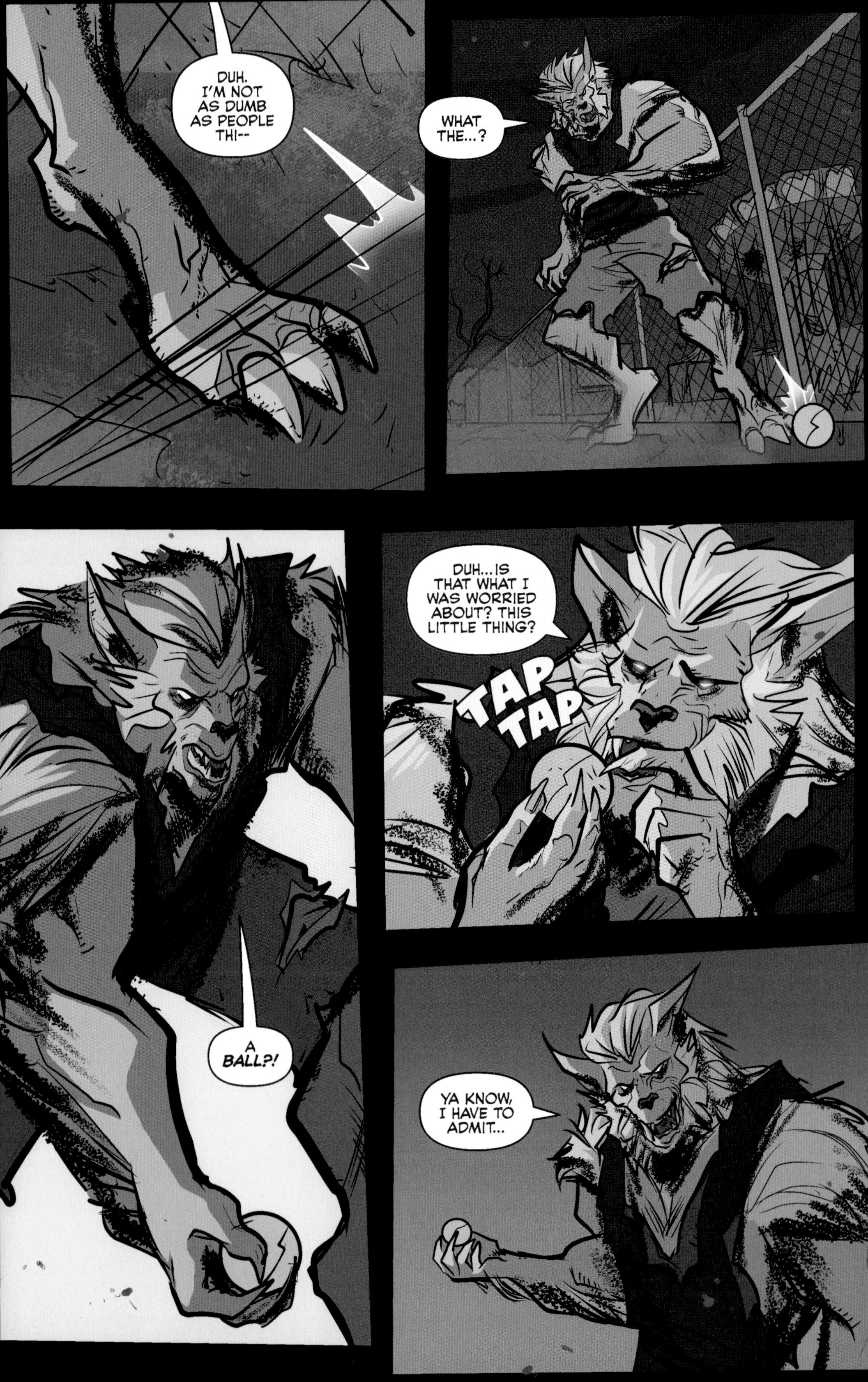
DUH. I'M NOT AS DUMB AS PEOPLE THI--
WHAT THE...?
A BALL?!
DUH...IS THAT WHAT I WAS WORRIED ABOUT? THIS LITTLE THING?
TAP TAP
YA KNOW, I HAVE TO ADMIT...

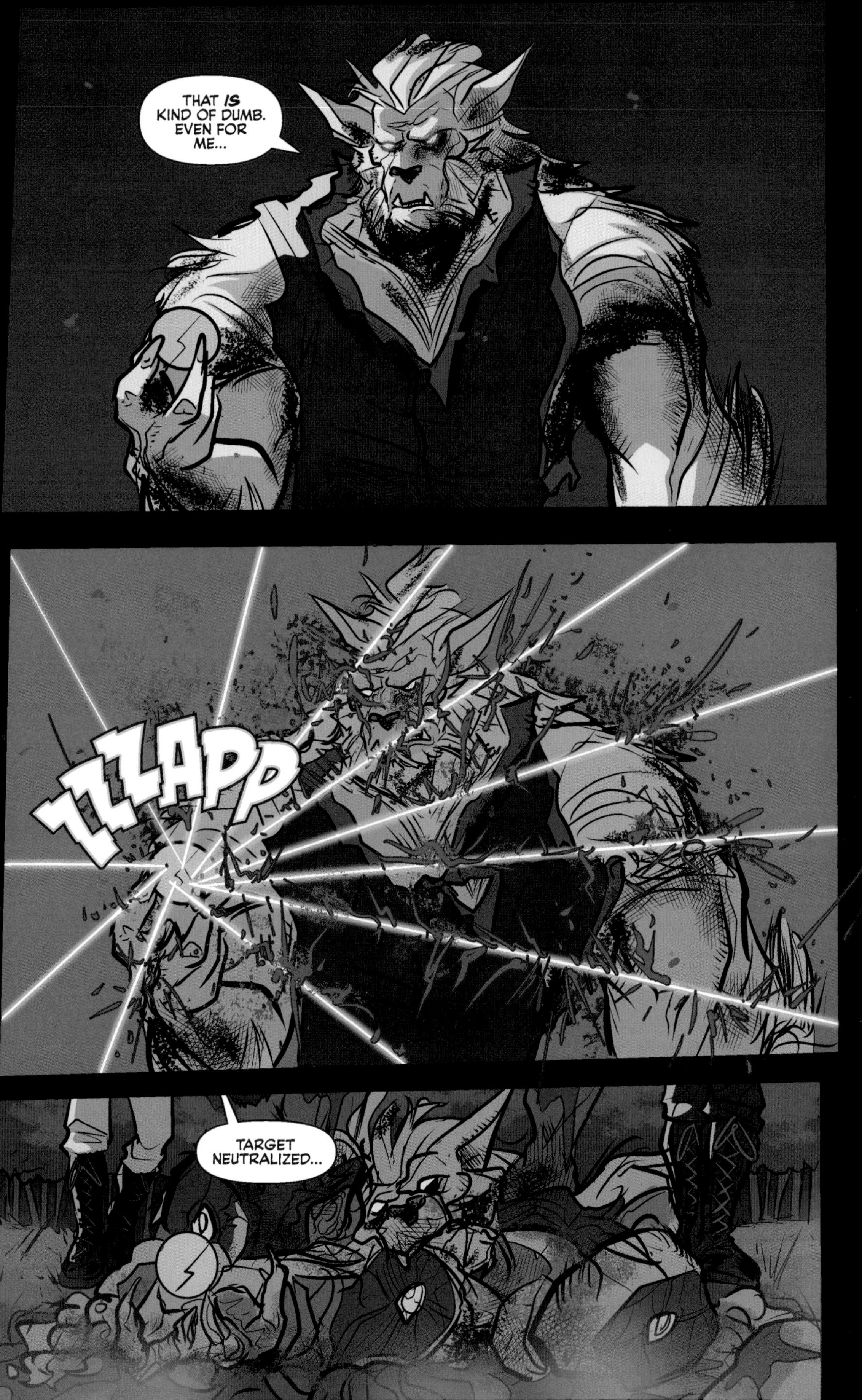
THAT *IS* KIND OF DUMB. EVEN FOR ME...
ZZZAPP
TARGET NEUTRALIZED...

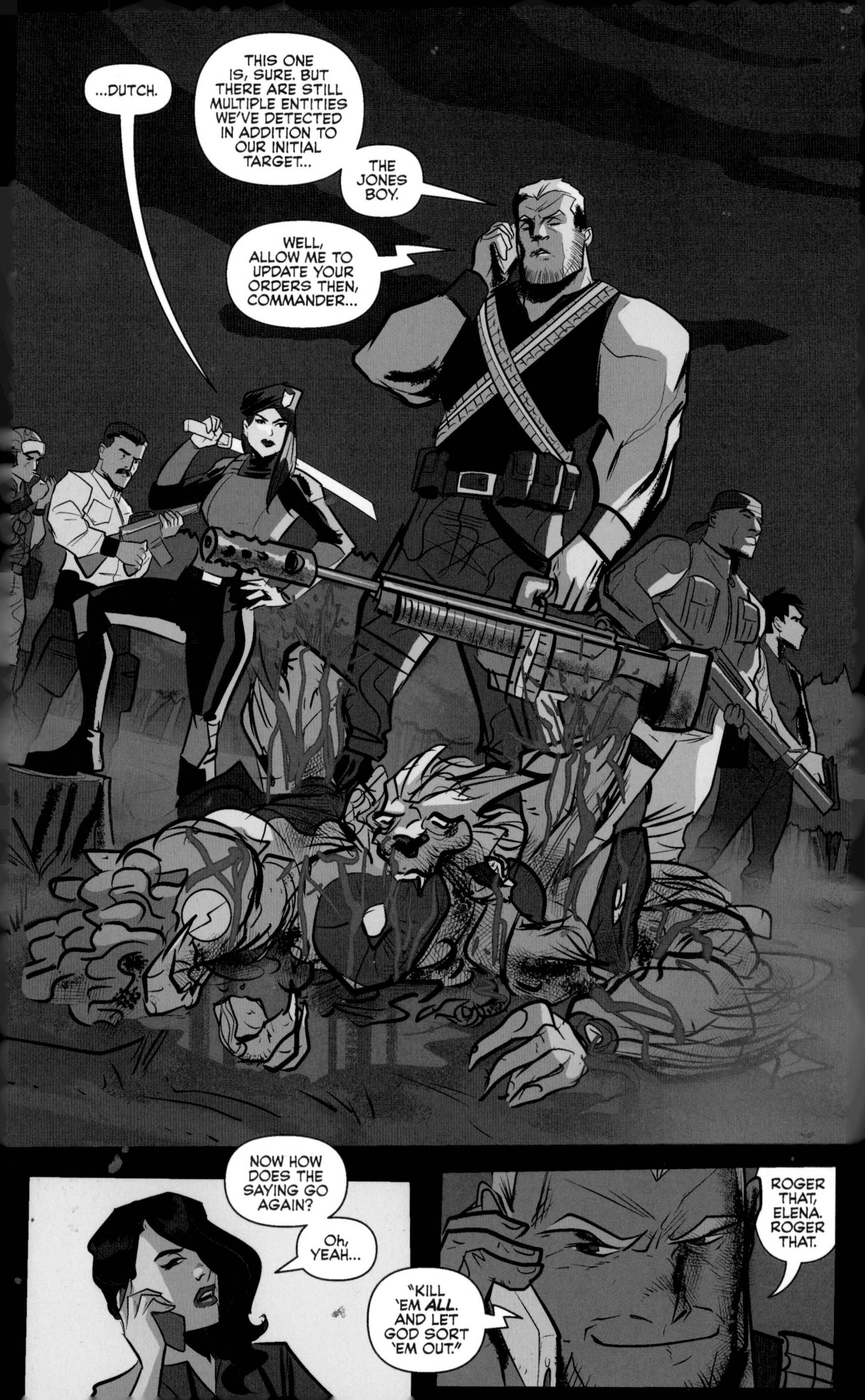
...DUTCH.
THIS ONE IS, SURE. BUT THERE ARE STILL MULTIPLE ENTITIES WE'VE DETECTED IN ADDITION TO OUR INITIAL TARGET...
THE JONES BOY.
WELL, ALLOW ME TO UPDATE YOUR ORDERS THEN, COMMANDER...
NOW HOW DOES THE SAYING GO AGAIN?
Oh, YEAH...
"KILL 'EM ALL. AND LET GOD SORT 'EM OUT."
ROGER THAT, ELENA. ROGER THAT.

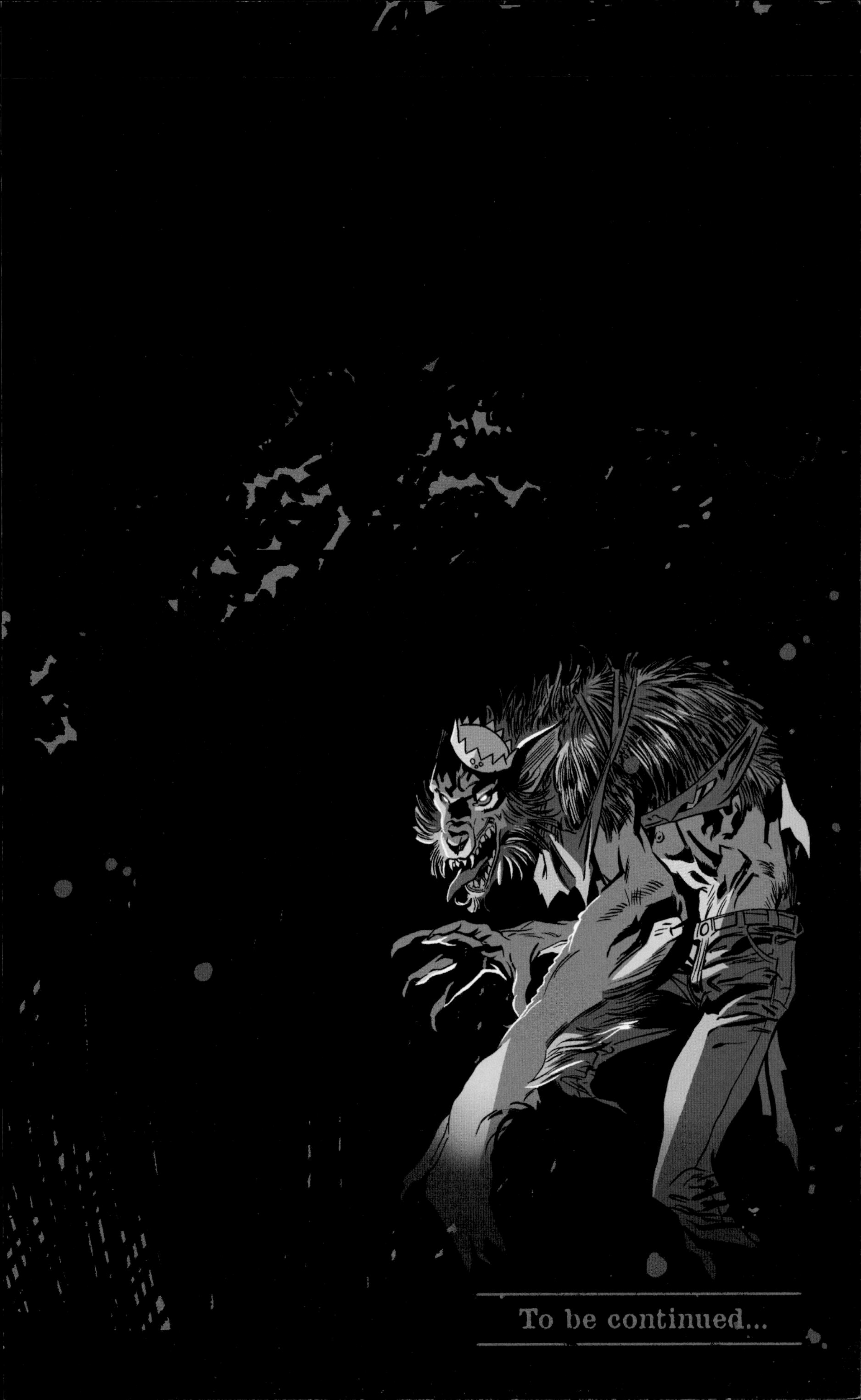
To be continued...

ISSUE SEVEN

COVER ART **Adam Gorham**

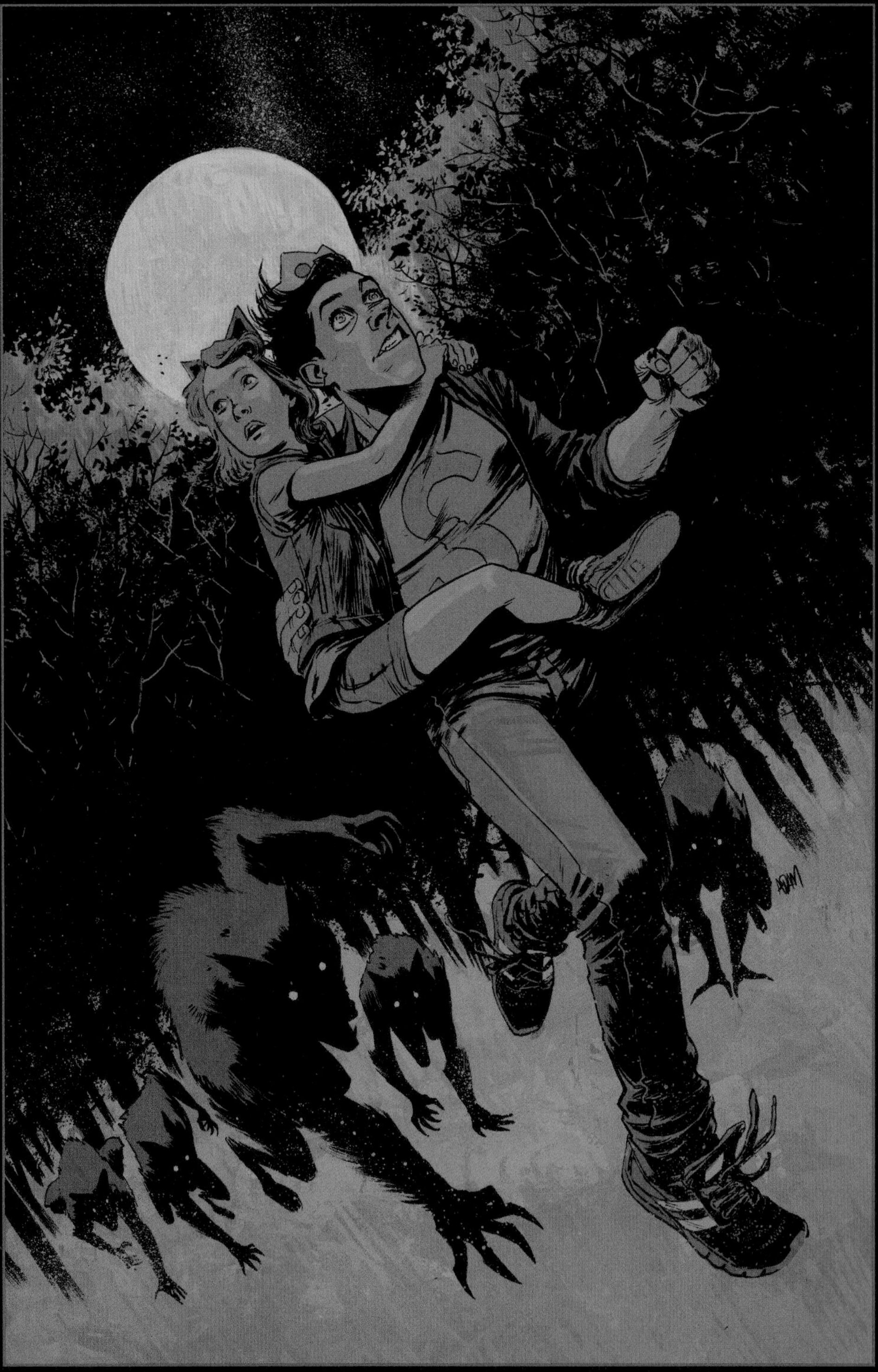

STORY **Frank Tieri** ART **Pat & Tim Kennedy** (p. 1-10) **Joe Eisma** (p. 11-20)
COLORS **Matt Herms** INKS **Bob Smith** (p. 1-6, 10) **Ryan Jampole** (p. 7-9)
LETTERING **Jack Morelli**

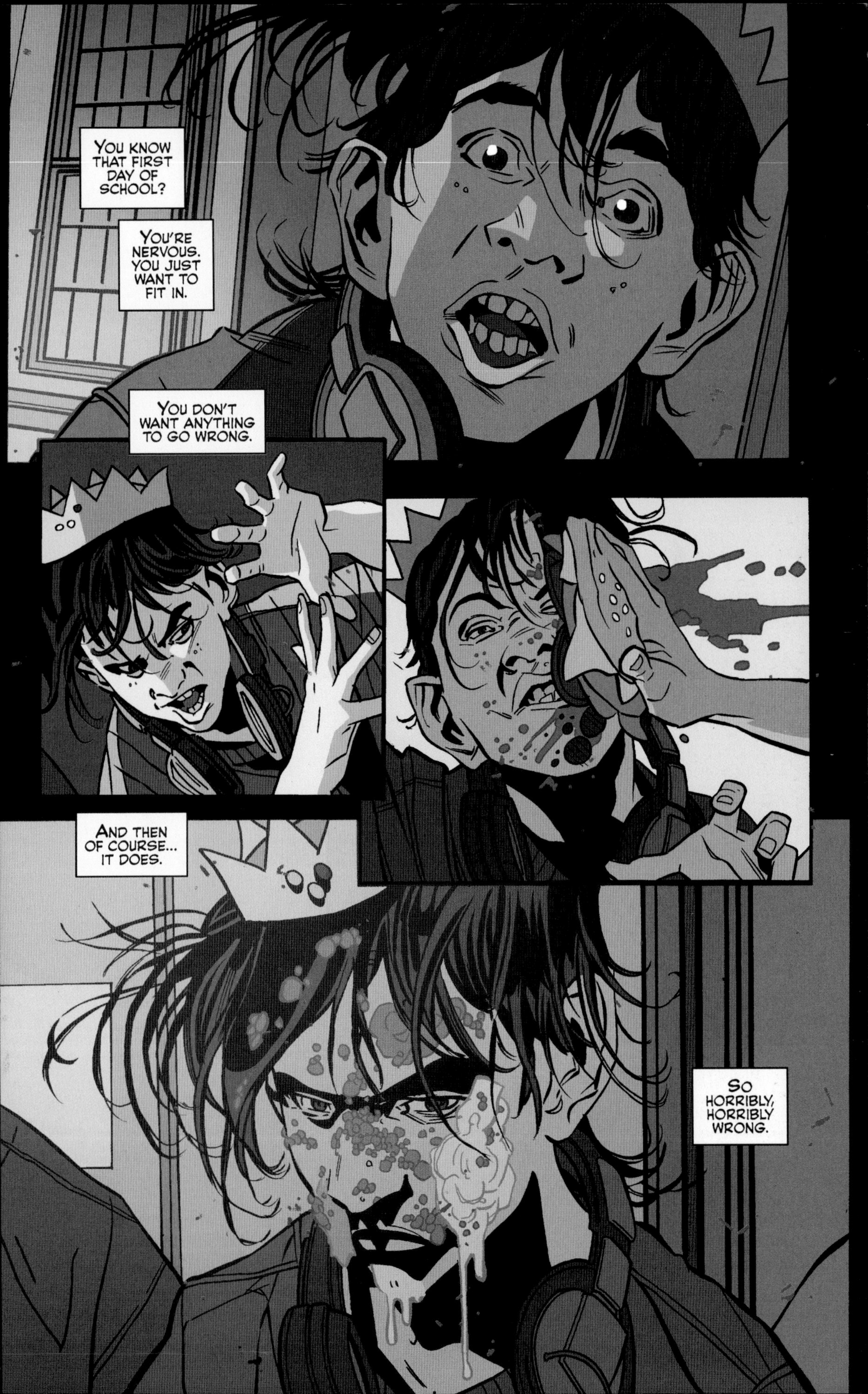

YOU KNOW THAT FIRST DAY OF SCHOOL?
YOU'RE NERVOUS. YOU JUST WANT TO FIT IN.
YOU DON'T WANT ANYTHING TO GO WRONG.
AND THEN OF COURSE... IT DOES.
SO HORRIBLY, HORRIBLY WRONG.

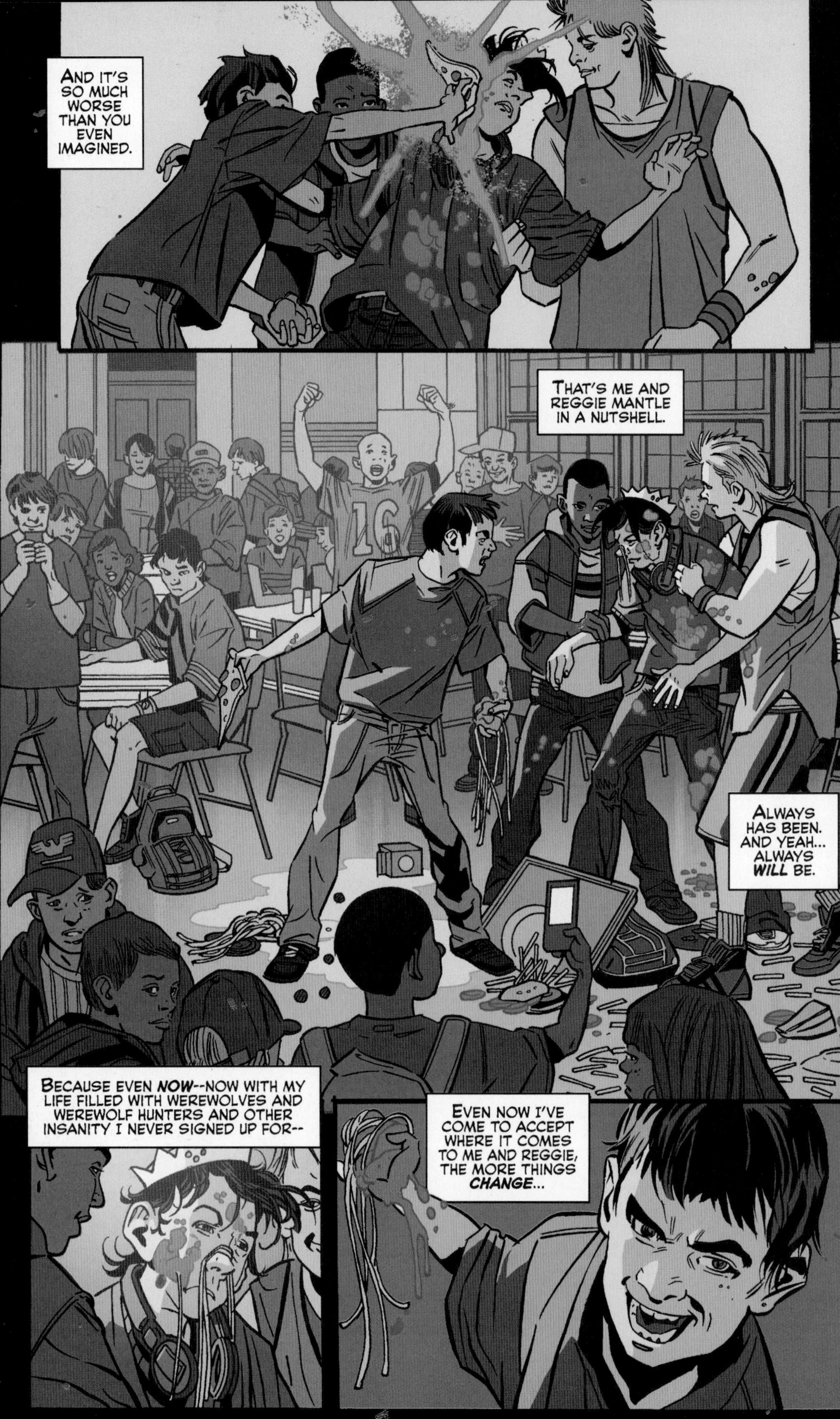
AND IT'S SO MUCH WORSE THAN YOU EVEN IMAGINED.
THAT'S ME AND REGGIE MANTLE IN A NUTSHELL.
16
ALWAYS HAS BEEN. AND YEAH... ALWAYS *WILL* BE.
BECAUSE EVEN *NOW*--NOW WITH MY LIFE FILLED WITH WEREWOLVES AND WEREWOLF HUNTERS AND OTHER INSANITY I NEVER SIGNED UP FOR--
EVEN NOW I'VE COME TO ACCEPT WHERE IT COMES TO ME AND REGGIE, THE MORE THINGS *CHANGE*...

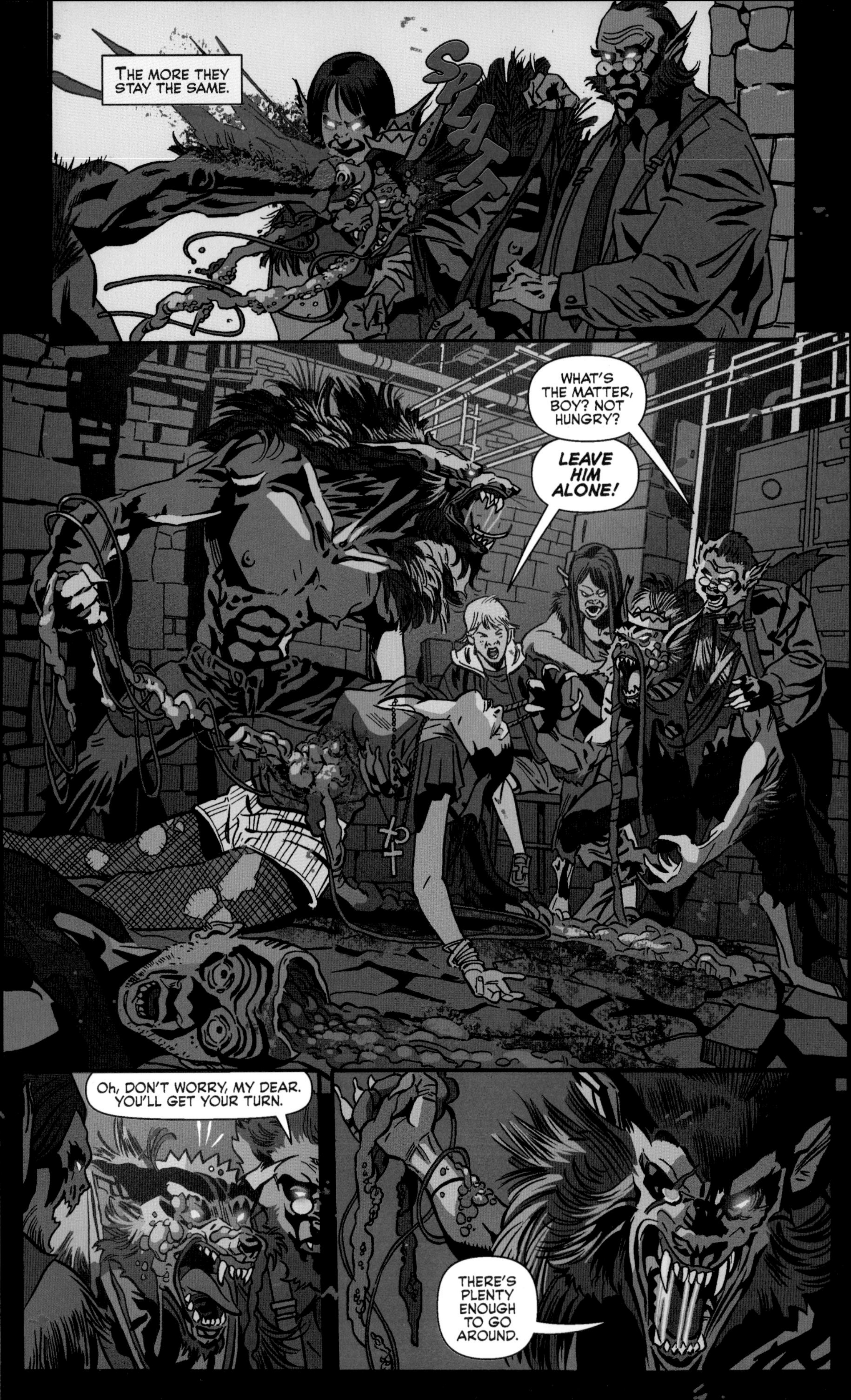

THE MORE THEY STAY THE SAME.
SPLATT
WHAT'S THE MATTER, BOY? NOT HUNGRY?
LEAVE HIM ALONE!
Oh, DON'T WORRY, MY DEAR. YOU'LL GET YOUR TURN.
THERE'S PLENTY ENOUGH TO GO AROUND.

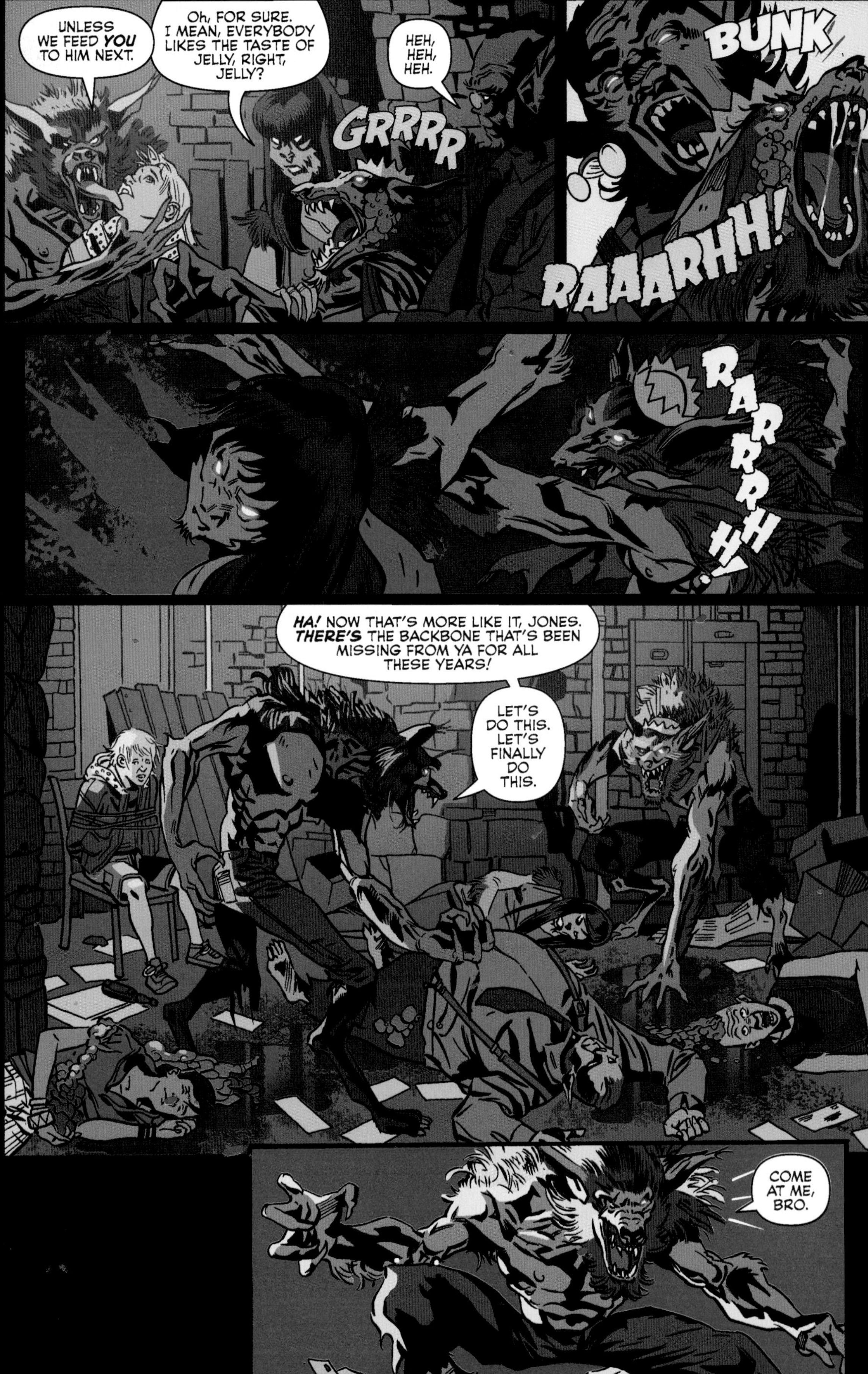
UNLESS WE FEED *YOU* TO HIM NEXT.
Oh, FOR SURE. I MEAN, EVERYBODY LIKES THE TASTE OF JELLY, RIGHT, JELLY?
HEH, HEH, HEH.
GRRRR
BUNK
RAAARHH!
RARRRRH!
HA! NOW THAT'S MORE LIKE IT, JONES. *THERE'S* THE BACKBONE THAT'S BEEN MISSING FROM YA FOR ALL THESE YEARS!
LET'S DO THIS. LET'S FINALLY DO THIS.
COME AT ME, BRO.

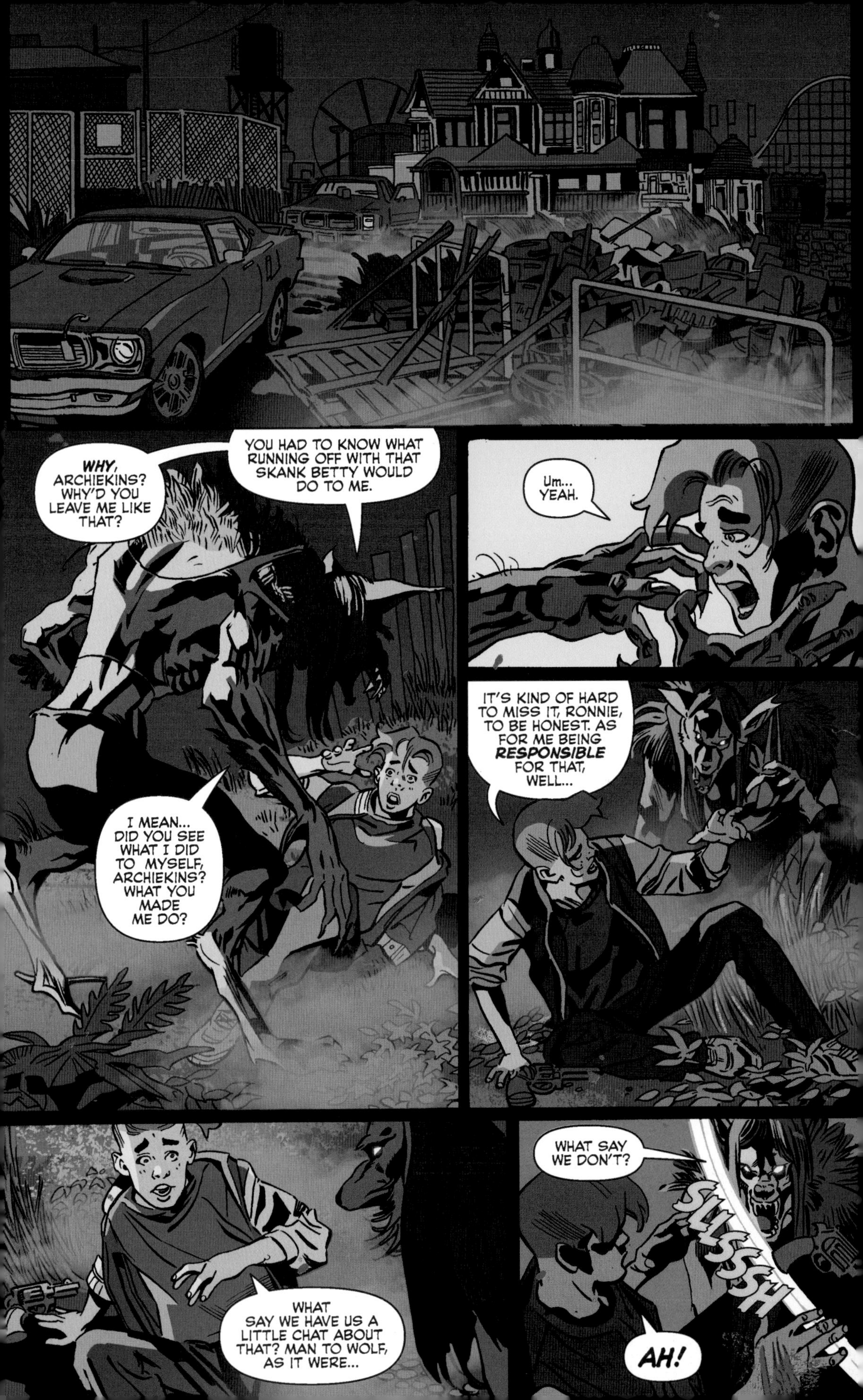

WHY, ARCHIEKINS? WHY'D YOU LEAVE ME LIKE THAT?
YOU HAD TO KNOW WHAT RUNNING OFF WITH THAT SKANK BETTY WOULD DO TO ME.
Um... YEAH.
I MEAN... DID YOU SEE WHAT I DID TO MYSELF, ARCHIEKINS? WHAT YOU MADE ME DO?
IT'S KIND OF HARD TO MISS IT, RONNIE, TO BE HONEST. AS FOR ME BEING **RESPONSIBLE** FOR THAT, WELL...
WHAT SAY WE HAVE US A LITTLE CHAT ABOUT THAT? MAN TO WOLF, AS IT WERE...
WHAT SAY WE DON'T?
SHLSSSH
AH!

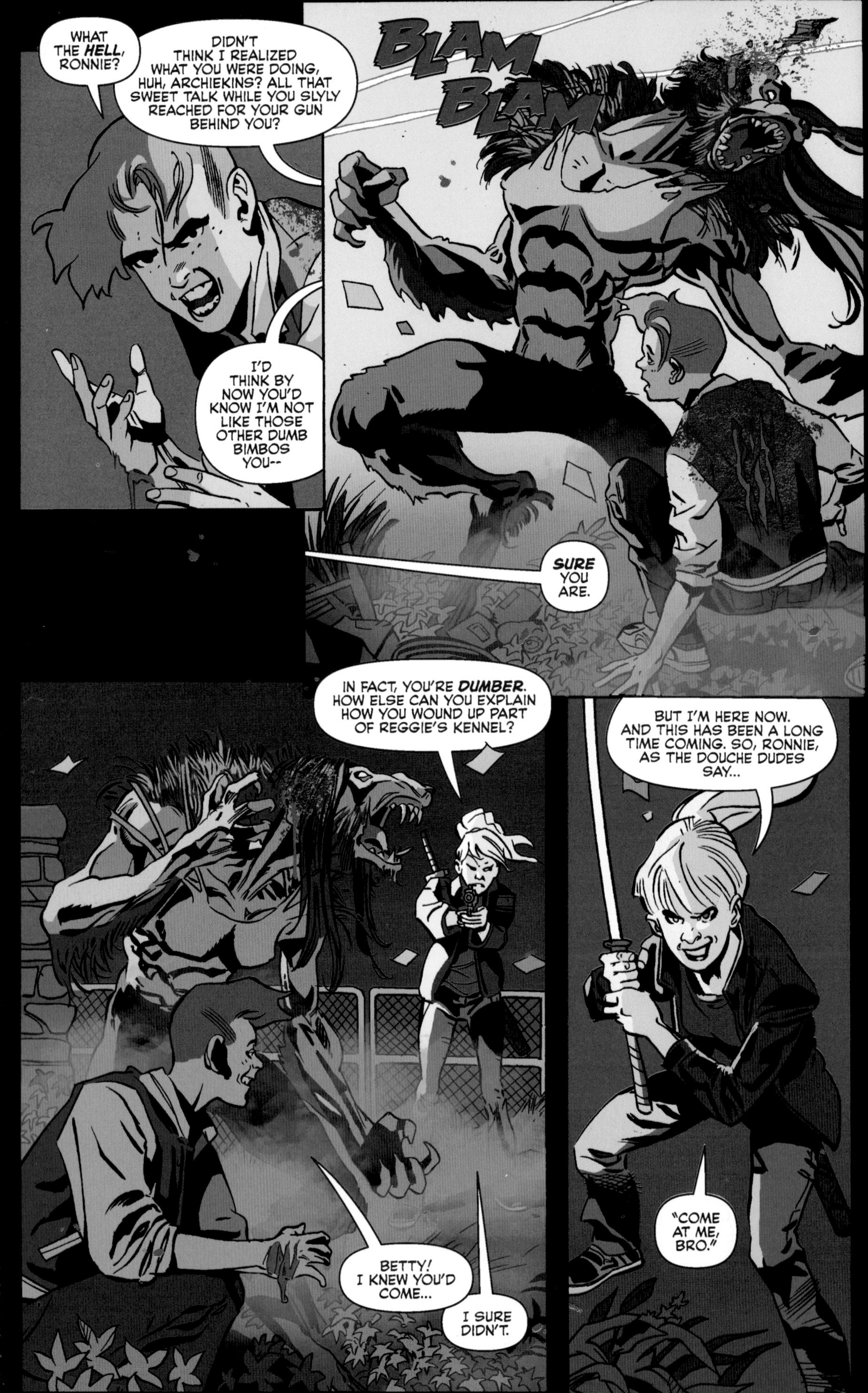
WHAT THE HELL, RONNIE?
DIDN'T THINK I REALIZED WHAT YOU WERE DOING, HUH, ARCHIEKINS? ALL THAT SWEET TALK WHILE YOU SLYLY REACHED FOR YOUR GUN BEHIND YOU?
I'D THINK BY NOW YOU'D KNOW I'M NOT LIKE THOSE OTHER DUMB BIMBOS YOU--
BLAM BLAM
SURE YOU ARE.
IN FACT, YOU'RE DUMBER. HOW ELSE CAN YOU EXPLAIN HOW YOU WOUND UP PART OF REGGIE'S KENNEL?
BETTY! I KNEW YOU'D COME...
I SURE DIDN'T.
BUT I'M HERE NOW. AND THIS HAS BEEN A LONG TIME COMING. SO, RONNIE, AS THE DOUCHE DUDES SAY...
"COME AT ME, BRO."

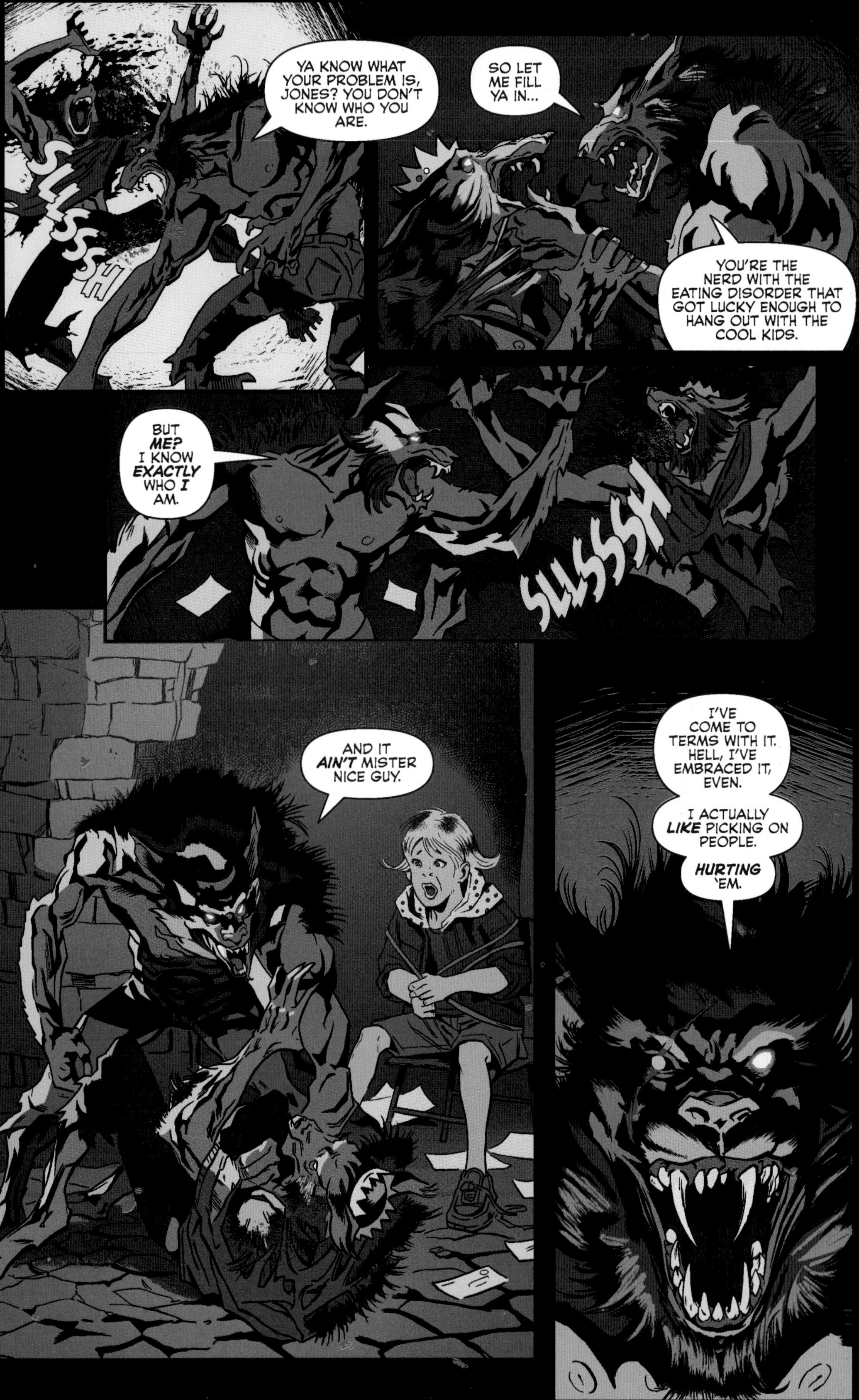
SLISSSH
YA KNOW WHAT YOUR PROBLEM IS, JONES? YOU DON'T KNOW WHO YOU ARE.
SO LET ME FILL YA IN...
YOU'RE THE NERD WITH THE EATING DISORDER THAT GOT LUCKY ENOUGH TO HANG OUT WITH THE COOL KIDS.
BUT ME? I KNOW EXACTLY WHO I AM.
SLISSSH
AND IT AIN'T MISTER NICE GUY.
I'VE COME TO TERMS WITH IT. HELL, I'VE EMBRACED IT, EVEN.
I ACTUALLY LIKE PICKING ON PEOPLE.
HURTING 'EM.

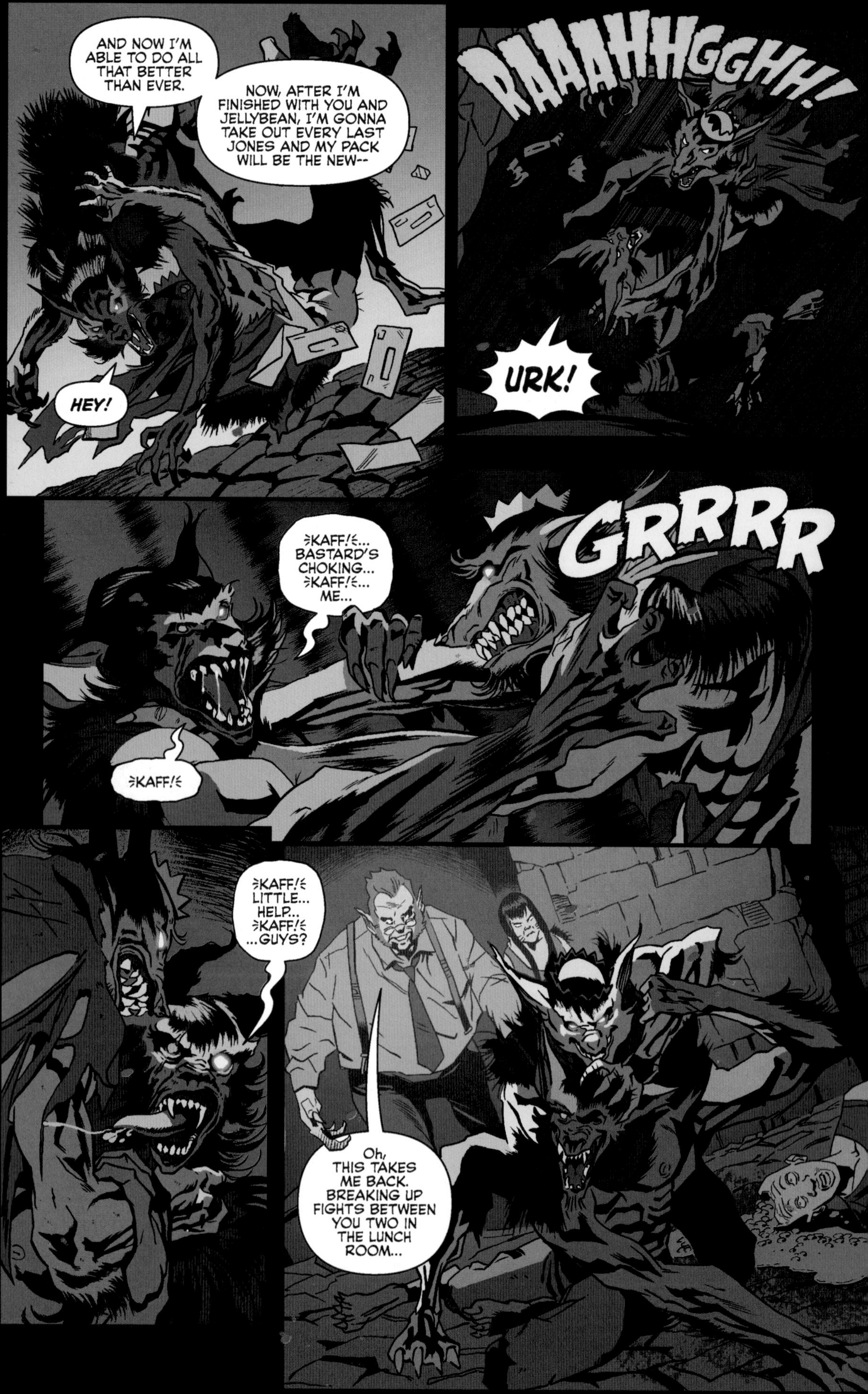
AND NOW I'M ABLE TO DO ALL THAT BETTER THAN EVER.
NOW, AFTER I'M FINISHED WITH YOU AND JELLYBEAN, I'M GONNA TAKE OUT EVERY LAST JONES AND MY PACK WILL BE THE NEW--
HEY!
RAAAHHGGHH!
URK!
KAFF!... BASTARD'S CHOKING... *KAFF!*... ME...
KAFF!
GRRRR
KAFF! LITTLE... HELP... *KAFF!* ...GUYS?
Oh, THIS TAKES ME BACK. BREAKING UP FIGHTS BETWEEN YOU TWO IN THE LUNCH ROOM...

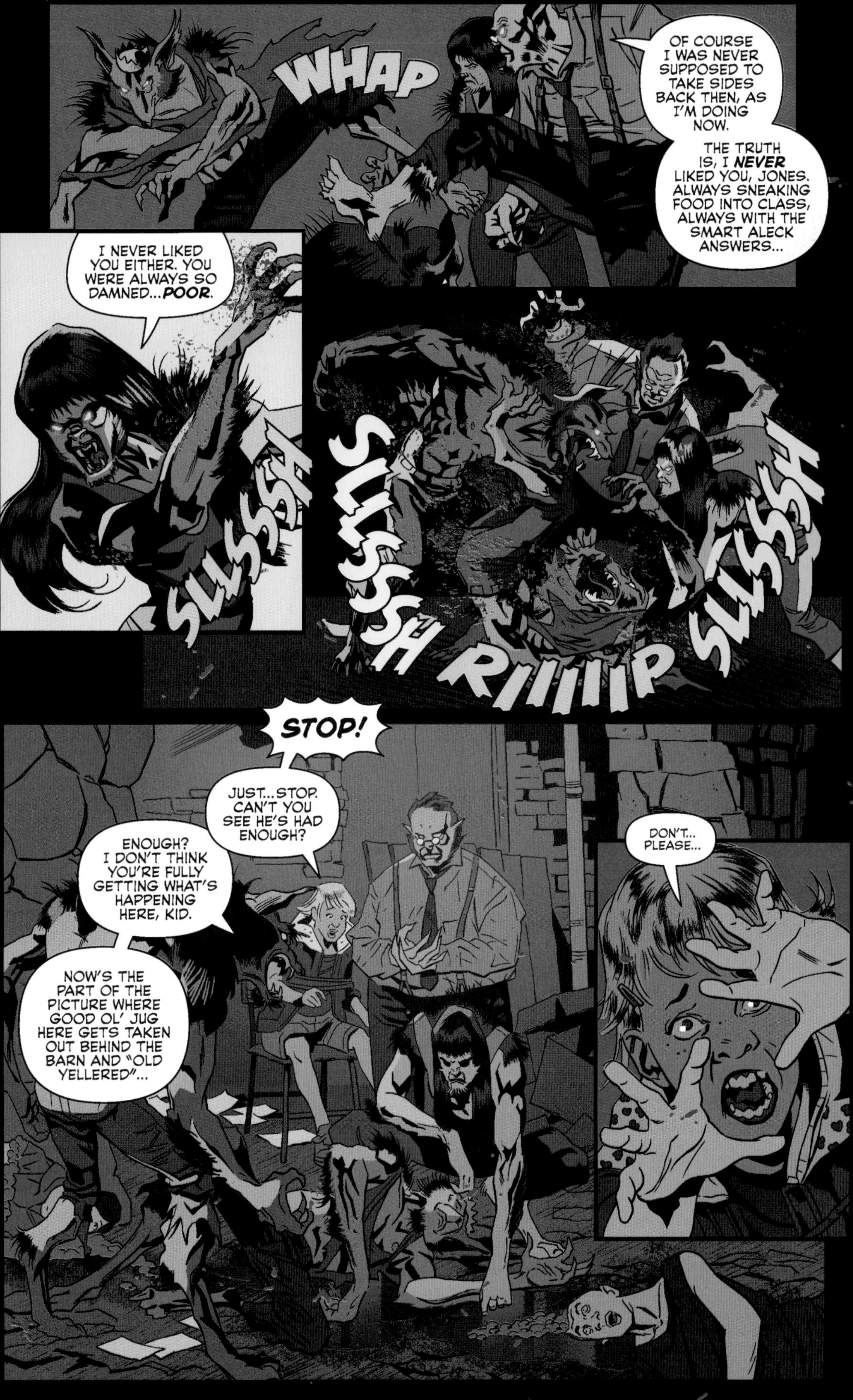

WHAP
OF COURSE I WAS NEVER SUPPOSED TO TAKE SIDES BACK THEN, AS I'M DOING NOW.
THE TRUTH IS, I **NEVER** LIKED YOU, JONES. ALWAYS SNEAKING FOOD INTO CLASS, ALWAYS WITH THE SMART ALECK ANSWERS...
I NEVER LIKED YOU EITHER. YOU WERE ALWAYS SO DAMNED...**POOR**.
SLISSSH
SLISSSH
RIIIIIP
SLISSSH
STOP!
JUST...STOP. CAN'T YOU SEE HE'S HAD ENOUGH?
ENOUGH? I DON'T THINK YOU'RE FULLY GETTING WHAT'S HAPPENING HERE, KID.
NOW'S THE PART OF THE PICTURE WHERE GOOD OL' JUG HERE GETS TAKEN OUT BEHIND THE BARN AND "OLD YELLERED"...
DON'T... PLEASE...

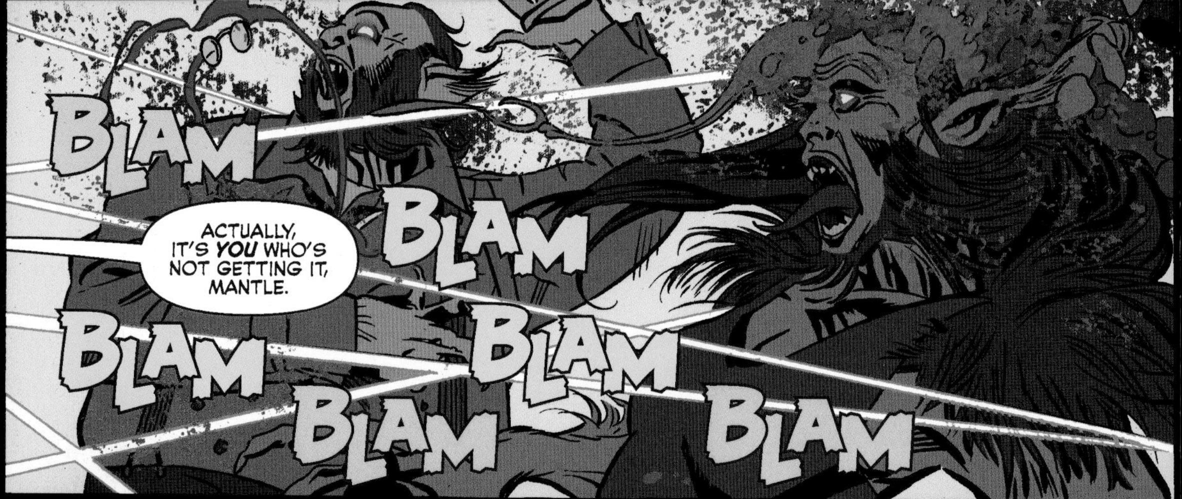
BLAM
ACTUALLY, IT'S YOU WHO'S NOT GETTING IT, MANTLE.
BLAM
BLAM
BLAM
BLAM
BLAM
BLAM

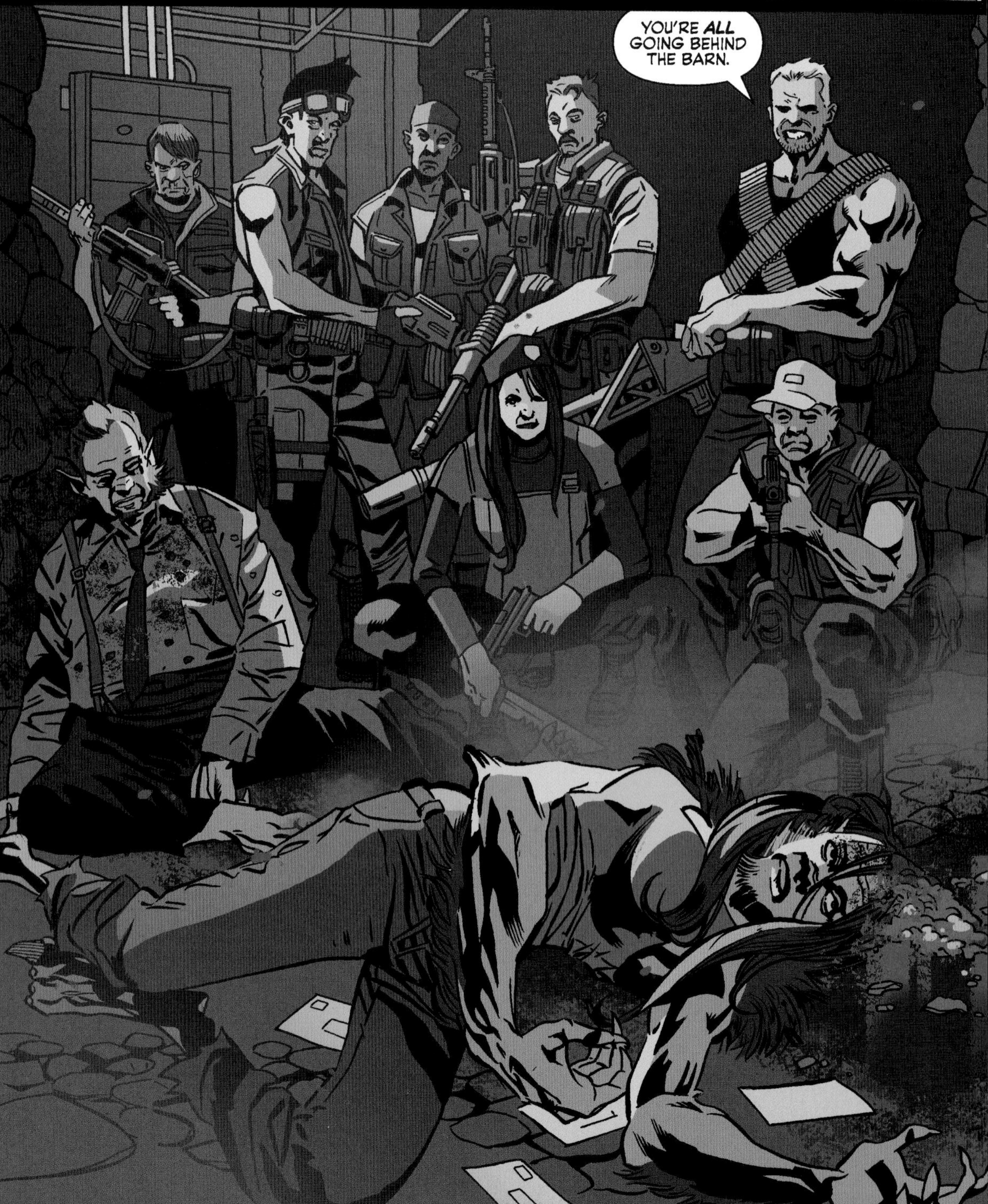
YOU'RE ALL GOING BEHIND THE BARN.

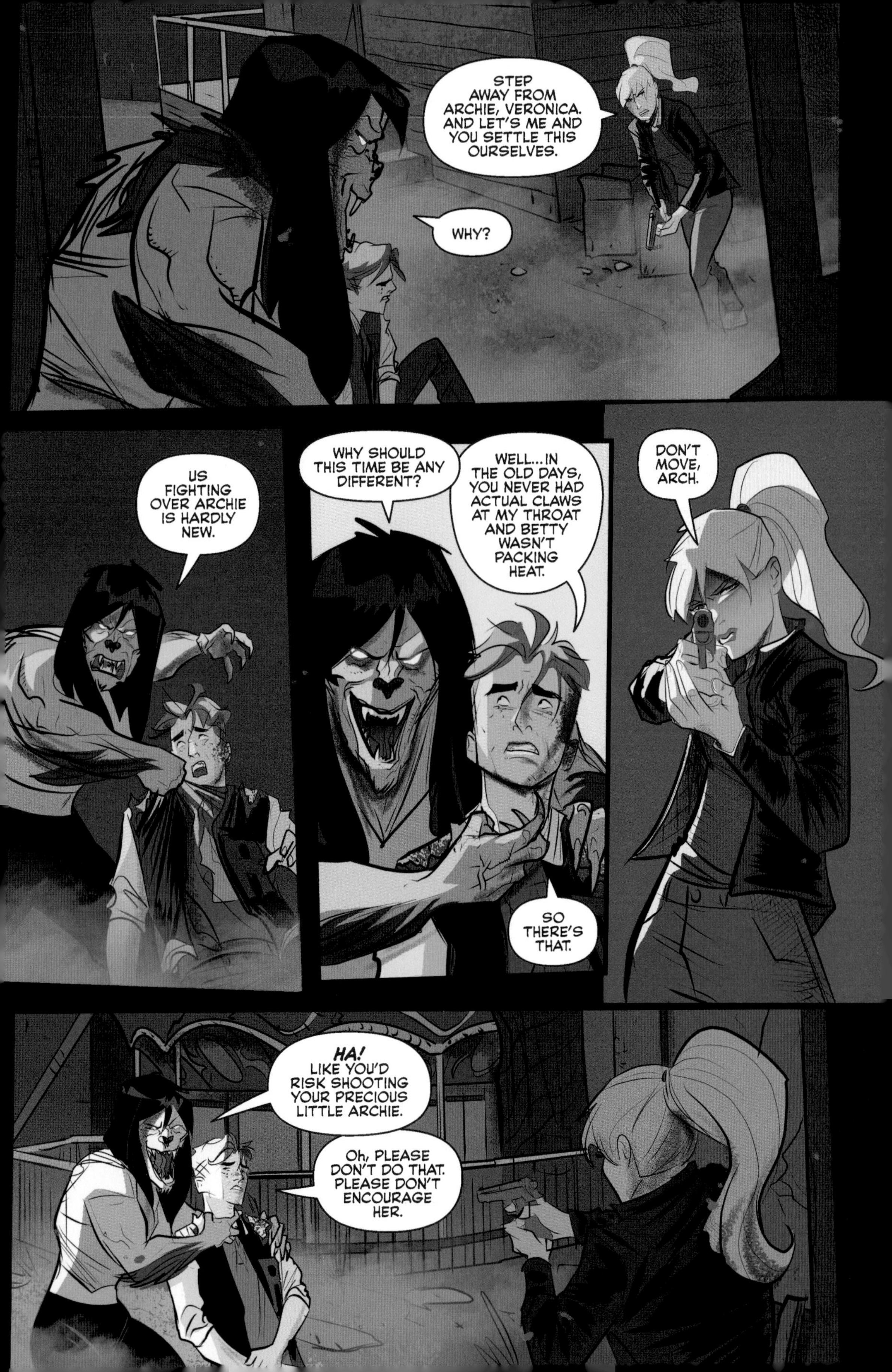
STEP AWAY FROM ARCHIE, VERONICA. AND LET'S ME AND YOU SETTLE THIS OURSELVES.
WHY?
US FIGHTING OVER ARCHIE IS HARDLY NEW.
WHY SHOULD THIS TIME BE ANY DIFFERENT?
WELL...IN THE OLD DAYS, YOU NEVER HAD ACTUAL CLAWS AT MY THROAT AND BETTY WASN'T PACKING HEAT.
SO THERE'S THAT.
DON'T MOVE, ARCH.
HA! LIKE YOU'D RISK SHOOTING YOUR PRECIOUS LITTLE ARCHIE.
Oh, PLEASE DON'T DO THAT. PLEASE DON'T ENCOURAGE HER.

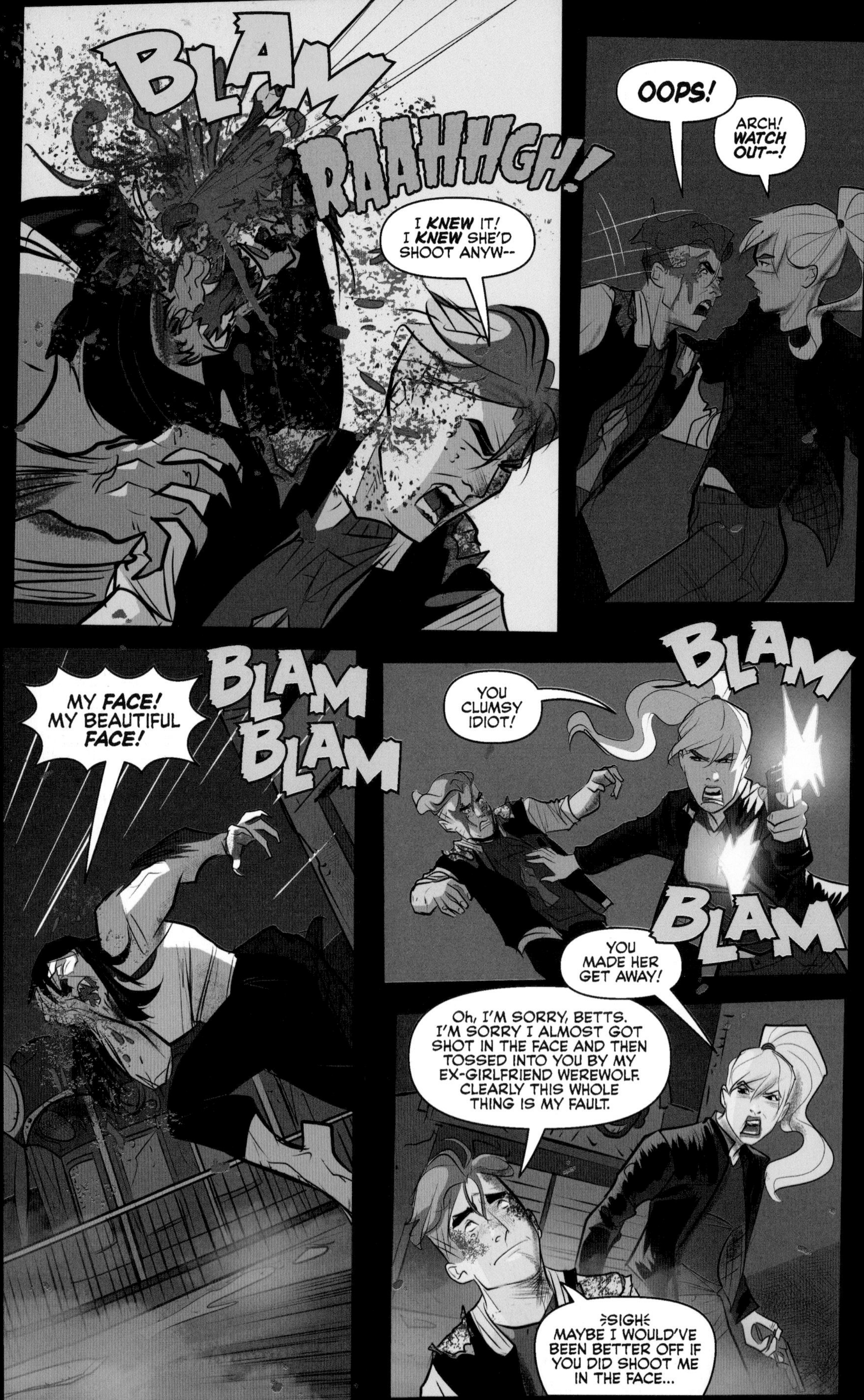
BLAM
RAAHHGH!
I KNEW IT! I KNEW SHE'D SHOOT ANYW--
OOPS!
ARCH! WATCH OUT--!
MY FACE! MY BEAUTIFUL FACE!
BLAM BLAM
YOU CLUMSY IDIOT!
BLAM
BLAM
YOU MADE HER GET AWAY!
Oh, I'M SORRY, BETTS. I'M SORRY I ALMOST GOT SHOT IN THE FACE AND THEN TOSSED INTO YOU BY MY EX-GIRLFRIEND WEREWOLF. CLEARLY THIS WHOLE THING IS MY FAULT.
SIGH
MAYBE I WOULD'VE BEEN BETTER OFF IF YOU DID SHOOT ME IN THE FACE...

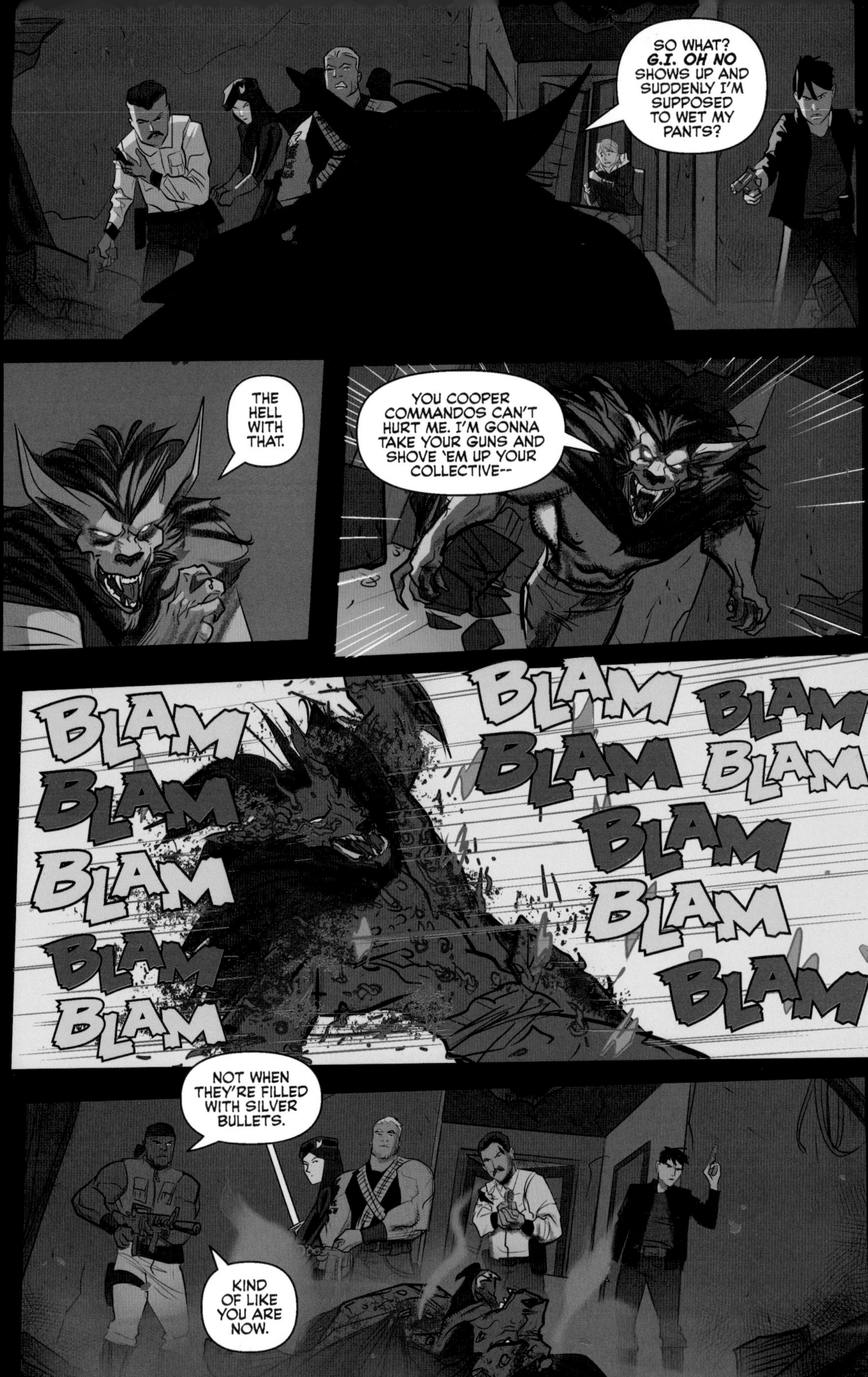
SO WHAT? G.I. OH NO SHOWS UP AND SUDDENLY I'M SUPPOSED TO WET MY PANTS?
THE HELL WITH THAT.
YOU COOPER COMMANDOS CAN'T HURT ME. I'M GONNA TAKE YOUR GUNS AND SHOVE 'EM UP YOUR COLLECTIVE--
BLAM BLAM BLAM BLAM BLAM
BLAM BLAM BLAM BLAM BLAM BLAM BLAM BLAM
NOT WHEN THEY'RE FILLED WITH SILVER BULLETS.
KIND OF LIKE YOU ARE NOW.

SO NOW THAT *THAT'S* OVER WITH...

TIME TO TAKE CARE OF OUR ACTUAL TARGET.

NO! IT WAS REGGIE AND HIS PACK WHO CAUSED ALL THE TROUBLE, NOT HIM!

DOESN'T MATTER.

OUR ORDERS ARE TO TAKE OUT THE WEREWOLVES IN THE AREA.

ALL THE WEREWOLVES.

KLIK

W-WHAT? BUT... *I'M* NOT A WEREWOLF...

NOT YET.

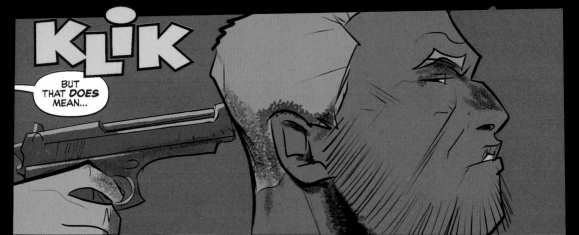

KLIK

BUT THAT *DOES* MEAN...

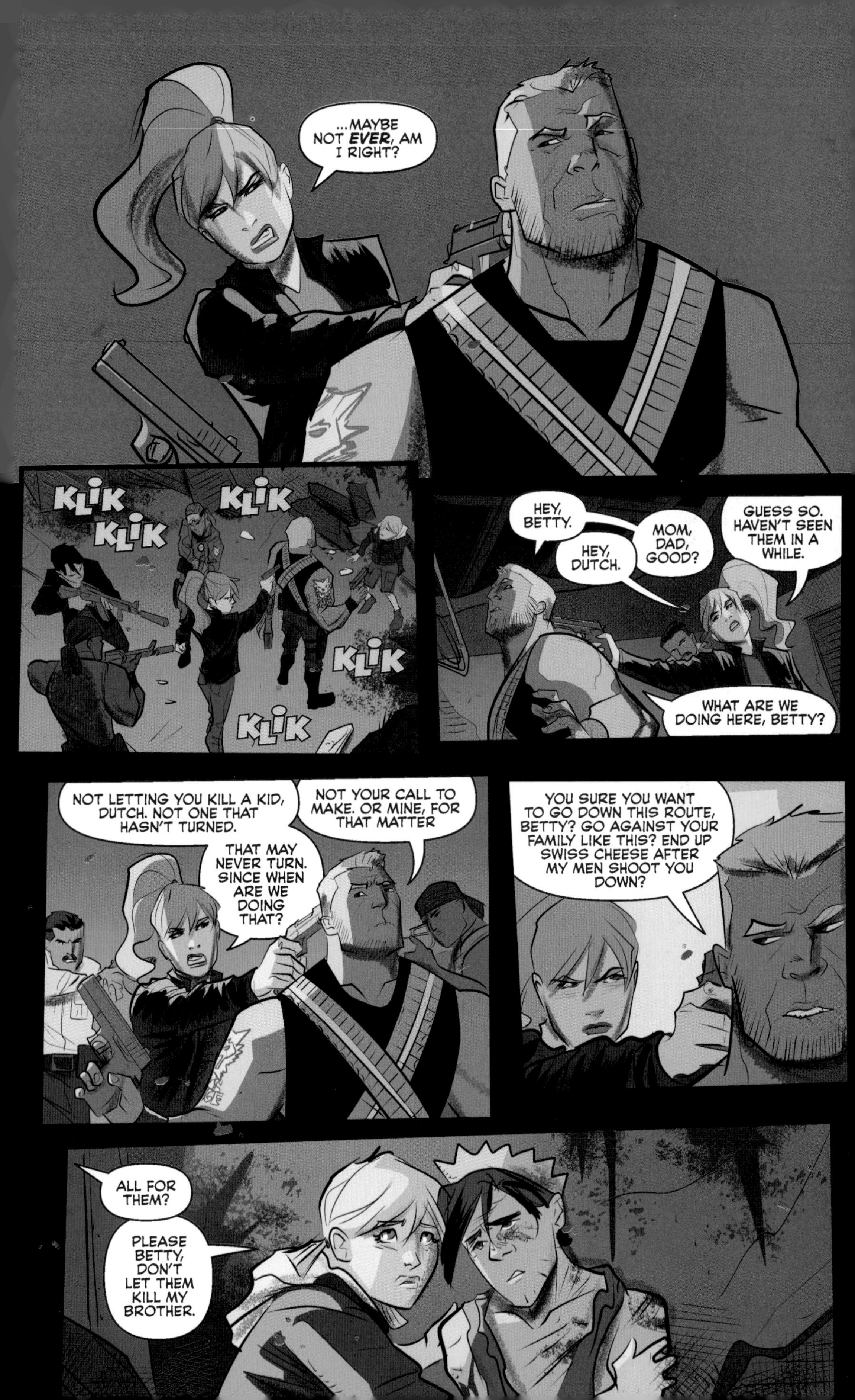
...MAYBE NOT EVER, AM I RIGHT?
KLIK
KLIK
KLIK
KLIK
KLIK
HEY, BETTY.
HEY, DUTCH.
MOM, DAD, GOOD?
GUESS SO. HAVEN'T SEEN THEM IN A WHILE.
WHAT ARE WE DOING HERE, BETTY?
NOT LETTING YOU KILL A KID, DUTCH. NOT ONE THAT HASN'T TURNED.
NOT YOUR CALL TO MAKE. OR MINE, FOR THAT MATTER
THAT MAY NEVER TURN. SINCE WHEN ARE WE DOING THAT?
YOU SURE YOU WANT TO GO DOWN THIS ROUTE, BETTY? GO AGAINST YOUR FAMILY LIKE THIS? END UP SWISS CHEESE AFTER MY MEN SHOOT YOU DOWN?
ALL FOR THEM?
PLEASE BETTY, DON'T LET THEM KILL MY BROTHER.

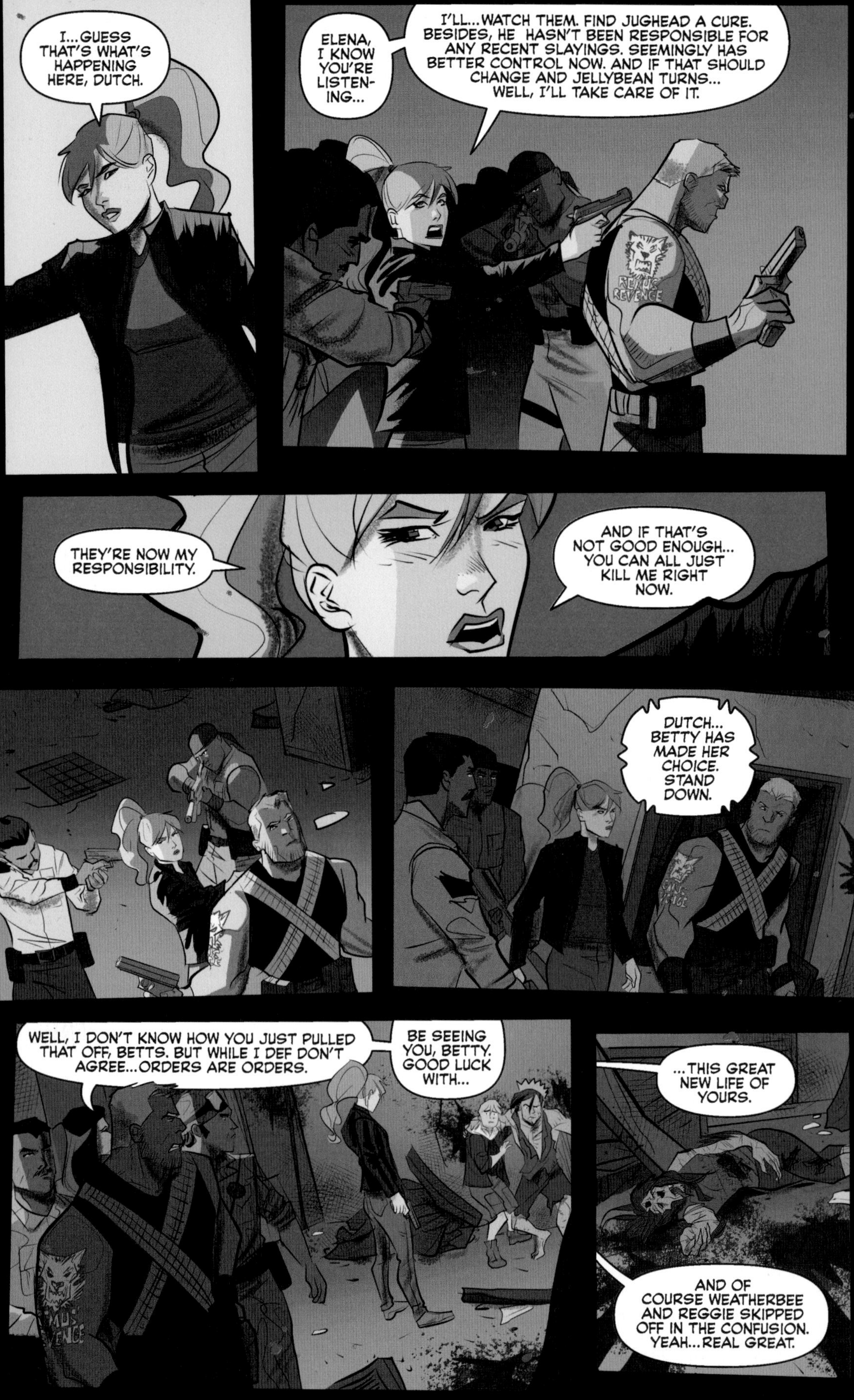
I...GUESS THAT'S WHAT'S HAPPENING HERE, DUTCH.
ELENA, I KNOW YOU'RE LISTEN-ING...
I'LL...WATCH THEM. FIND JUGHEAD A CURE. BESIDES, HE HASN'T BEEN RESPONSIBLE FOR ANY RECENT SLAYINGS. SEEMINGLY HAS BETTER CONTROL NOW. AND IF THAT SHOULD CHANGE AND JELLYBEAN TURNS... WELL, I'LL TAKE CARE OF IT.
THEY'RE NOW MY RESPONSIBILITY.
AND IF THAT'S NOT GOOD ENOUGH... YOU CAN ALL JUST KILL ME RIGHT NOW.
DUTCH... BETTY HAS MADE HER CHOICE. STAND DOWN.
WELL, I DON'T KNOW HOW YOU JUST PULLED THAT OFF, BETTS. BUT WHILE I DEF DON'T AGREE...ORDERS ARE ORDERS.
BE SEEING YOU, BETTY. GOOD LUCK WITH...
...THIS GREAT NEW LIFE OF YOURS.
AND OF COURSE WEATHERBEE AND REGGIE SKIPPED OFF IN THE CONFUSION. YEAH...REAL GREAT.

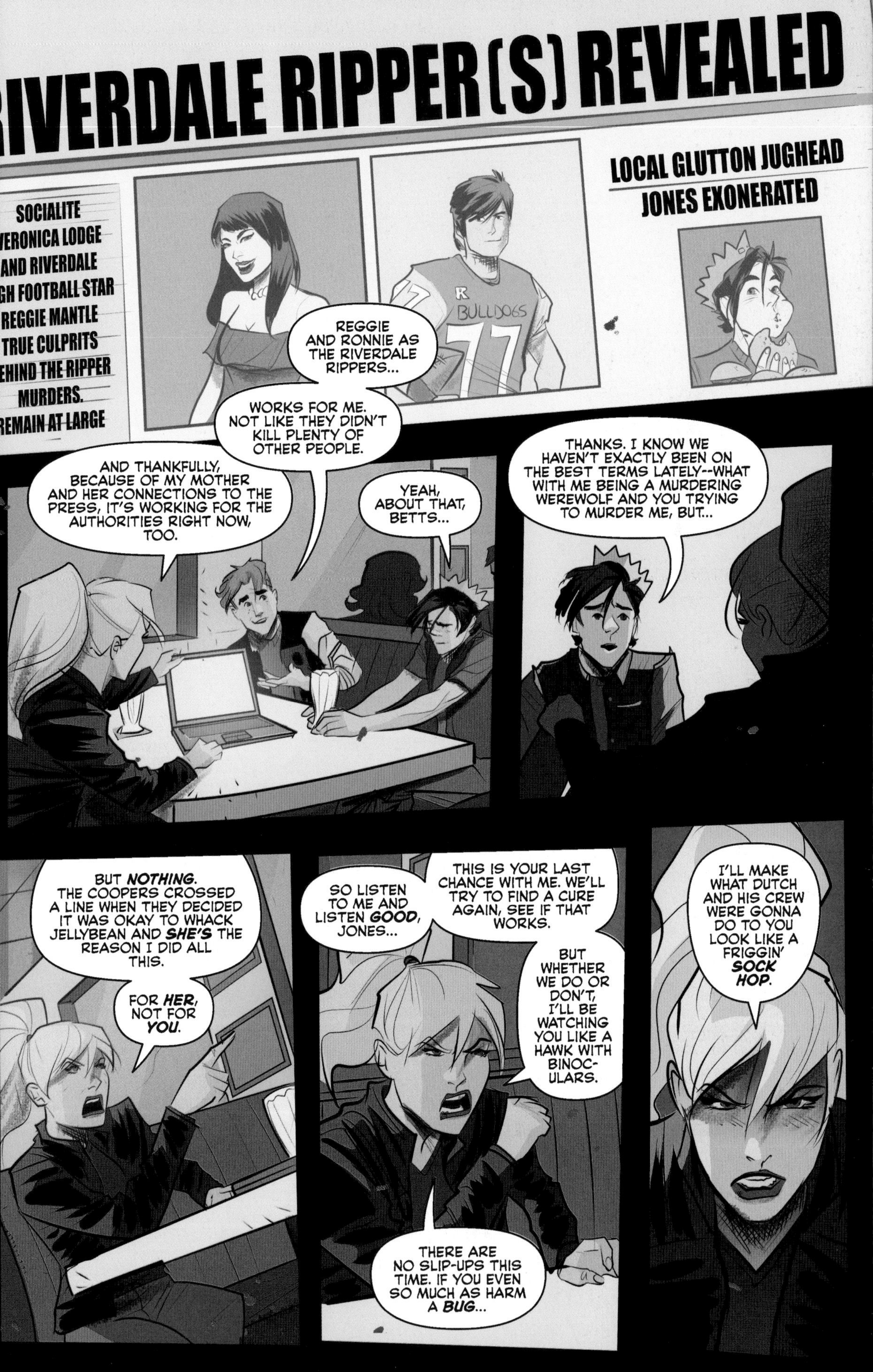
RIVERDALE RIPPER(S) REVEALED
SOCIALITE VERONICA LODGE AND RIVERDALE HIGH FOOTBALL STAR REGGIE MANTLE TRUE CULPRITS BEHIND THE RIPPER MURDERS.
REMAIN AT LARGE
LOCAL GLUTTON JUGHEAD JONES EXONERATED
BULLDOGS
77
REGGIE AND RONNIE AS THE RIVERDALE RIPPERS...
WORKS FOR ME. NOT LIKE THEY DIDN'T KILL PLENTY OF OTHER PEOPLE.
AND THANKFULLY, BECAUSE OF MY MOTHER AND HER CONNECTIONS TO THE PRESS, IT'S WORKING FOR THE AUTHORITIES RIGHT NOW, TOO.
YEAH, ABOUT THAT, BETTS...
THANKS. I KNOW WE HAVEN'T EXACTLY BEEN ON THE BEST TERMS LATELY--WHAT WITH ME BEING A MURDERING WEREWOLF AND YOU TRYING TO MURDER ME, BUT...
BUT NOTHING. THE COOPERS CROSSED A LINE WHEN THEY DECIDED IT WAS OKAY TO WHACK JELLYBEAN AND SHE'S THE REASON I DID ALL THIS.
FOR HER, NOT FOR YOU.
SO LISTEN TO ME AND LISTEN GOOD, JONES...
THIS IS YOUR LAST CHANCE WITH ME. WE'LL TRY TO FIND A CURE AGAIN, SEE IF THAT WORKS.
BUT WHETHER WE DO OR DON'T, I'LL BE WATCHING YOU LIKE A HAWK WITH BINOC-ULARS.
THERE ARE NO SLIP-UPS THIS TIME. IF YOU EVEN SO MUCH AS HARM A BUG...
I'LL MAKE WHAT DUTCH AND HIS CREW WERE GONNA DO TO YOU LOOK LIKE A FRIGGIN' SOCK HOP.

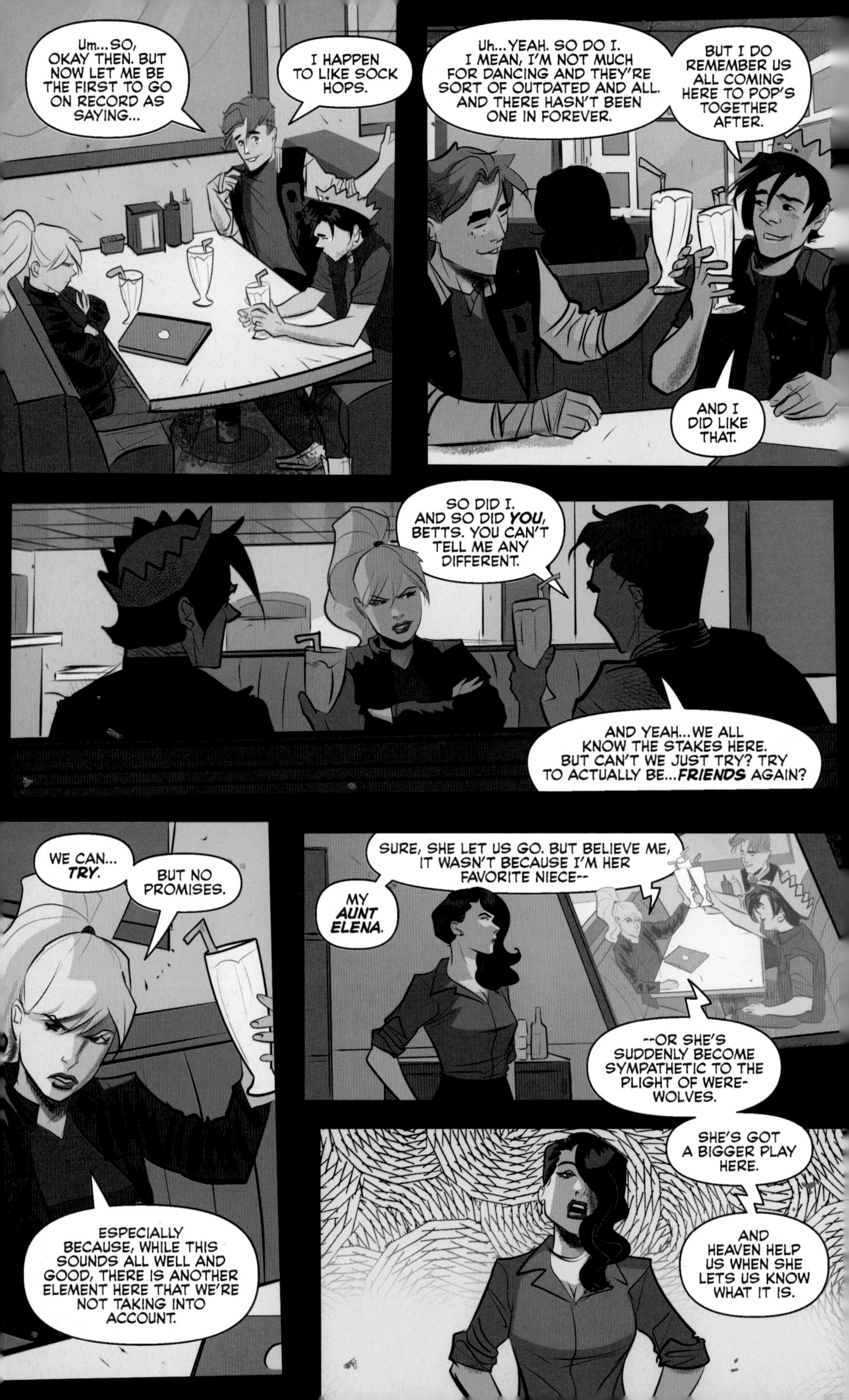
Um...SO, OKAY THEN. BUT NOW LET ME BE THE FIRST TO GO ON RECORD AS SAYING...
I HAPPEN TO LIKE SOCK HOPS.
Uh...YEAH. SO DO I. I MEAN, I'M NOT MUCH FOR DANCING AND THEY'RE SORT OF OUTDATED AND ALL. AND THERE HASN'T BEEN ONE IN FOREVER.
BUT I DO REMEMBER US ALL COMING HERE TO POP'S TOGETHER AFTER.
AND I DID LIKE THAT.
SO DID I. AND SO DID *YOU*, BETTS. YOU CAN'T TELL ME ANY DIFFERENT.
AND YEAH...WE ALL KNOW THE STAKES HERE. BUT CAN'T WE JUST TRY? TRY TO ACTUALLY BE...*FRIENDS* AGAIN?
WE CAN... *TRY*.
BUT NO PROMISES.
ESPECIALLY BECAUSE, WHILE THIS SOUNDS ALL WELL AND GOOD, THERE IS ANOTHER ELEMENT HERE THAT WE'RE NOT TAKING INTO ACCOUNT.
MY *AUNT ELENA*.
SURE, SHE LET US GO. BUT BELIEVE ME, IT WASN'T BECAUSE I'M HER FAVORITE NIECE--
--OR SHE'S SUDDENLY BECOME SYMPATHETIC TO THE PLIGHT OF WERE-WOLVES.
SHE'S GOT A BIGGER PLAY HERE.
AND HEAVEN HELP US WHEN SHE LETS US KNOW WHAT IT IS.

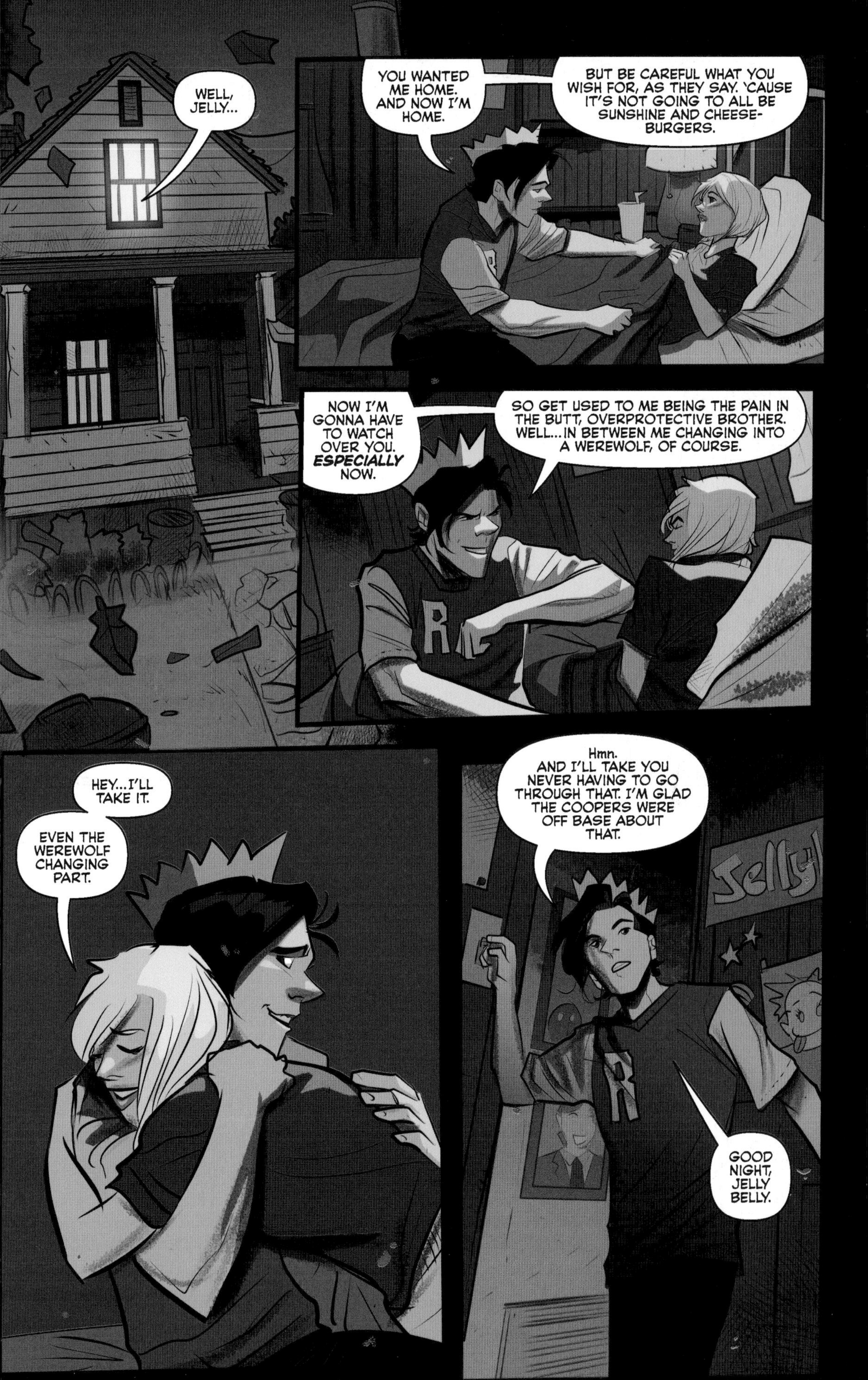
WELL, JELLY...
YOU WANTED ME HOME. AND NOW I'M HOME.
BUT BE CAREFUL WHAT YOU WISH FOR, AS THEY SAY. 'CAUSE IT'S NOT GOING TO ALL BE SUNSHINE AND CHEESE-BURGERS.
NOW I'M GONNA HAVE TO WATCH OVER YOU. *ESPECIALLY* NOW.
SO GET USED TO ME BEING THE PAIN IN THE BUTT, OVERPROTECTIVE BROTHER. WELL...IN BETWEEN ME CHANGING INTO A WEREWOLF, OF COURSE.
HEY...I'LL TAKE IT.
EVEN THE WEREWOLF CHANGING PART.
Hmn.
AND I'LL TAKE YOU NEVER HAVING TO GO THROUGH THAT. I'M GLAD THE COOPERS WERE OFF BASE ABOUT THAT.
GOOD NIGHT, JELLY BELLY.

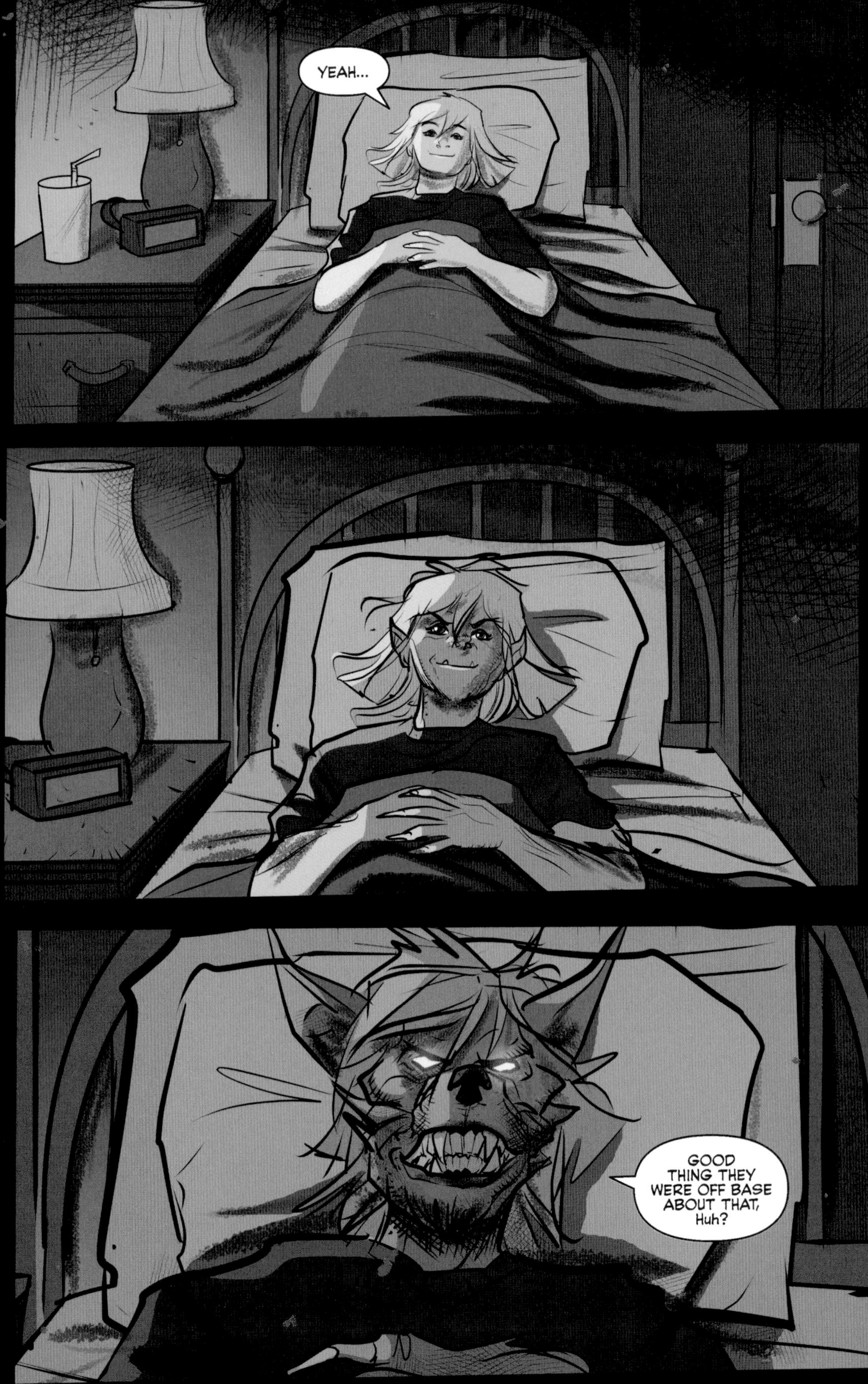
YEAH...
GOOD THING THEY WERE OFF BASE ABOUT THAT, Huh?

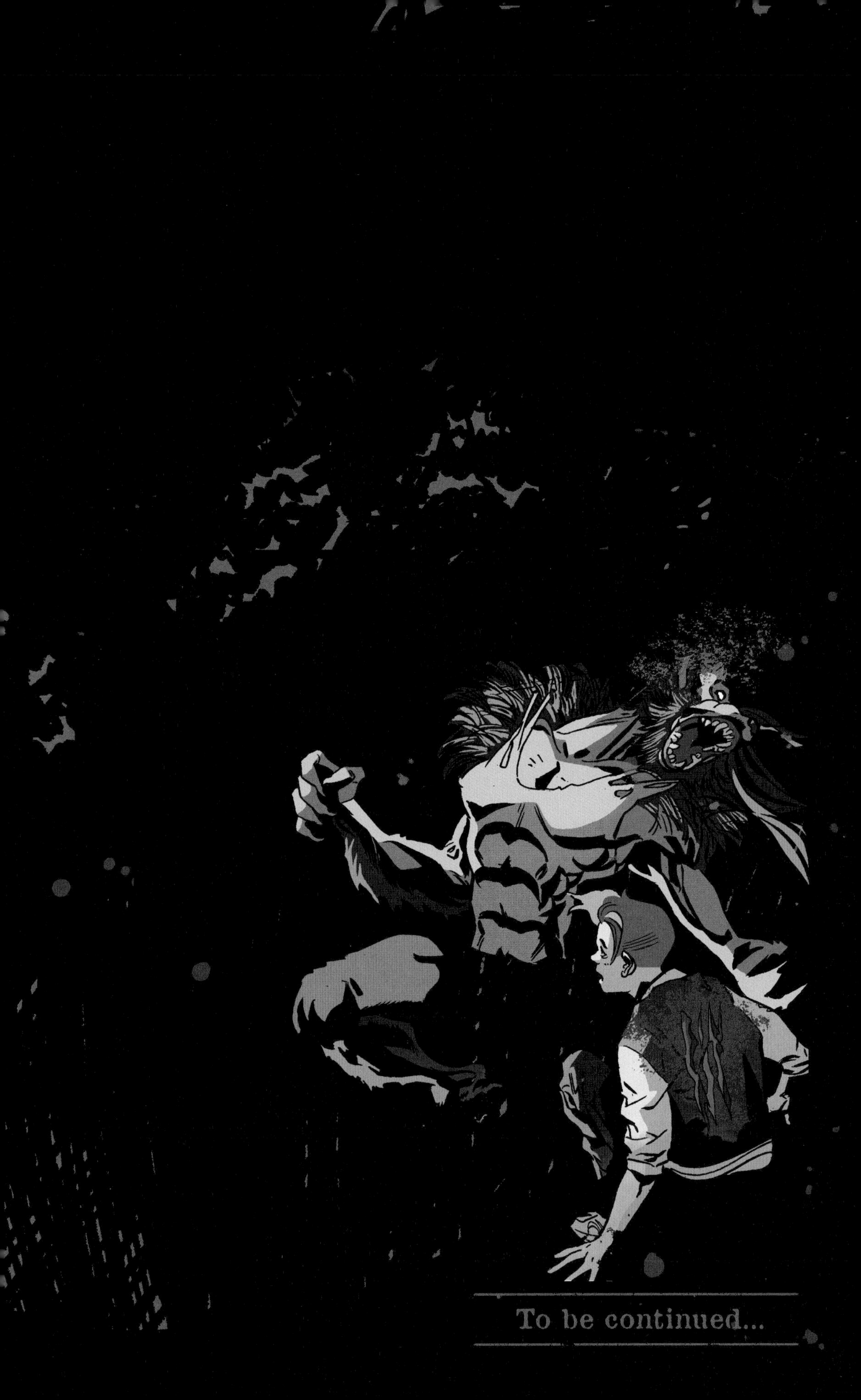
To be continued...

ISSUE EIGHT

COVER ART **Adam Gorham**

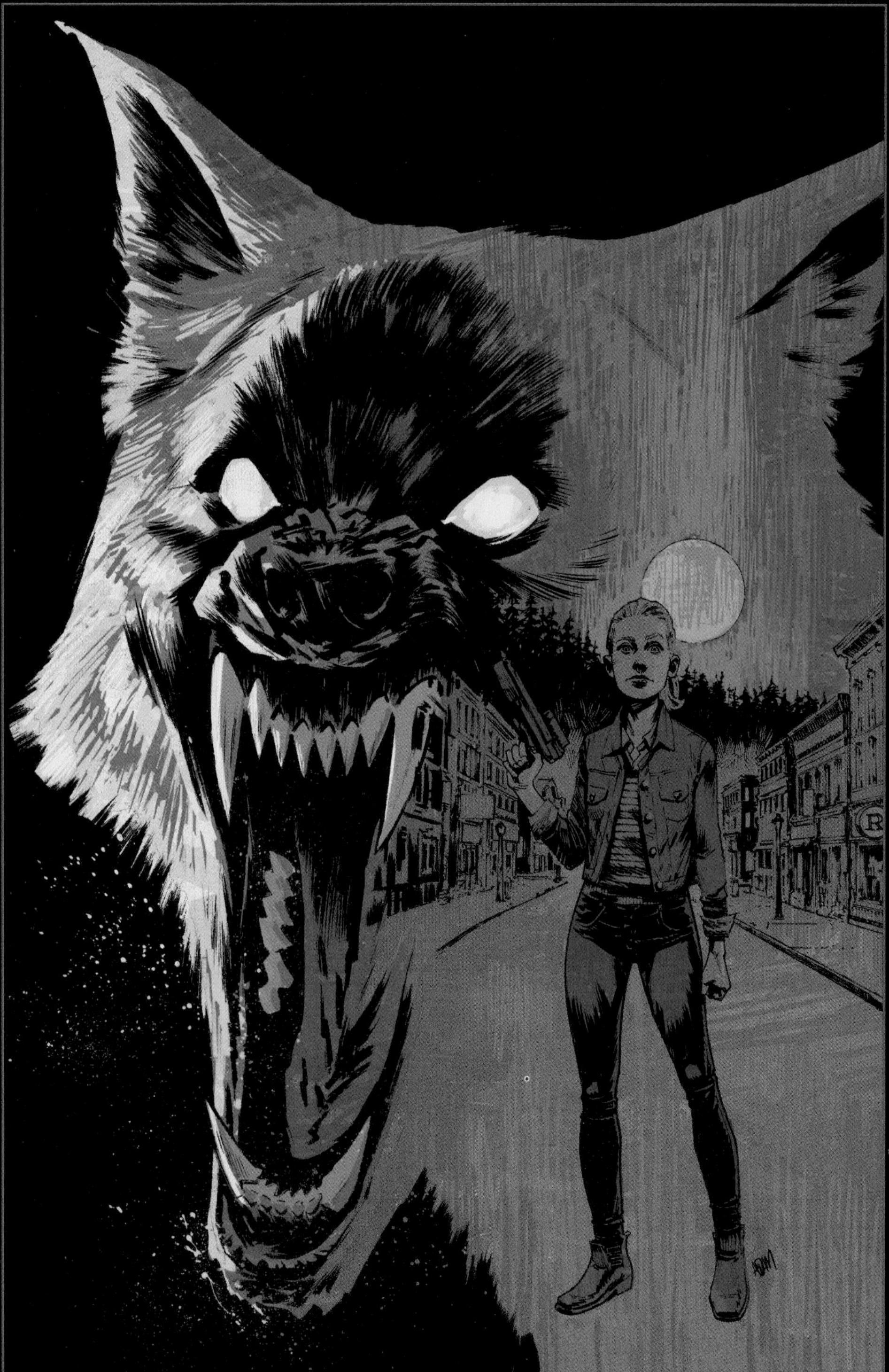
R

STORY **Frank Tieri** ART **Pat & Tim Kennedy** (p. 1-10) **Joe Eisma** (p. 11-20)
COLORS **Matt Herms** INKS **Bob Smith** (p. 1-10) LETTERING **Jack Morelli**

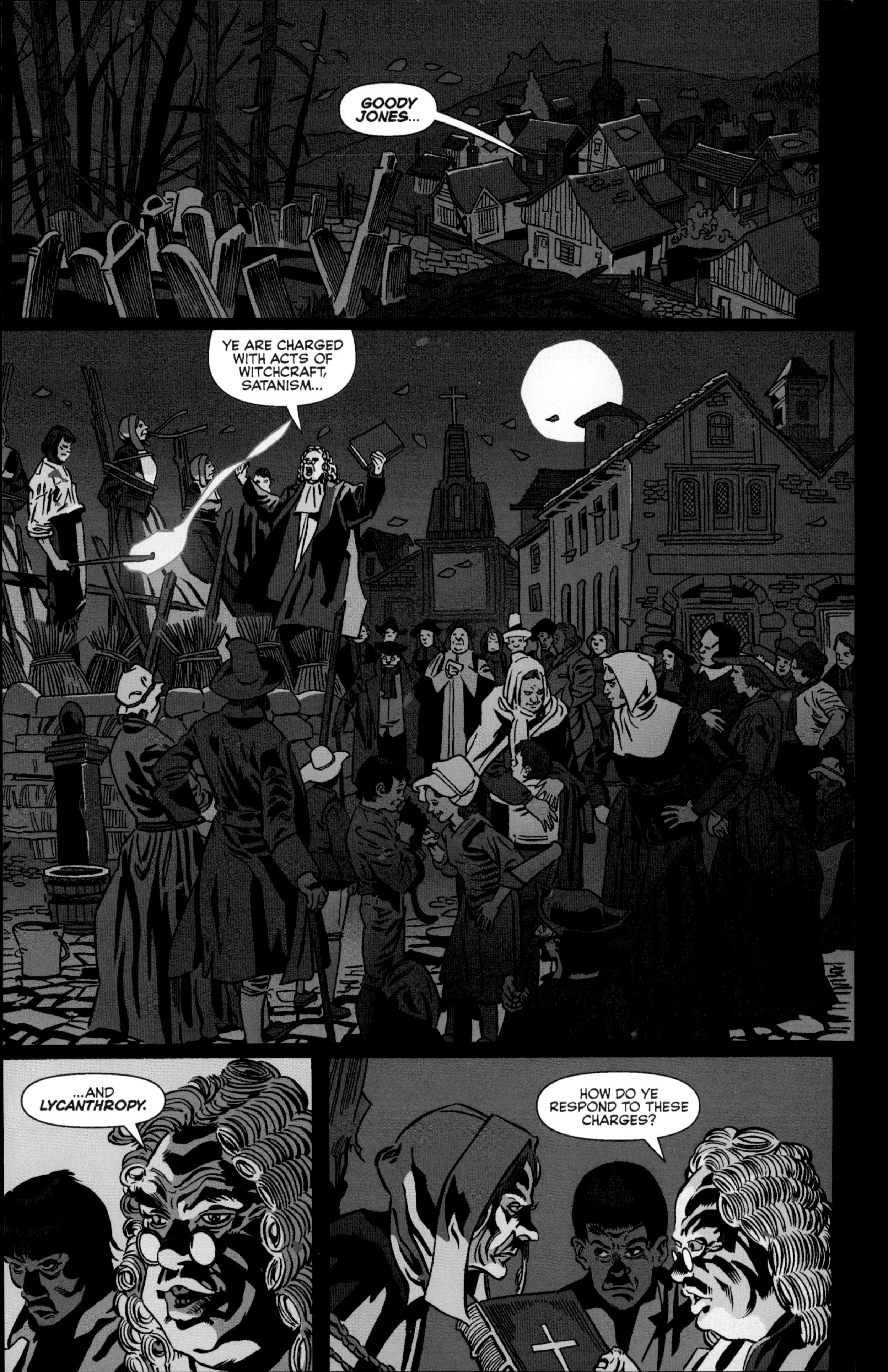
GOODY JONES...
YE ARE CHARGED WITH ACTS OF WITCHCRAFT, SATANISM...
...AND LYCANTHROPY.
HOW DO YE RESPOND TO THESE CHARGES?

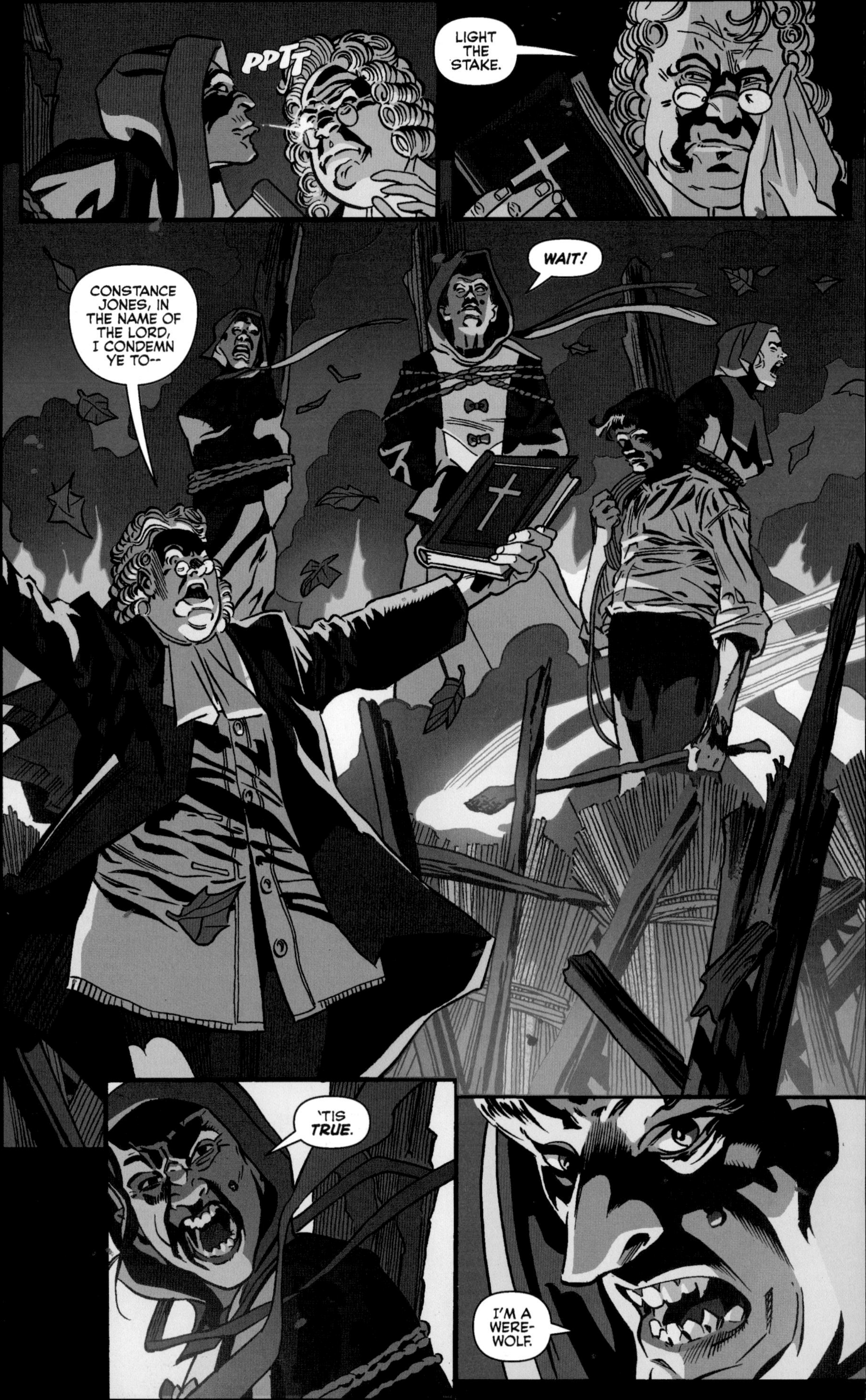
PPTT
LIGHT THE STAKE.
CONSTANCE JONES, IN THE NAME OF THE LORD, I CONDEMN YE TO--
WAIT!
'TIS TRUE.
I'M A WERE-WOLF.

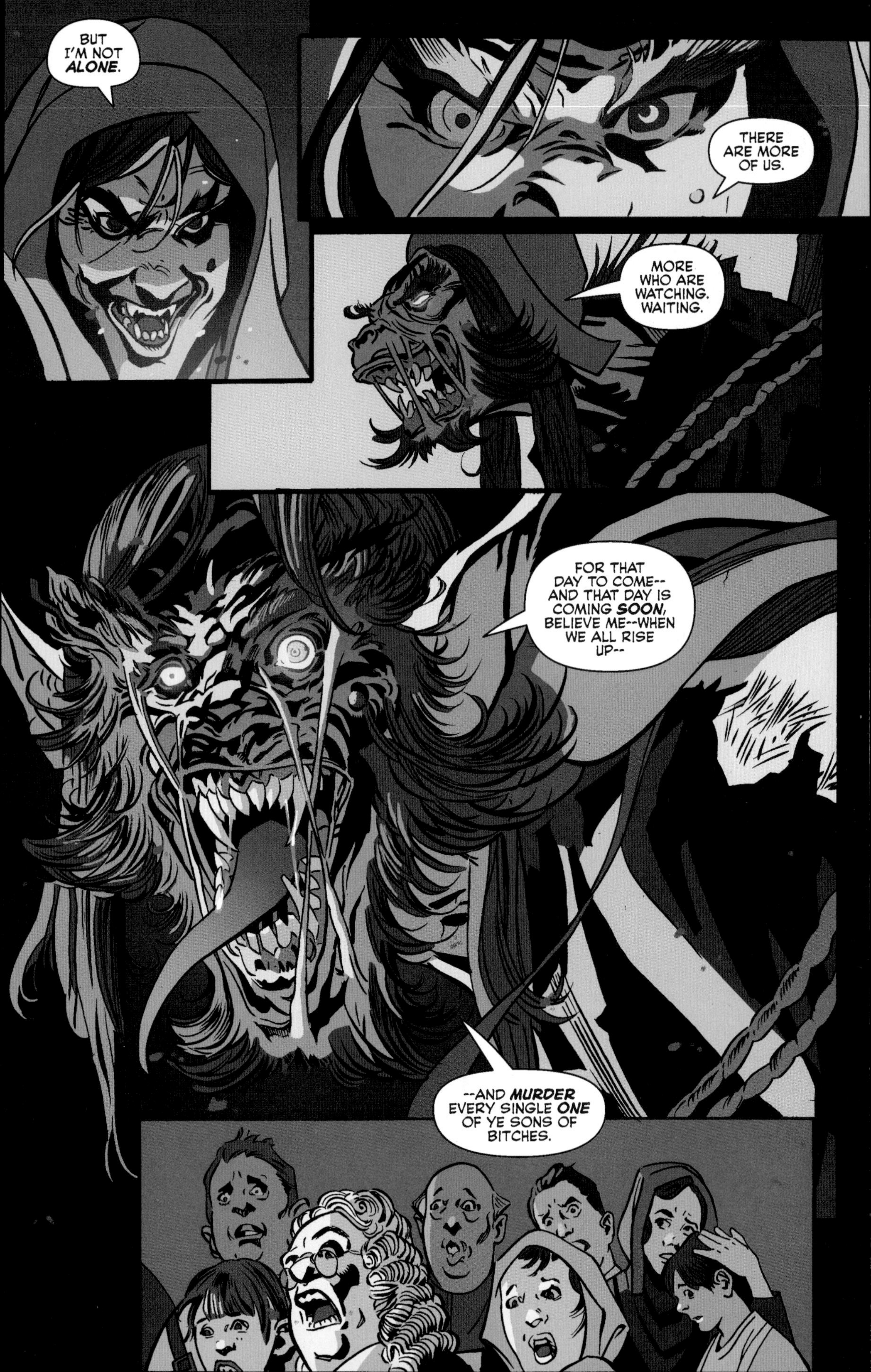
BUT I'M NOT ALONE.
THERE ARE MORE OF US.
MORE WHO ARE WATCHING. WAITING.
FOR THAT DAY TO COME-- AND THAT DAY IS COMING SOON, BELIEVE ME--WHEN WE ALL RISE UP--
--AND MURDER EVERY SINGLE ONE OF YE SONS OF BITCHES.

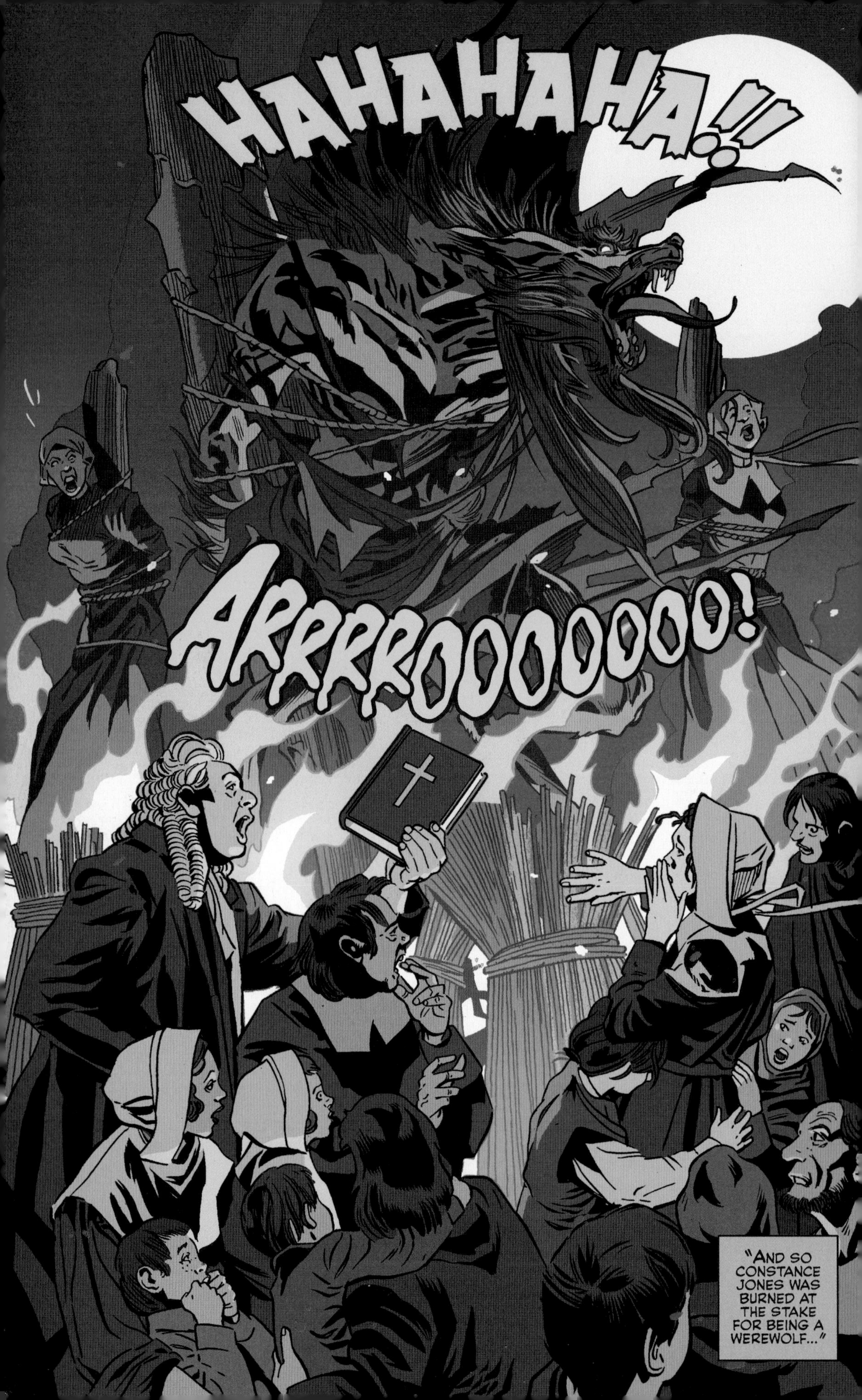
HAHAHAHA!!!
ARRRROOOOOOOO!
"AND SO CONSTANCE JONES WAS BURNED AT THE STAKE FOR BEING A WEREWOLF..."

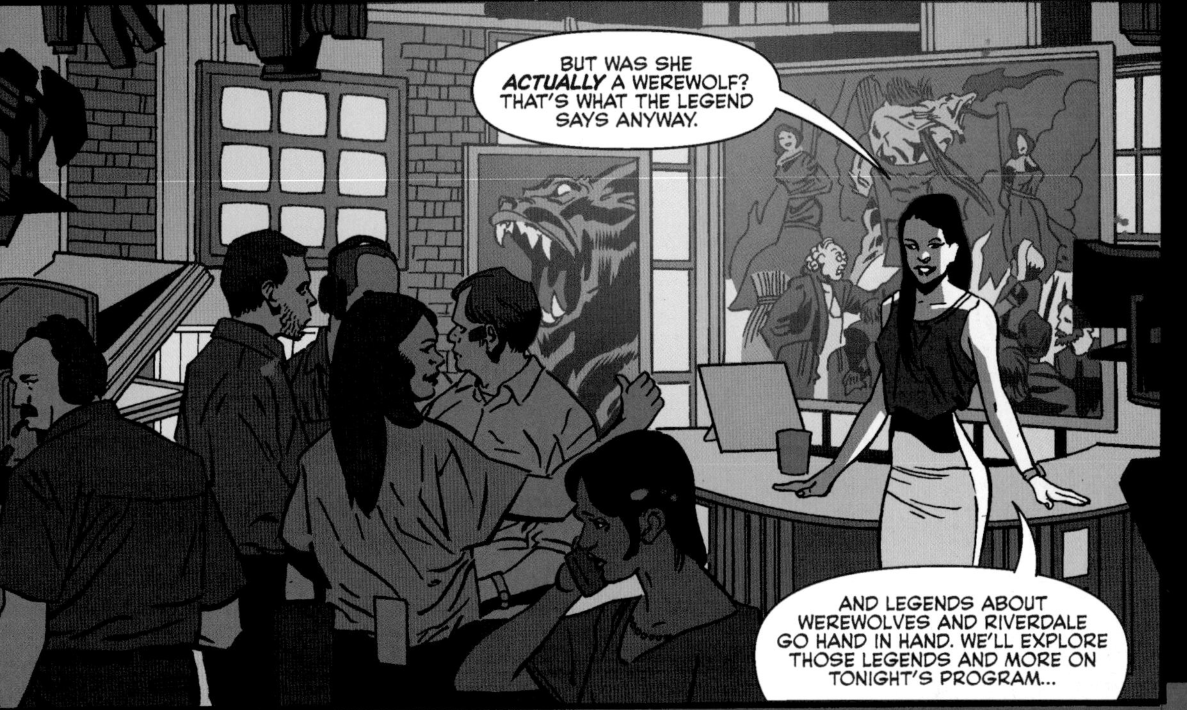
BUT WAS SHE ACTUALLY A WEREWOLF? THAT'S WHAT THE LEGEND SAYS ANYWAY.
AND LEGENDS ABOUT WEREWOLVES AND RIVERDALE GO HAND IN HAND. WE'LL EXPLORE THOSE LEGENDS AND MORE ON TONIGHT'S PROGRAM...

WEREWOLVES OF RIVERDALE: THE UNTOLD STORY

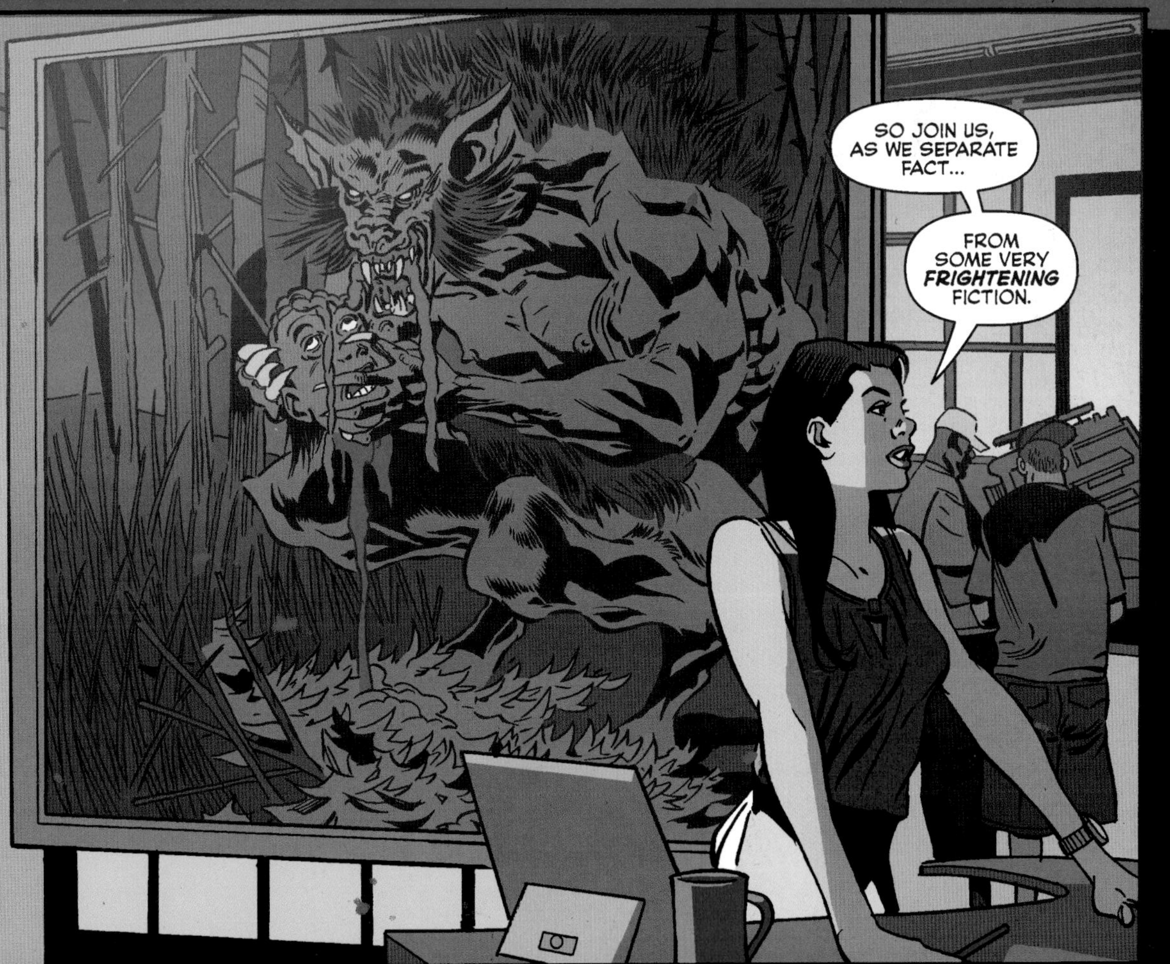
SO JOIN US, AS WE SEPARATE FACT...
FROM SOME VERY FRIGHTENING FICTION.

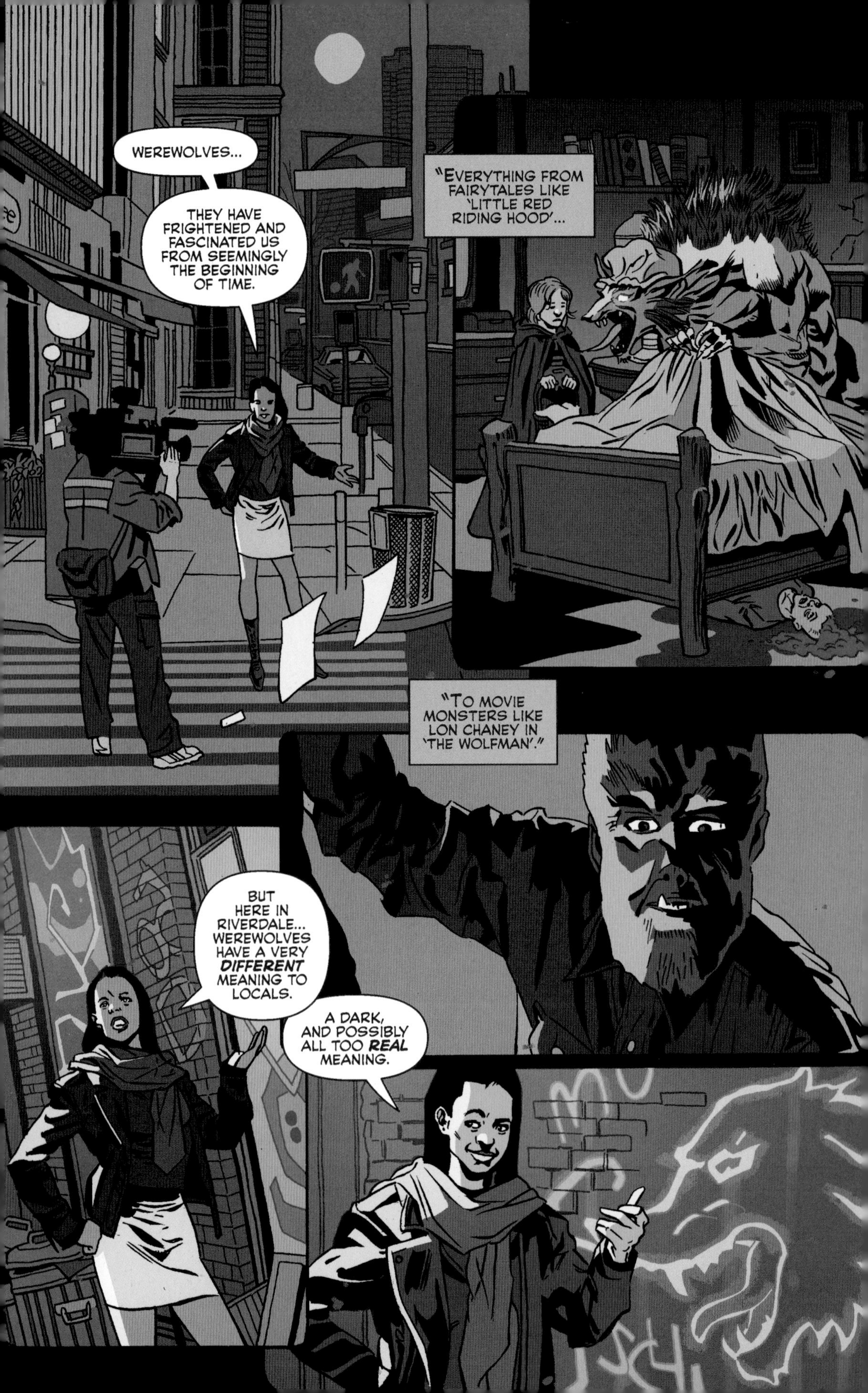
WEREWOLVES...
THEY HAVE FRIGHTENED AND FASCINATED US FROM SEEMINGLY THE BEGINNING OF TIME.
"EVERYTHING FROM FAIRYTALES LIKE 'LITTLE RED RIDING HOOD'...
"TO MOVIE MONSTERS LIKE LON CHANEY IN 'THE WOLFMAN'."
BUT HERE IN RIVERDALE... WEREWOLVES HAVE A VERY *DIFFERENT* MEANING TO LOCALS.
A DARK, AND POSSIBLY ALL TOO *REAL* MEANING.

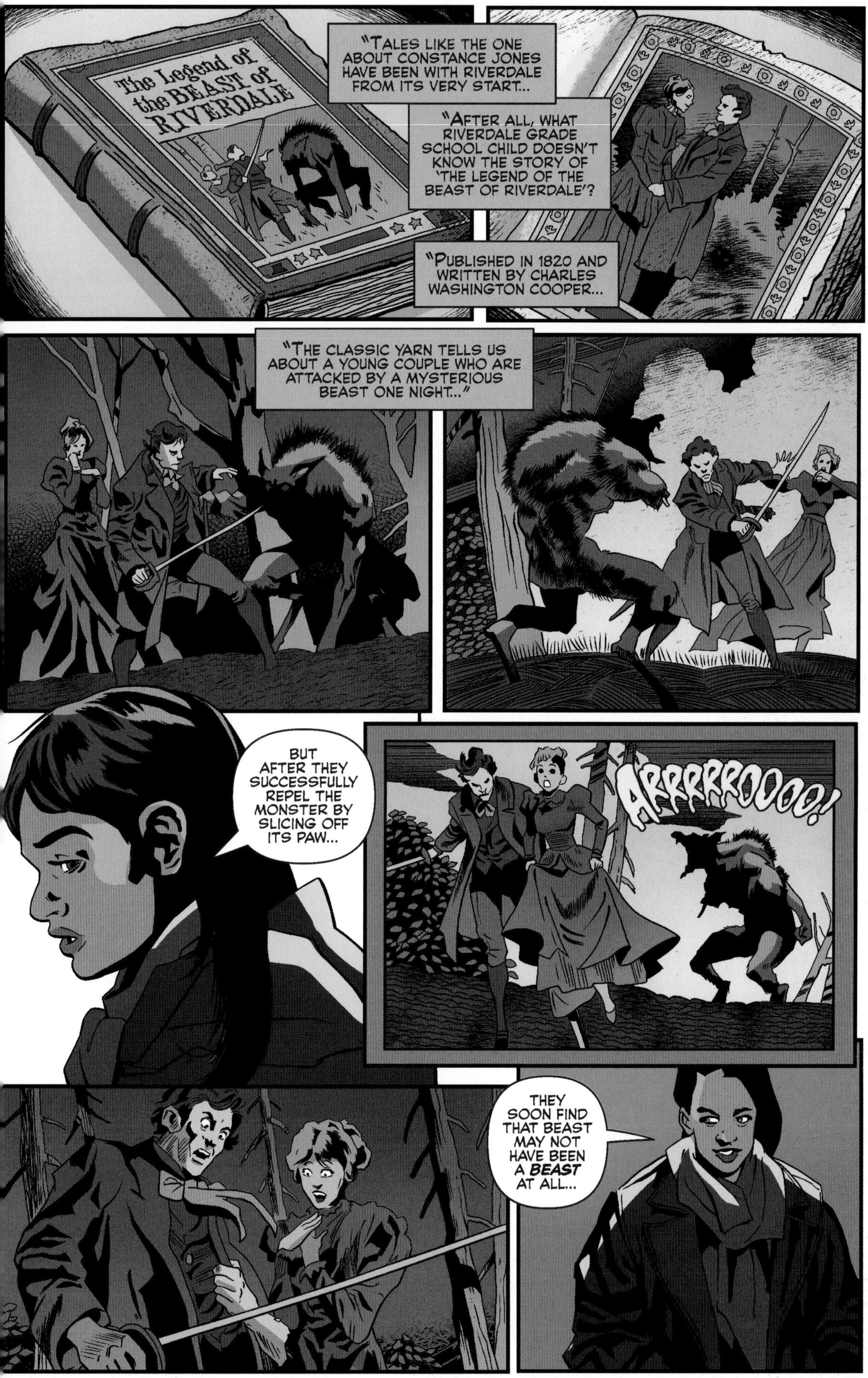
The Legend of the BEAST of RIVERDALE
"TALES LIKE THE ONE ABOUT CONSTANCE JONES HAVE BEEN WITH RIVERDALE FROM ITS VERY START...
"AFTER ALL, WHAT RIVERDALE GRADE SCHOOL CHILD DOESN'T KNOW THE STORY OF 'THE LEGEND OF THE BEAST OF RIVERDALE'?
"PUBLISHED IN 1820 AND WRITTEN BY CHARLES WASHINGTON COOPER...
"THE CLASSIC YARN TELLS US ABOUT A YOUNG COUPLE WHO ARE ATTACKED BY A MYSTERIOUS BEAST ONE NIGHT..."
BUT AFTER THEY SUCCESSFULLY REPEL THE MONSTER BY SLICING OFF ITS PAW...
ARRRRROOOO!
THEY SOON FIND THAT BEAST MAY NOT HAVE BEEN A ***BEAST*** AT ALL...

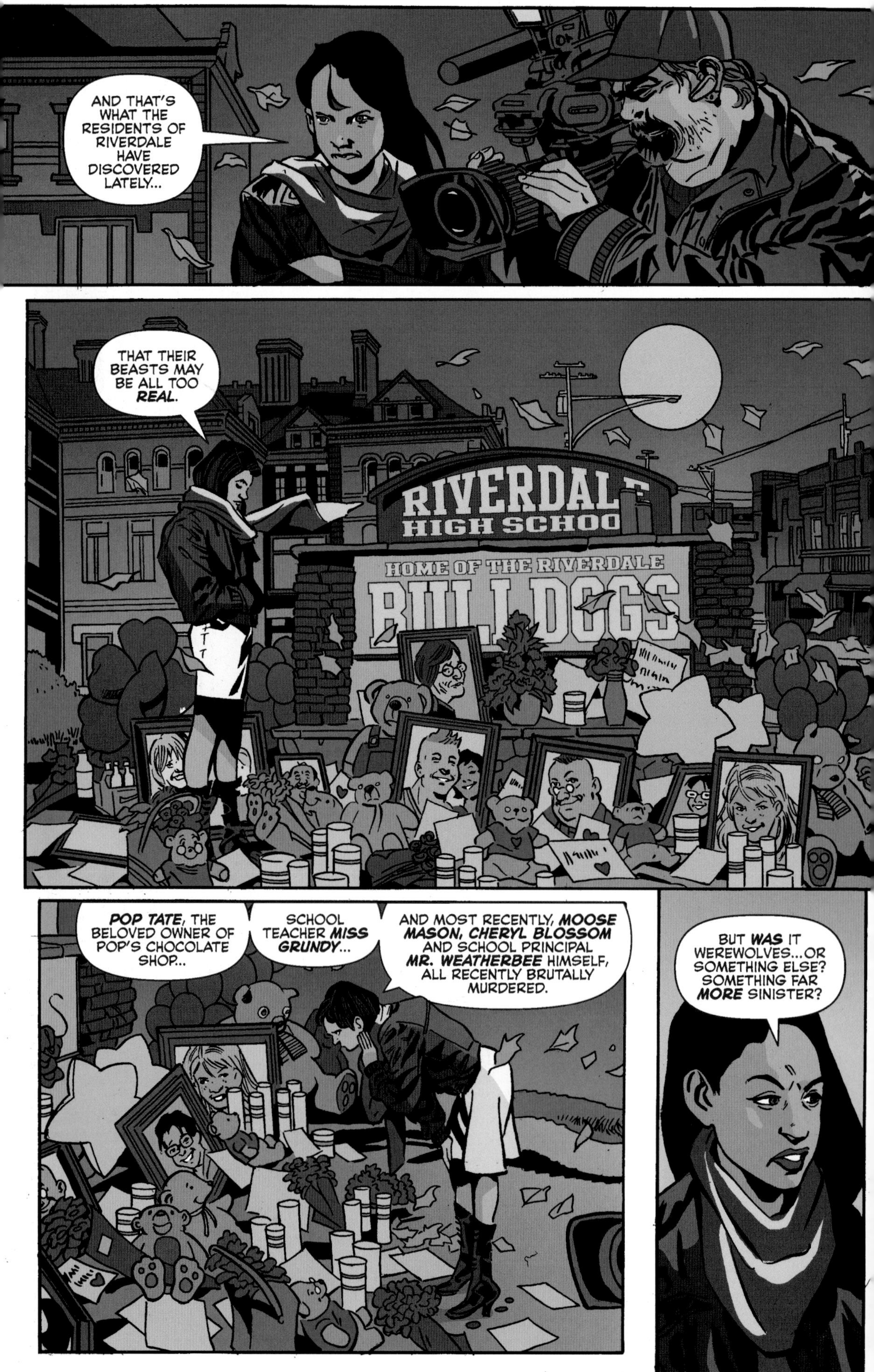
AND THAT'S WHAT THE RESIDENTS OF RIVERDALE HAVE DISCOVERED LATELY...
THAT THEIR BEASTS MAY BE ALL TOO REAL.
RIVERDALE HIGH SCHOO
HOME OF THE RIVERDALE
BULLDOGS
POP TATE, THE BELOVED OWNER OF POP'S CHOCOLATE SHOP...
SCHOOL TEACHER MISS GRUNDY...
AND MOST RECENTLY, MOOSE MASON, CHERYL BLOSSOM AND SCHOOL PRINCIPAL MR. WEATHERBEE HIMSELF, ALL RECENTLY BRUTALLY MURDERED.
BUT WAS IT WEREWOLVES...OR SOMETHING ELSE? SOMETHING FAR MORE SINISTER?

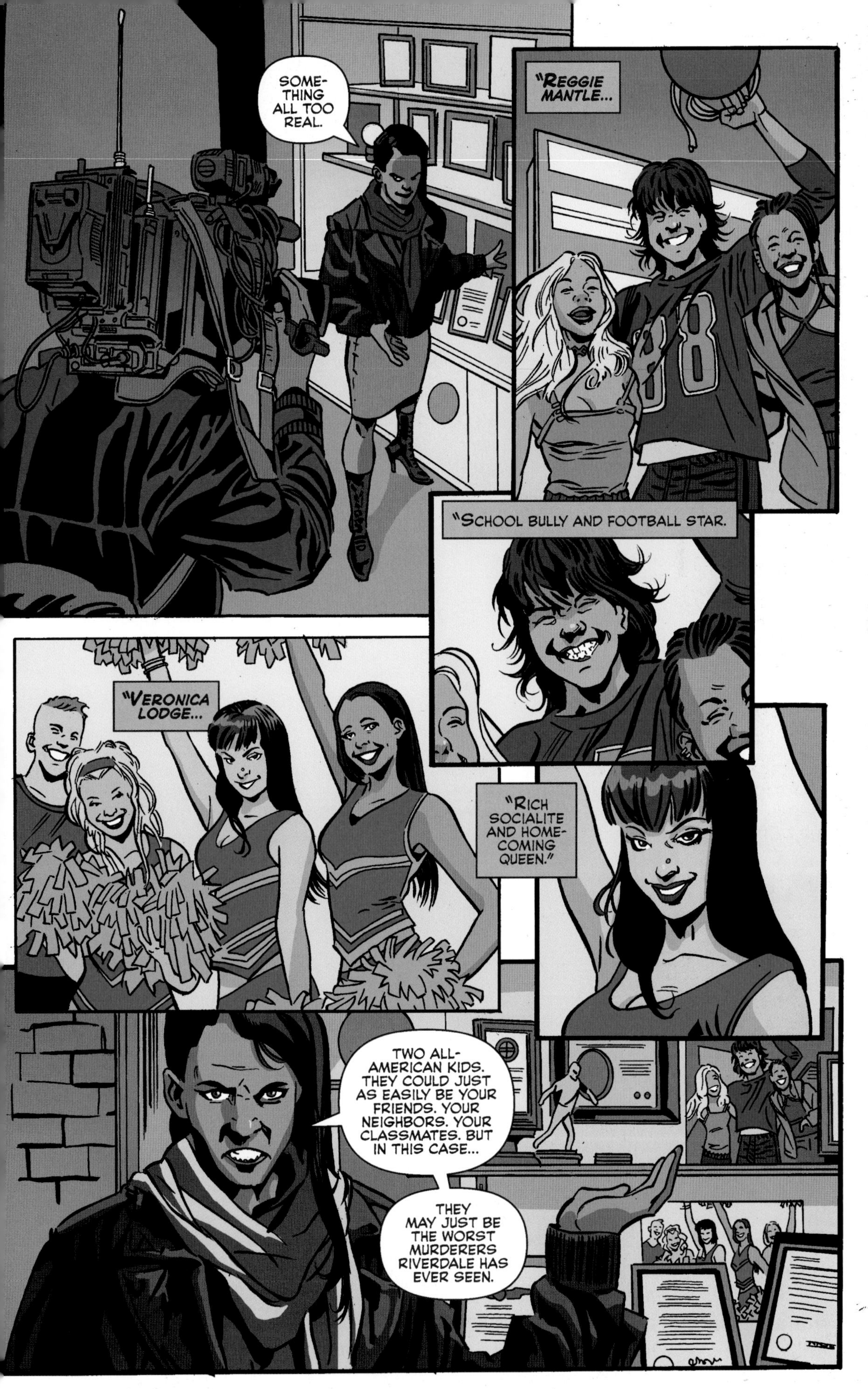
SOME-THING ALL TOO REAL.
"REGGIE MANTLE...
"SCHOOL BULLY AND FOOTBALL STAR.
"VERONICA LODGE...
"RICH SOCIALITE AND HOME-COMING QUEEN."
TWO ALL-AMERICAN KIDS. THEY COULD JUST AS EASILY BE YOUR FRIENDS. YOUR NEIGHBORS. YOUR CLASSMATES. BUT IN THIS CASE...
THEY MAY JUST BE THE WORST MURDERERS RIVERDALE HAS EVER SEEN.

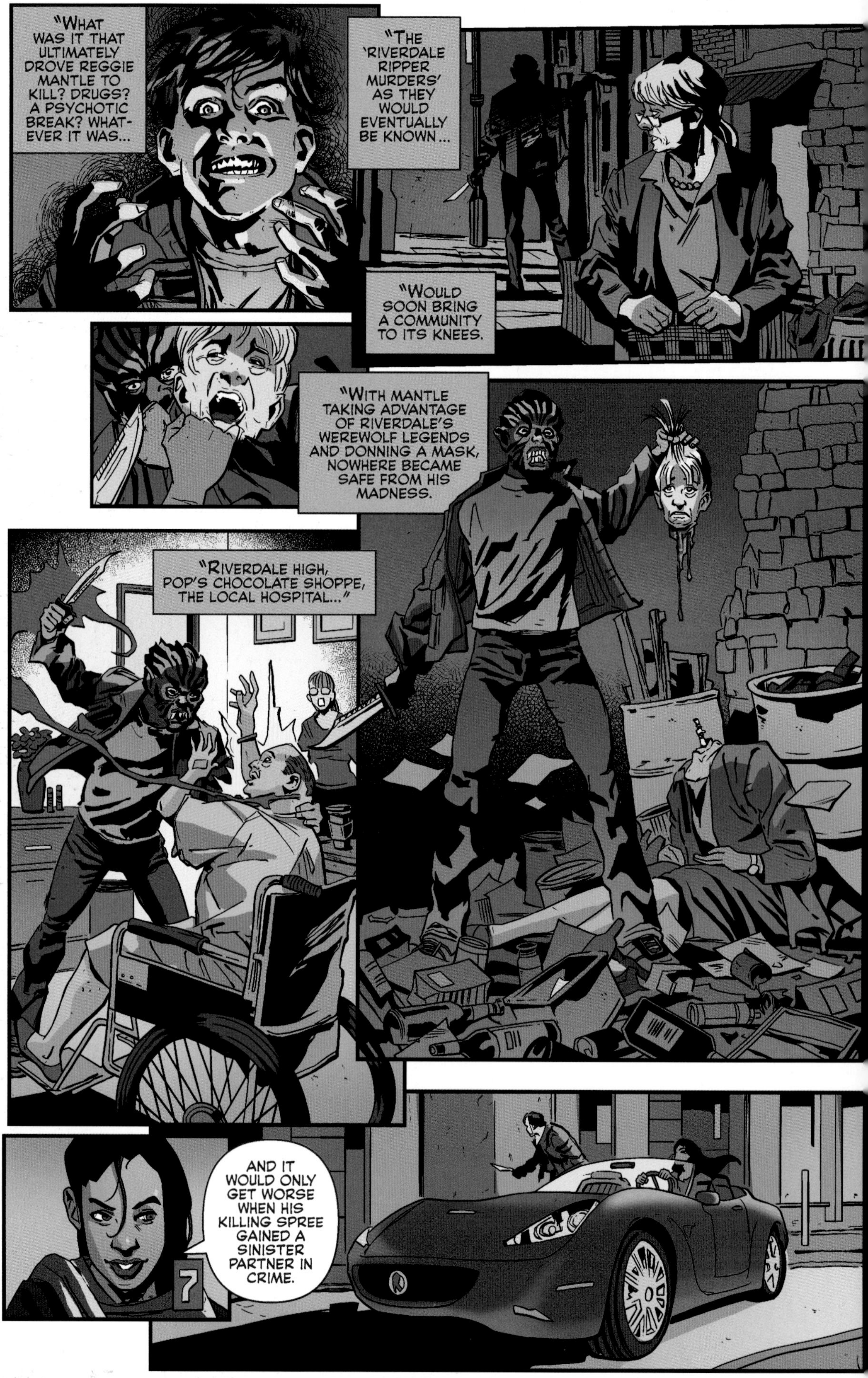
"WHAT WAS IT THAT ULTIMATELY DROVE REGGIE MANTLE TO KILL? DRUGS? A PSYCHOTIC BREAK? WHAT-EVER IT WAS...
"THE 'RIVERDALE RIPPER MURDERS' AS THEY WOULD EVENTUALLY BE KNOWN...
"WOULD SOON BRING A COMMUNITY TO ITS KNEES.
"WITH MANTLE TAKING ADVANTAGE OF RIVERDALE'S WEREWOLF LEGENDS AND DONNING A MASK, NOWHERE BECAME SAFE FROM HIS MADNESS.
"RIVERDALE HIGH, POP'S CHOCOLATE SHOPPE, THE LOCAL HOSPITAL..."
AND IT WOULD ONLY GET WORSE WHEN HIS KILLING SPREE GAINED A SINISTER PARTNER IN CRIME.
7

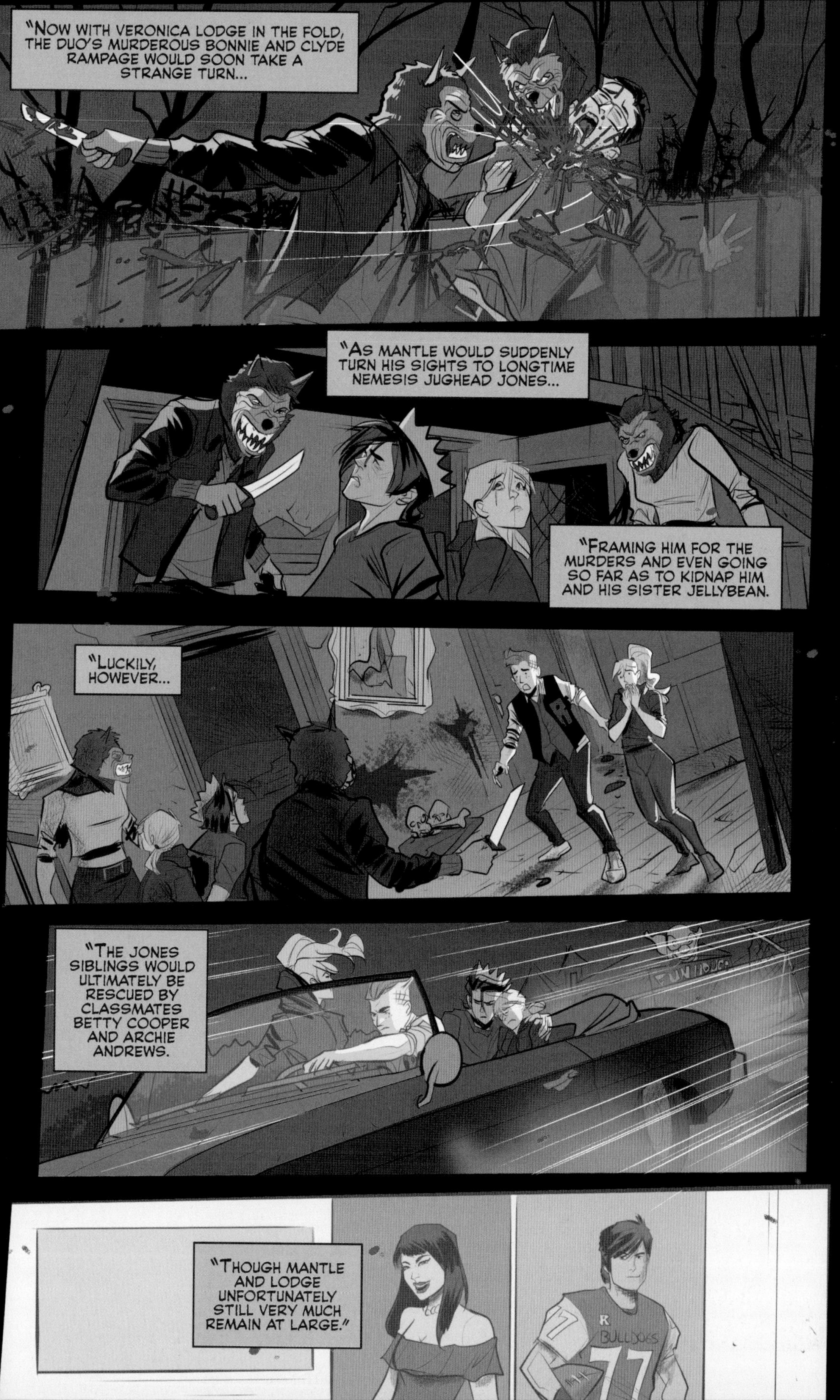
"NOW WITH VERONICA LODGE IN THE FOLD, THE DUO'S MURDEROUS BONNIE AND CLYDE RAMPAGE WOULD SOON TAKE A STRANGE TURN...
"AS MANTLE WOULD SUDDENLY TURN HIS SIGHTS TO LONGTIME NEMESIS JUGHEAD JONES...
"FRAMING HIM FOR THE MURDERS AND EVEN GOING SO FAR AS TO KIDNAP HIM AND HIS SISTER JELLYBEAN.
"LUCKILY, HOWEVER...
"THE JONES SIBLINGS WOULD ULTIMATELY BE RESCUED BY CLASSMATES BETTY COOPER AND ARCHIE ANDREWS.
"THOUGH MANTLE AND LODGE UNFORTUNATELY STILL VERY MUCH REMAIN AT LARGE."

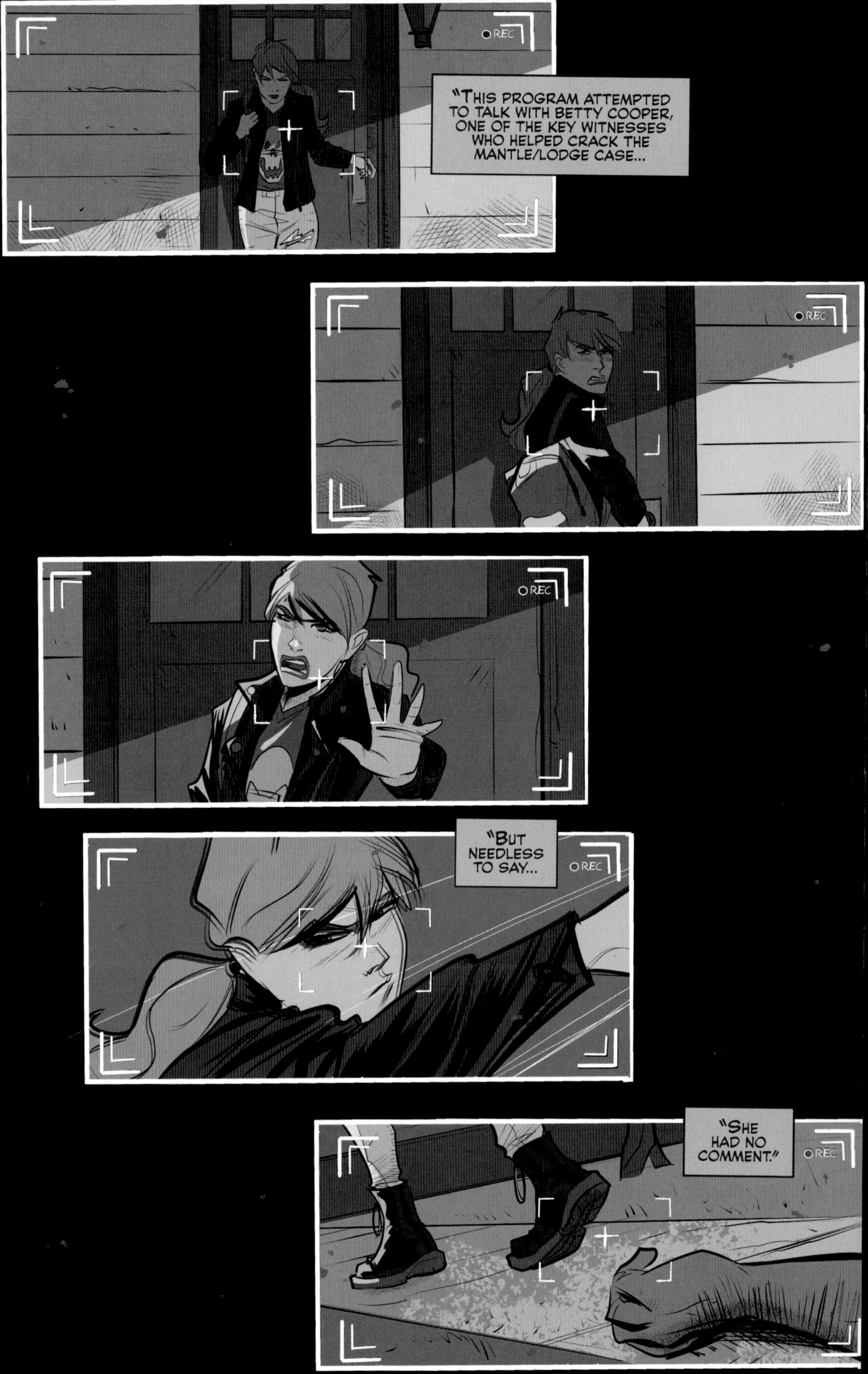
REC
"THIS PROGRAM ATTEMPTED TO TALK WITH BETTY COOPER, ONE OF THE KEY WITNESSES WHO HELPED CRACK THE MANTLE/LODGE CASE...
REC
REC
"BUT NEEDLESS TO SAY...
REC
"SHE HAD NO COMMENT."
REC

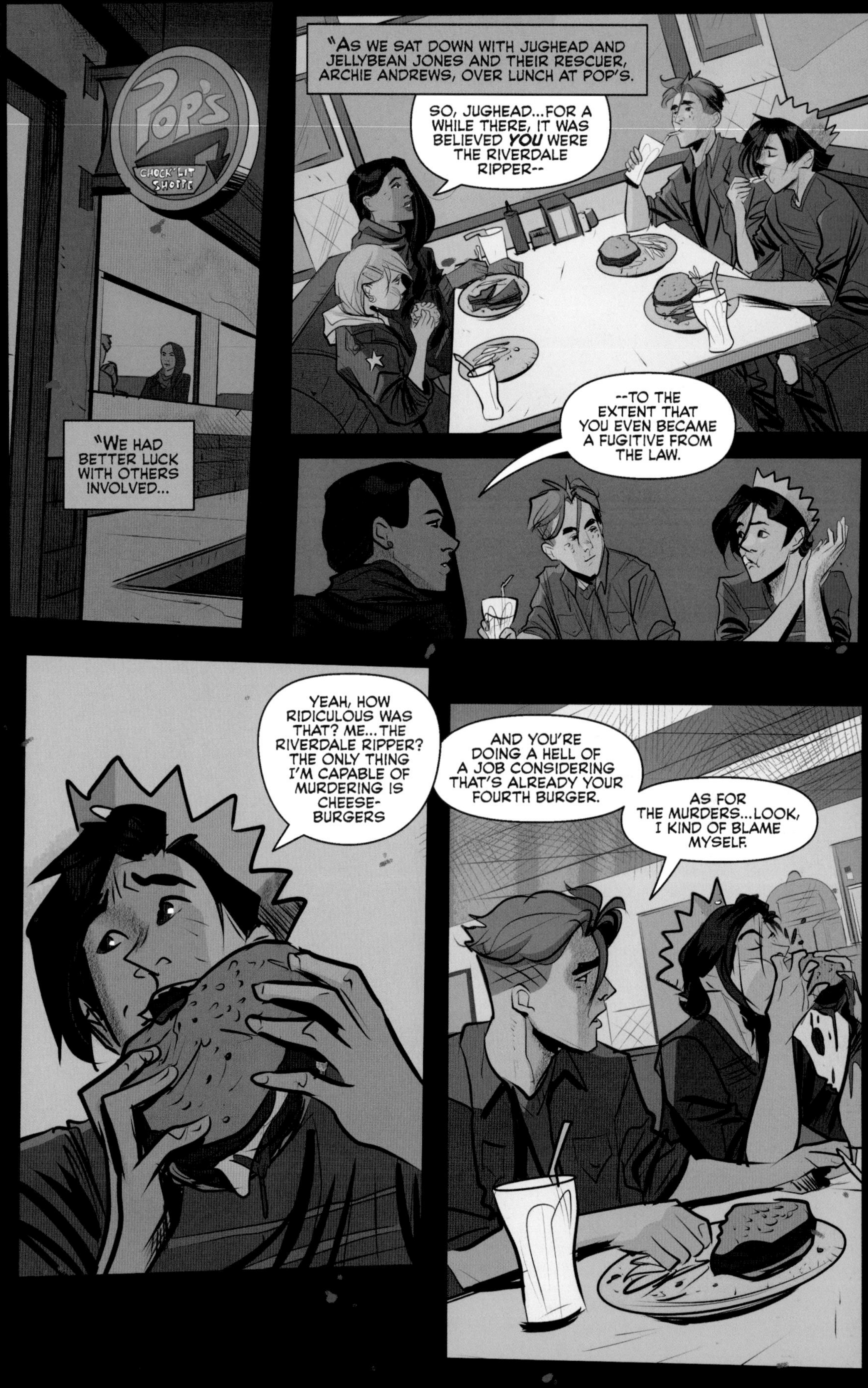
POP'S
CHOCK'LIT SHOPPE
"AS WE SAT DOWN WITH JUGHEAD AND JELLYBEAN JONES AND THEIR RESCUER, ARCHIE ANDREWS, OVER LUNCH AT POP'S.
SO, JUGHEAD...FOR A WHILE THERE, IT WAS BELIEVED YOU WERE THE RIVERDALE RIPPER--
"WE HAD BETTER LUCK WITH OTHERS INVOLVED...
--TO THE EXTENT THAT YOU EVEN BECAME A FUGITIVE FROM THE LAW.
YEAH, HOW RIDICULOUS WAS THAT? ME...THE RIVERDALE RIPPER? THE ONLY THING I'M CAPABLE OF MURDERING IS CHEESE-BURGERS
AND YOU'RE DOING A HELL OF A JOB CONSIDERING THAT'S ALREADY YOUR FOURTH BURGER.
AS FOR THE MURDERS...LOOK, I KIND OF BLAME MYSELF.

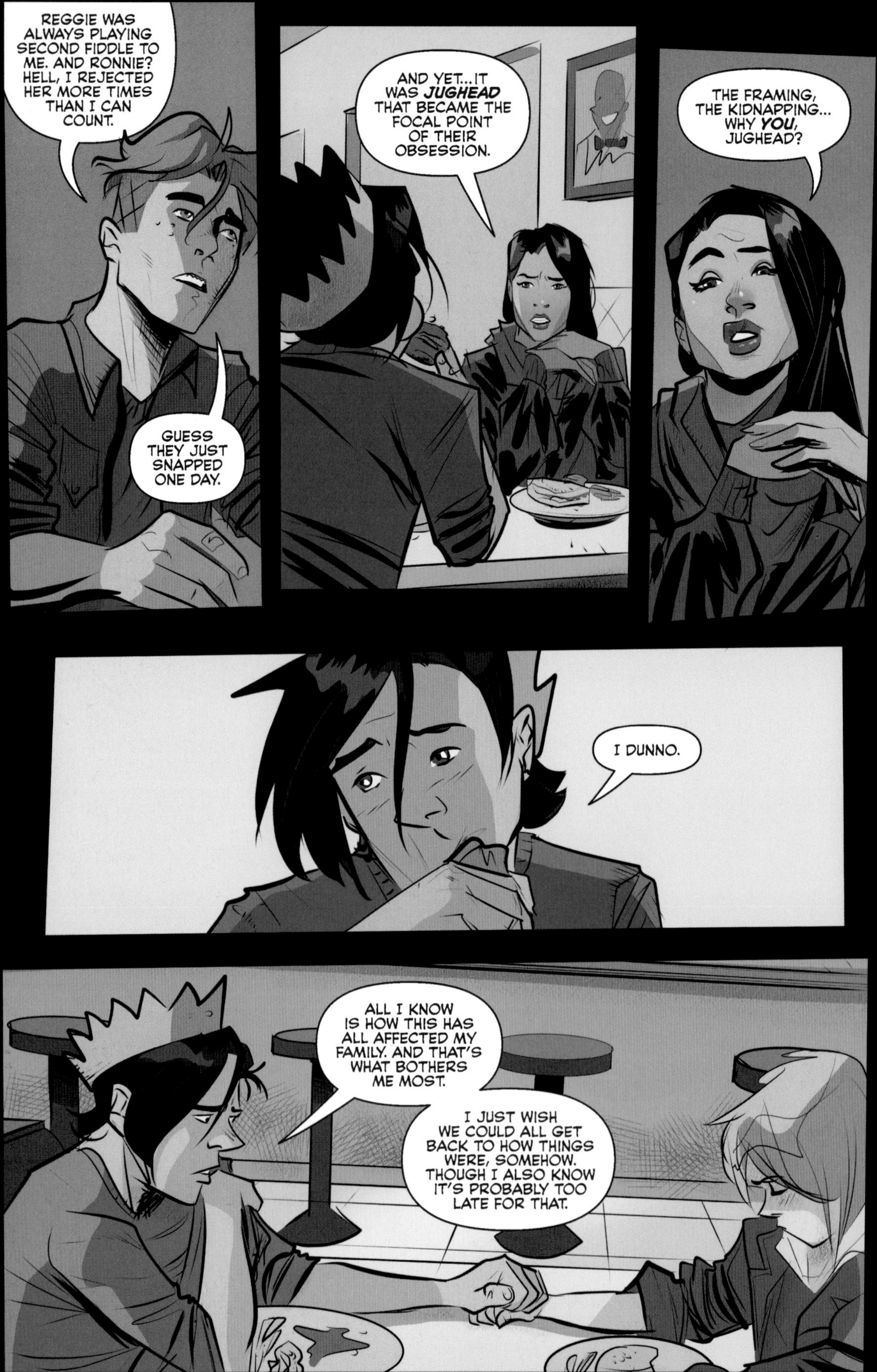
REGGIE WAS ALWAYS PLAYING SECOND FIDDLE TO ME. AND RONNIE? HELL, I REJECTED HER MORE TIMES THAN I CAN COUNT.
GUESS THEY JUST SNAPPED ONE DAY.
AND YET...IT WAS *JUGHEAD* THAT BECAME THE FOCAL POINT OF THEIR OBSESSION.
THE FRAMING, THE KIDNAPPING... WHY *YOU*, JUGHEAD?
I DUNNO.
ALL I KNOW IS HOW THIS HAS ALL AFFECTED MY FAMILY. AND THAT'S WHAT BOTHERS ME MOST.
I JUST WISH WE COULD ALL GET BACK TO HOW THINGS WERE, SOMEHOW. THOUGH I ALSO KNOW IT'S PROBABLY TOO LATE FOR THAT.

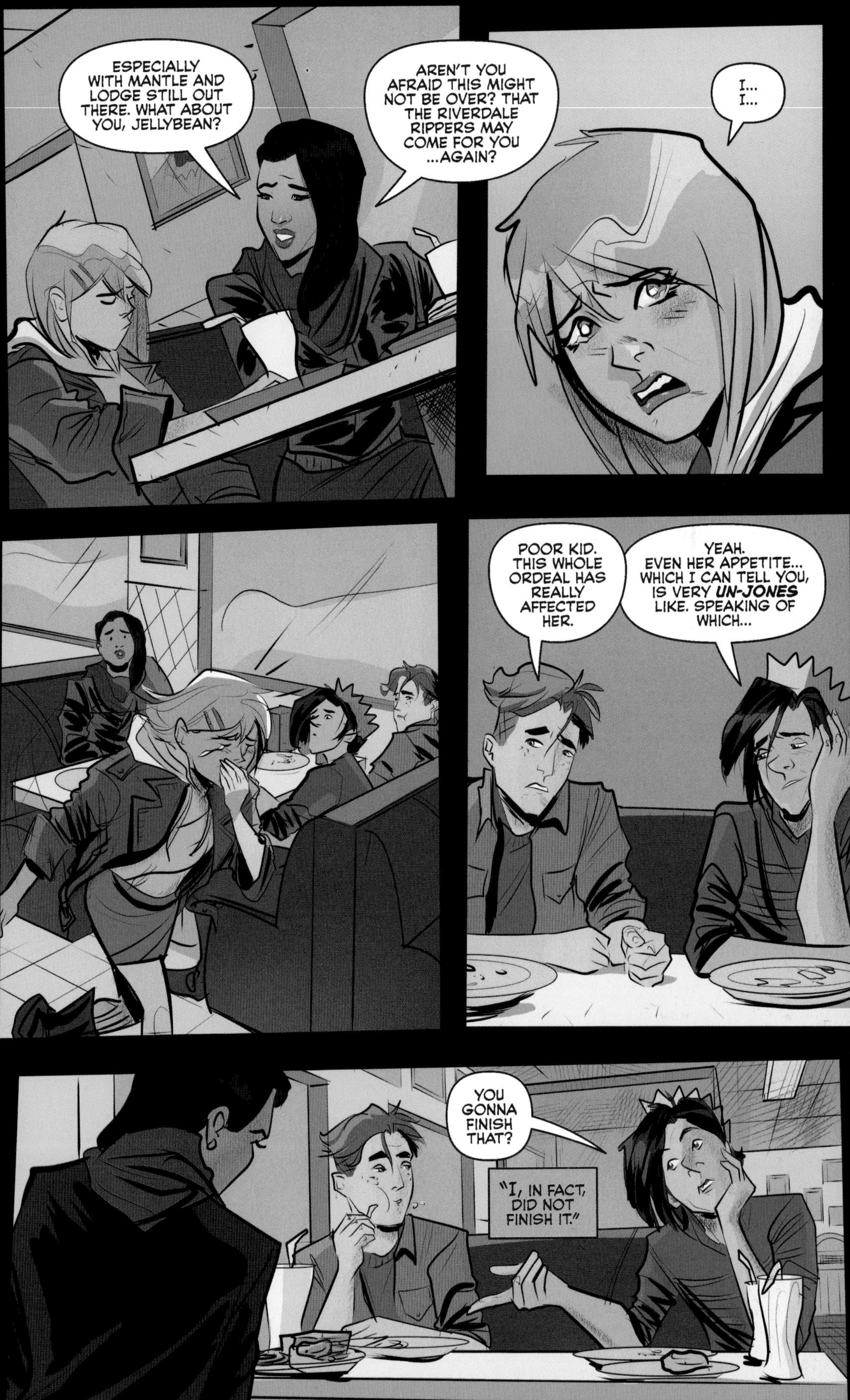
ESPECIALLY WITH MANTLE AND LODGE STILL OUT THERE. WHAT ABOUT YOU, JELLYBEAN?
AREN'T YOU AFRAID THIS MIGHT NOT BE OVER? THAT THE RIVERDALE RIPPERS MAY COME FOR YOU ...AGAIN?
I... I...
POOR KID. THIS WHOLE ORDEAL HAS REALLY AFFECTED HER.
YEAH. EVEN HER APPETITE... WHICH I CAN TELL YOU, IS VERY UN-JONES LIKE. SPEAKING OF WHICH...
YOU GONNA FINISH THAT?
"I, IN FACT, DID NOT FINISH IT."

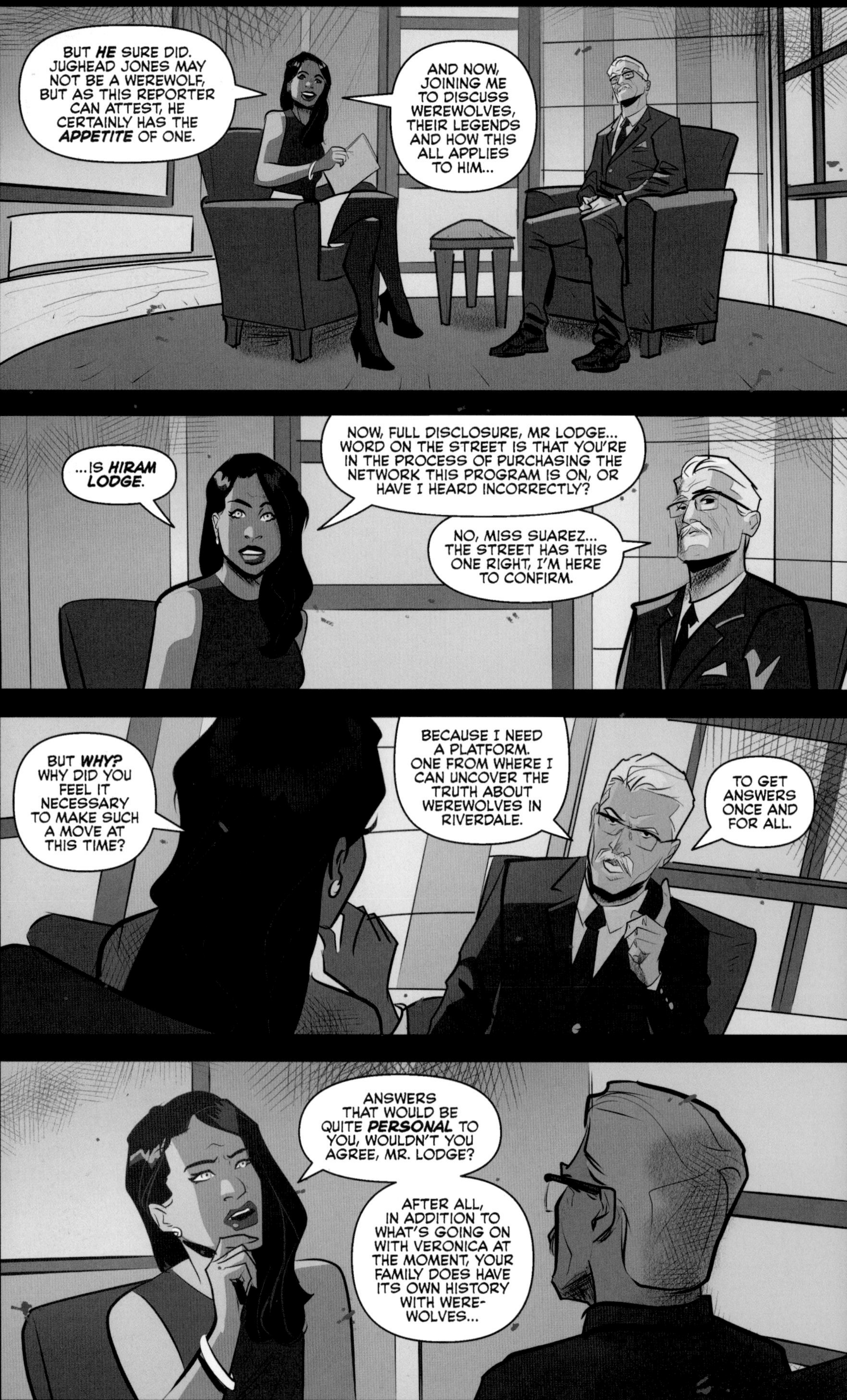

BUT HE SURE DID. JUGHEAD JONES MAY NOT BE A WEREWOLF, BUT AS THIS REPORTER CAN ATTEST, HE CERTAINLY HAS THE APPETITE OF ONE.
AND NOW, JOINING ME TO DISCUSS WEREWOLVES, THEIR LEGENDS AND HOW THIS ALL APPLIES TO HIM...
...IS HIRAM LODGE.
NOW, FULL DISCLOSURE, MR LODGE... WORD ON THE STREET IS THAT YOU'RE IN THE PROCESS OF PURCHASING THE NETWORK THIS PROGRAM IS ON, OR HAVE I HEARD INCORRECTLY?
NO, MISS SUAREZ... THE STREET HAS THIS ONE RIGHT, I'M HERE TO CONFIRM.
BUT WHY? WHY DID YOU FEEL IT NECESSARY TO MAKE SUCH A MOVE AT THIS TIME?
BECAUSE I NEED A PLATFORM. ONE FROM WHERE I CAN UNCOVER THE TRUTH ABOUT WEREWOLVES IN RIVERDALE.
TO GET ANSWERS ONCE AND FOR ALL.
ANSWERS THAT WOULD BE QUITE PERSONAL TO YOU, WOULDN'T YOU AGREE, MR. LODGE?
AFTER ALL, IN ADDITION TO WHAT'S GOING ON WITH VERONICA AT THE MOMENT, YOUR FAMILY DOES HAVE ITS OWN HISTORY WITH WERE-WOLVES...

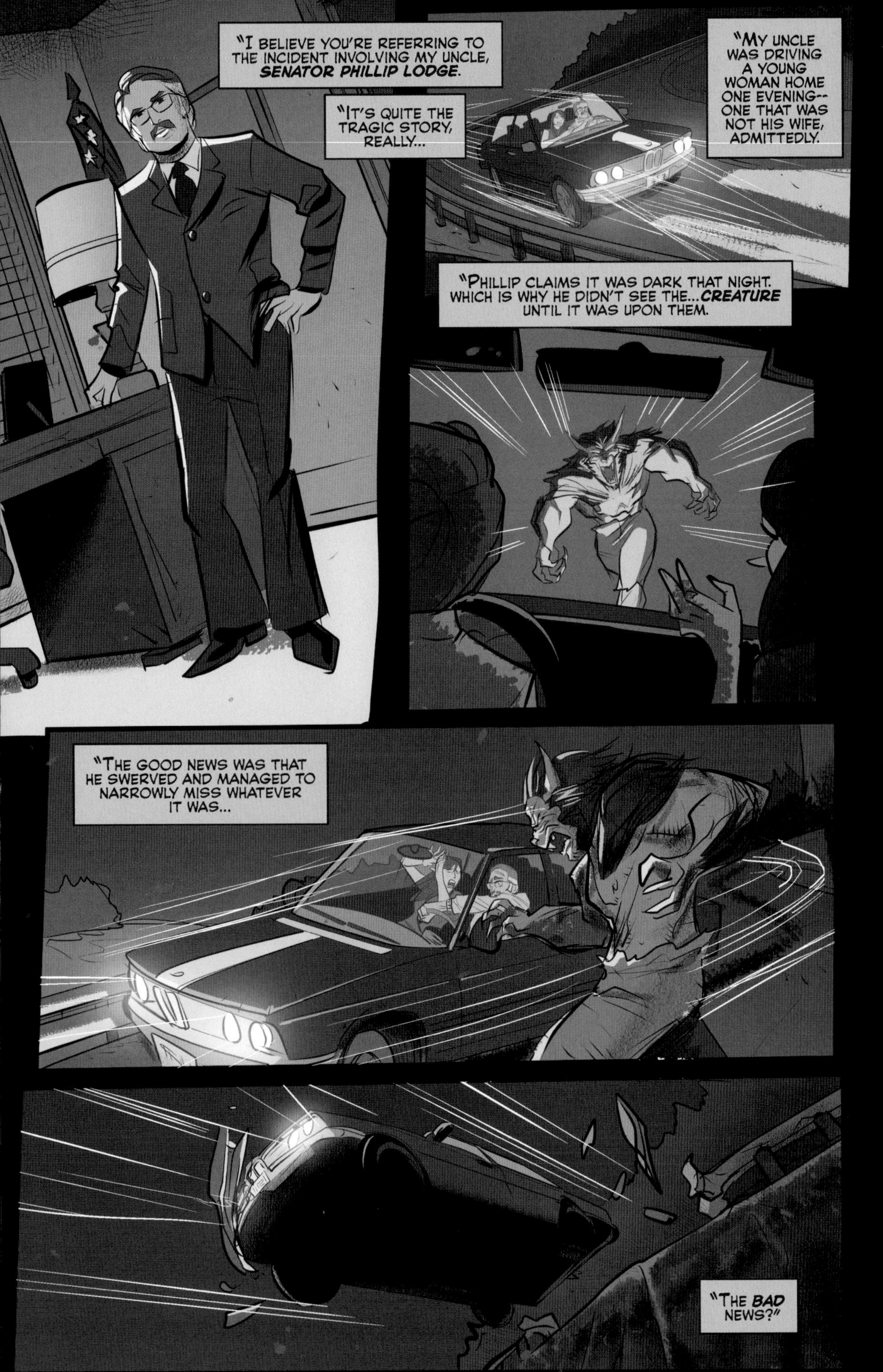
"I BELIEVE YOU'RE REFERRING TO THE INCIDENT INVOLVING MY UNCLE, **SENATOR PHILLIP LODGE**.
"IT'S QUITE THE TRAGIC STORY, REALLY...
"MY UNCLE WAS DRIVING A YOUNG WOMAN HOME ONE EVENING-- ONE THAT WAS NOT HIS WIFE, ADMITTEDLY.
"PHILLIP CLAIMS IT WAS DARK THAT NIGHT. WHICH IS WHY HE DIDN'T SEE THE...**CREATURE** UNTIL IT WAS UPON THEM.
"THE GOOD NEWS WAS THAT HE SWERVED AND MANAGED TO NARROWLY MISS WHATEVER IT WAS...
"THE **BAD** NEWS?"

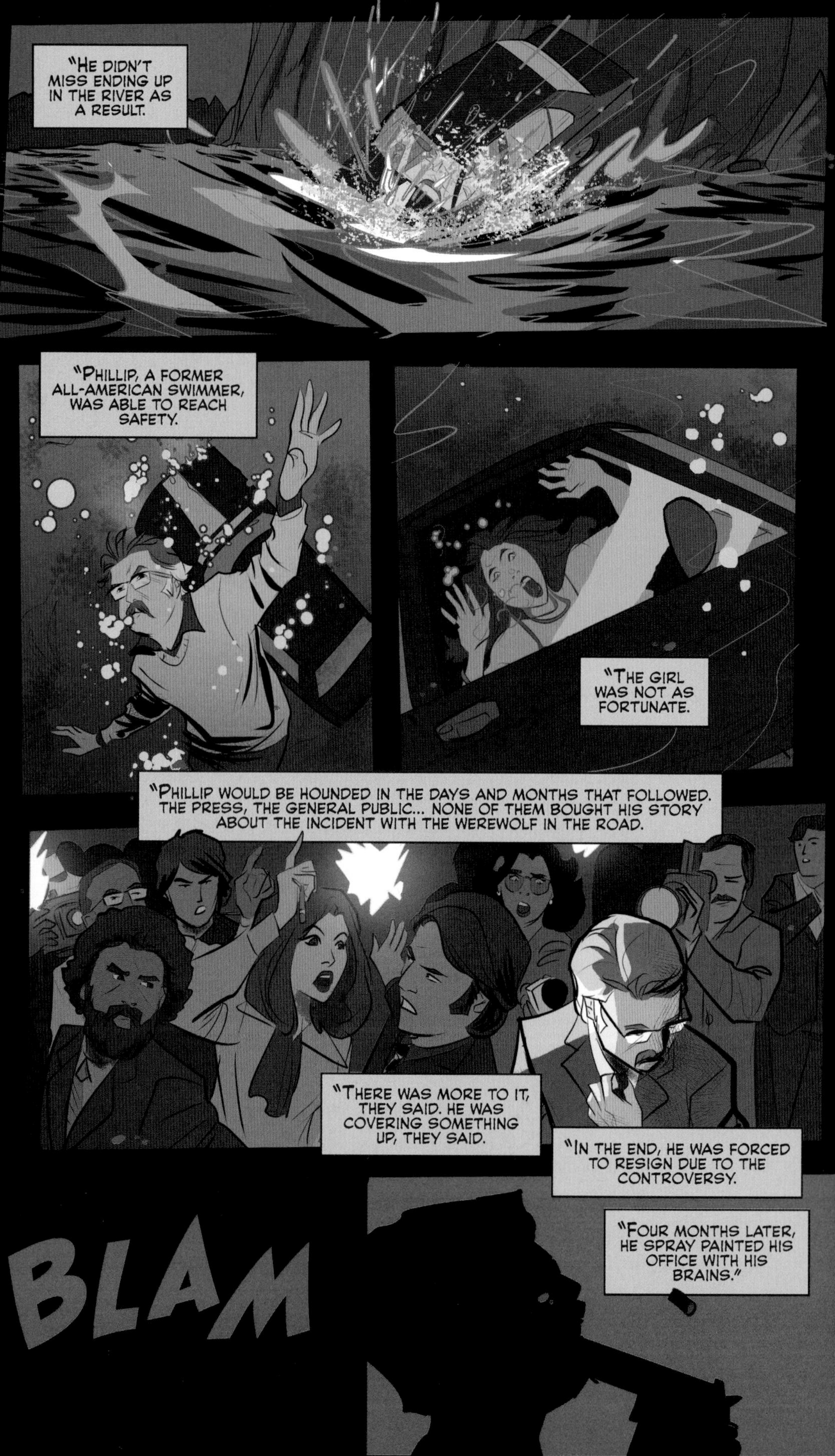
"HE DIDN'T MISS ENDING UP IN THE RIVER AS A RESULT.
"PHILLIP, A FORMER ALL-AMERICAN SWIMMER, WAS ABLE TO REACH SAFETY.
"THE GIRL WAS NOT AS FORTUNATE.
"PHILLIP WOULD BE HOUNDED IN THE DAYS AND MONTHS THAT FOLLOWED. THE PRESS, THE GENERAL PUBLIC... NONE OF THEM BOUGHT HIS STORY ABOUT THE INCIDENT WITH THE WEREWOLF IN THE ROAD.
"THERE WAS MORE TO IT, THEY SAID. HE WAS COVERING SOMETHING UP, THEY SAID.
"IN THE END, HE WAS FORCED TO RESIGN DUE TO THE CONTROVERSY.
"FOUR MONTHS LATER, HE SPRAY PAINTED HIS OFFICE WITH HIS BRAINS."
BLAM

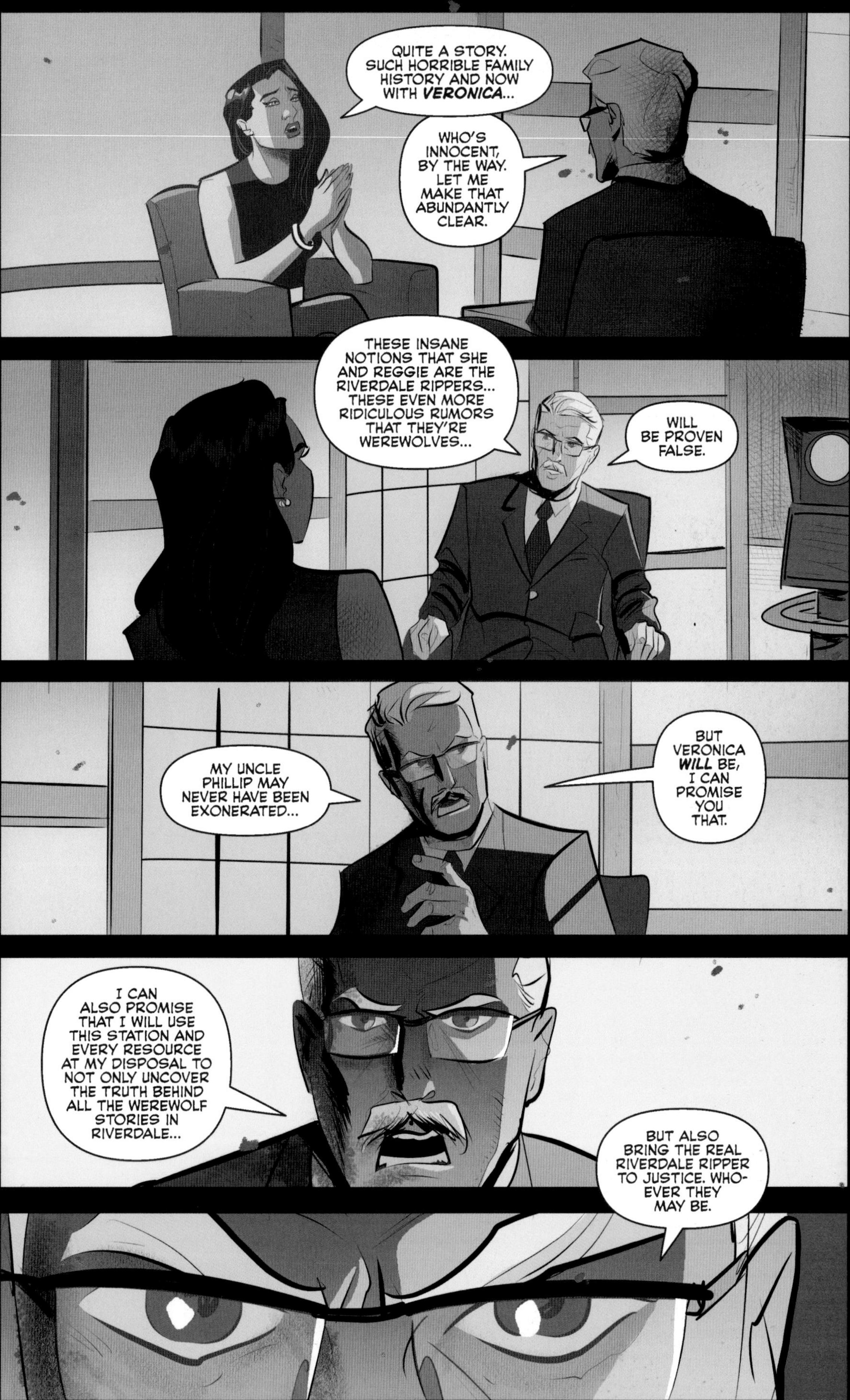
QUITE A STORY. SUCH HORRIBLE FAMILY HISTORY AND NOW WITH *VERONICA*...
WHO'S INNOCENT, BY THE WAY. LET ME MAKE THAT ABUNDANTLY CLEAR.
THESE INSANE NOTIONS THAT SHE AND REGGIE ARE THE RIVERDALE RIPPERS... THESE EVEN MORE RIDICULOUS RUMORS THAT THEY'RE WEREWOLVES...
WILL BE PROVEN FALSE.
MY UNCLE PHILLIP MAY NEVER HAVE BEEN EXONERATED...
BUT VERONICA *WILL* BE, I CAN PROMISE YOU THAT.
I CAN ALSO PROMISE THAT I WILL USE THIS STATION AND EVERY RESOURCE AT MY DISPOSAL TO NOT ONLY UNCOVER THE TRUTH BEHIND ALL THE WEREWOLF STORIES IN RIVERDALE...
BUT ALSO BRING THE REAL RIVERDALE RIPPER TO JUSTICE. WHO-EVER THEY MAY BE.

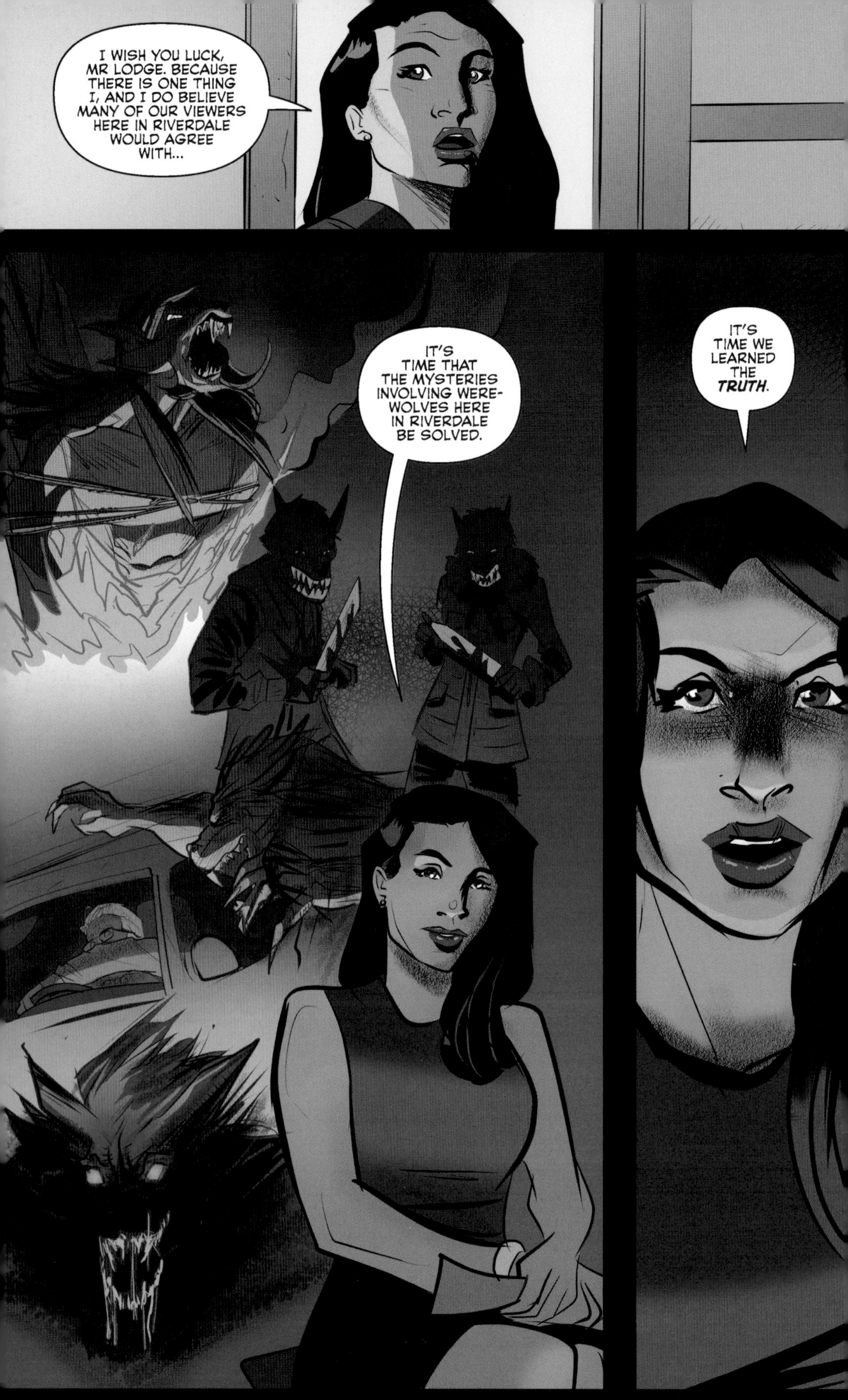
I WISH YOU LUCK, MR LODGE. BECAUSE THERE IS ONE THING I, AND I DO BELIEVE MANY OF OUR VIEWERS HERE IN RIVERDALE WOULD AGREE WITH...
IT'S TIME THAT THE MYSTERIES INVOLVING WERE-WOLVES HERE IN RIVERDALE BE SOLVED.
IT'S TIME WE LEARNED THE *TRUTH*.

Continued in the ongoing JUGHEAD THE HUNGER series on sale now!

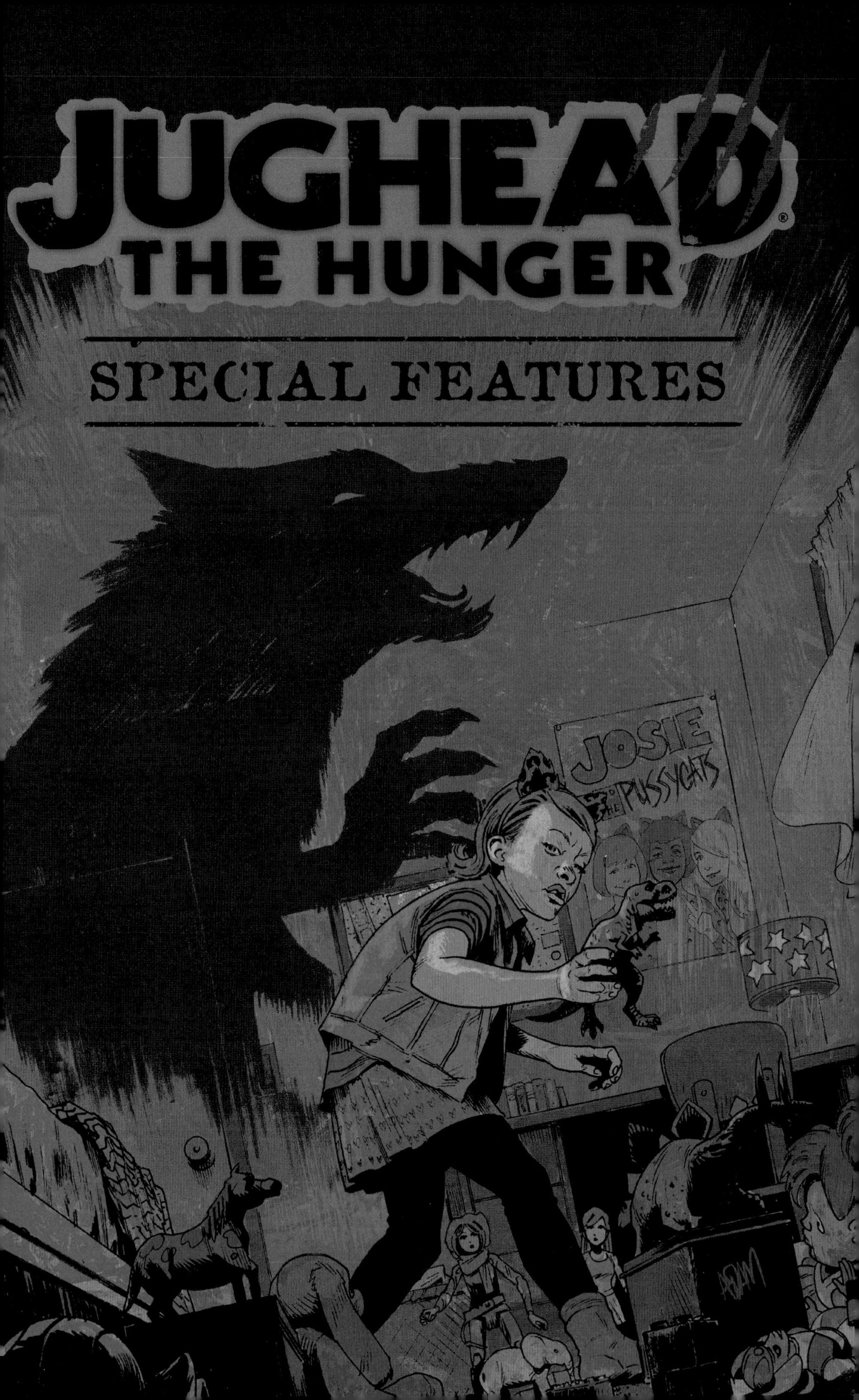
JUGHEAD
THE HUNGER
SPECIAL FEATURES
JOSIE
PUSSYCATS

JUGHEAD
THE HUNGER

VARIANT COVER GALLERY

Take a look at our eye-catching variant covers for the five issues included in this graphic novel collection.

ISSUE FOUR

(L)
T-Rex

(R)
Michael Walsh

ISSUE FIVE

(L)
Jamal Igle

(R)
Michael Walsh

ISSUE SIX

(L)
Derek Charm

(R)
Michael Walsh

ISSUE SEVEN

(L)
Tyler Boss

(R)
Michael Walsh

ISSUE EIGHT

(L)
Djibril Morrissette-Phan

(R)
Cary Nord

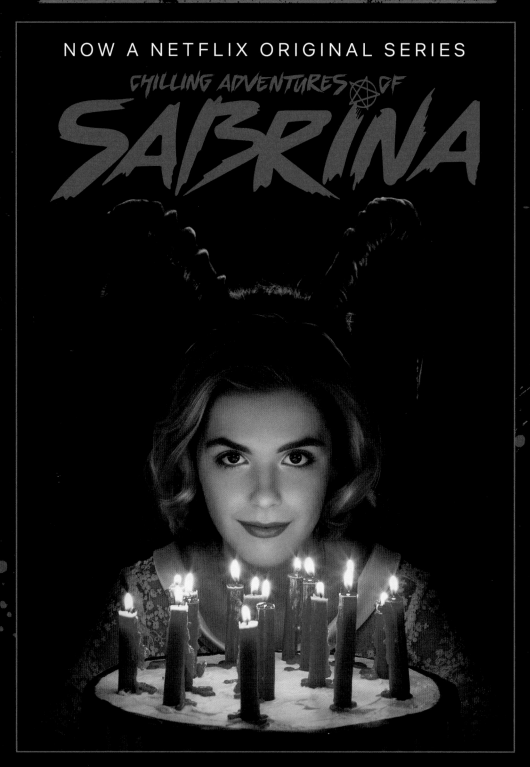

NOW A NETFLIX ORIGINAL SERIES

CHILLING ADVENTURES OF SABRINA

You've seen CHILLING ADVENTURES OF SABRINA, the brand new, hit NETFLIX series—now see where it all began! Written by ROBERTO AGUIRRE-SACASA with art by ROBERT HACK and lettering by JACK MORELLI.

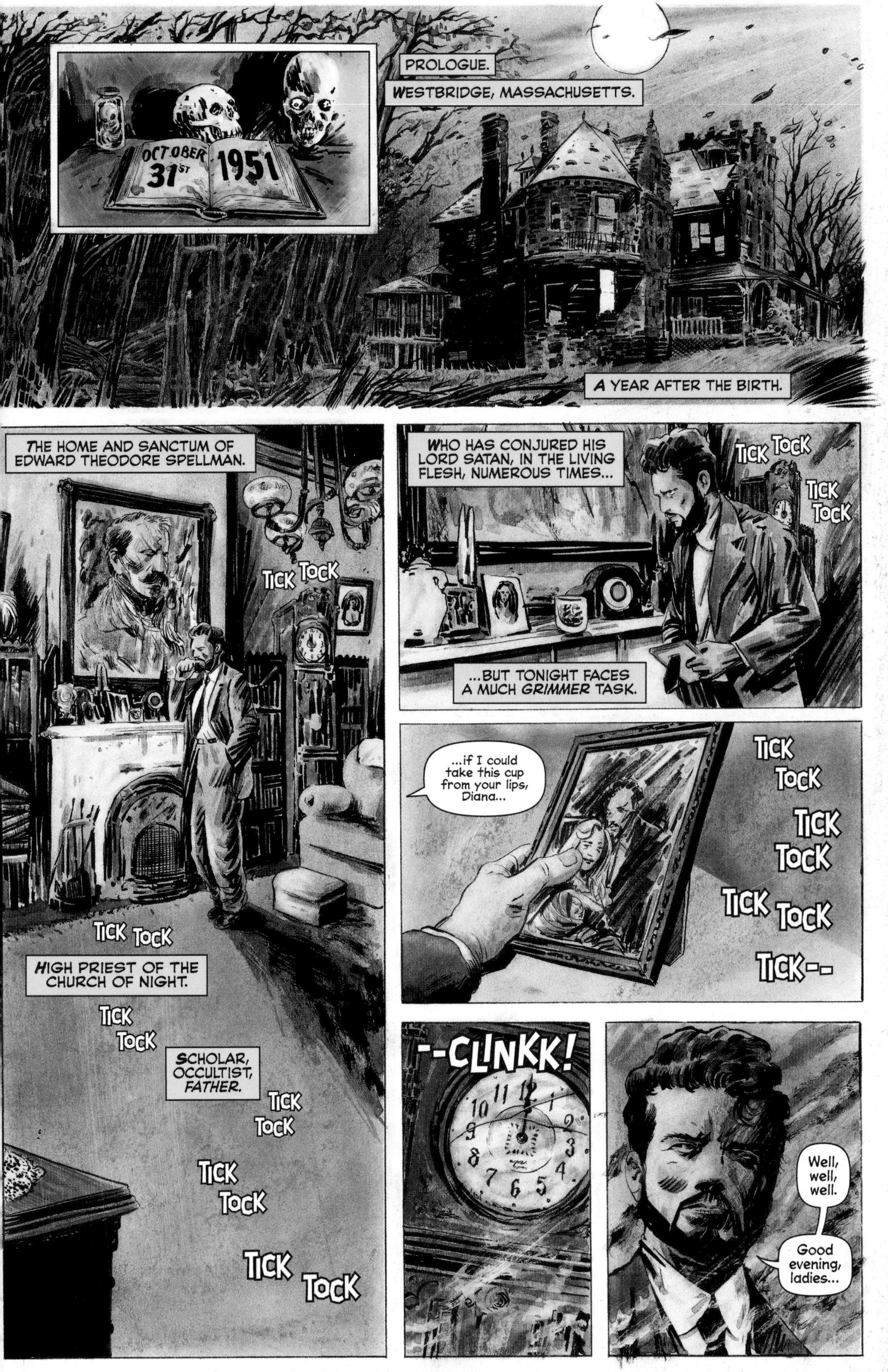
OCTOBER 31ST 1951
PROLOGUE.
WESTBRIDGE, MASSACHUSETTS.
A YEAR AFTER THE BIRTH.
THE HOME AND SANCTUM OF EDWARD THEODORE SPELLMAN.
TICK TOCK
TICK TOCK
HIGH PRIEST OF THE CHURCH OF NIGHT.
TICK TOCK
SCHOLAR, OCCULTIST, FATHER.
TICK TOCK
TICK TOCK
TICK TOCK
WHO HAS CONJURED HIS LORD SATAN, IN THE LIVING FLESH, NUMEROUS TIMES...
TICK TOCK
TICK TOCK
...BUT TONIGHT FACES A MUCH GRIMMER TASK.
...if I could take this cup from your lips, Diana...
TICK TOCK
TICK TOCK
TICK TOCK
TICK--
--CLINKK!
Well, well, well.
Good evening, ladies...

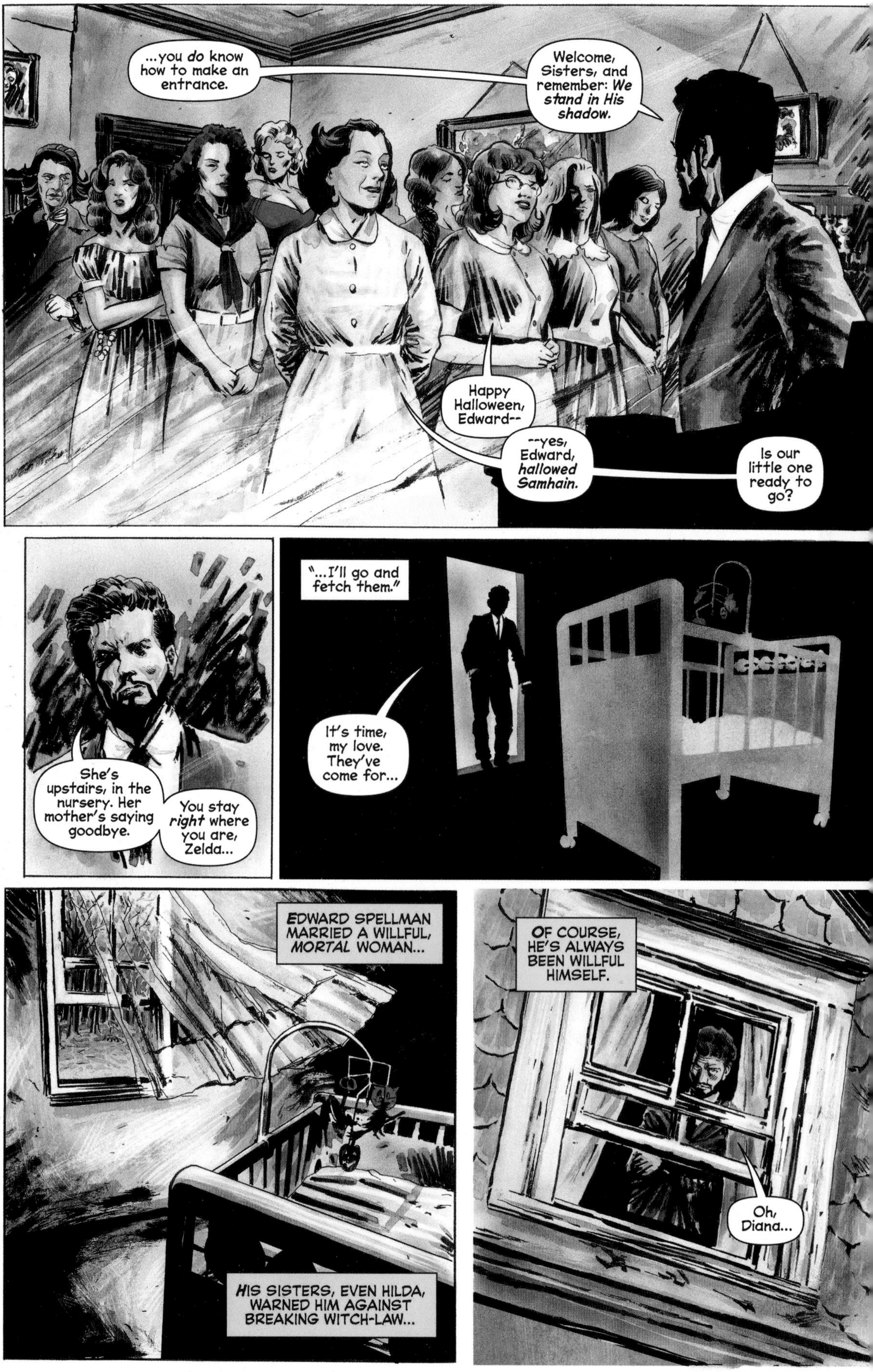
...you *do* know how to make an entrance.
Welcome, Sisters, and remember: *We stand in His shadow.*
Happy Halloween, Edward--
--yes, Edward, *hallowed Samhain.*
Is our little one ready to go?
She's upstairs, in the nursery. Her mother's saying goodbye.
You stay *right* where you are, Zelda...
"...I'll go and fetch them."
It's time, my love. They've come for...
EDWARD SPELLMAN MARRIED A WILLFUL, *MORTAL* WOMAN...
HIS SISTERS, EVEN HILDA, WARNED HIM AGAINST BREAKING WITCH-LAW...
OF COURSE, HE'S ALWAYS BEEN WILLFUL HIMSELF.
Oh, Diana...

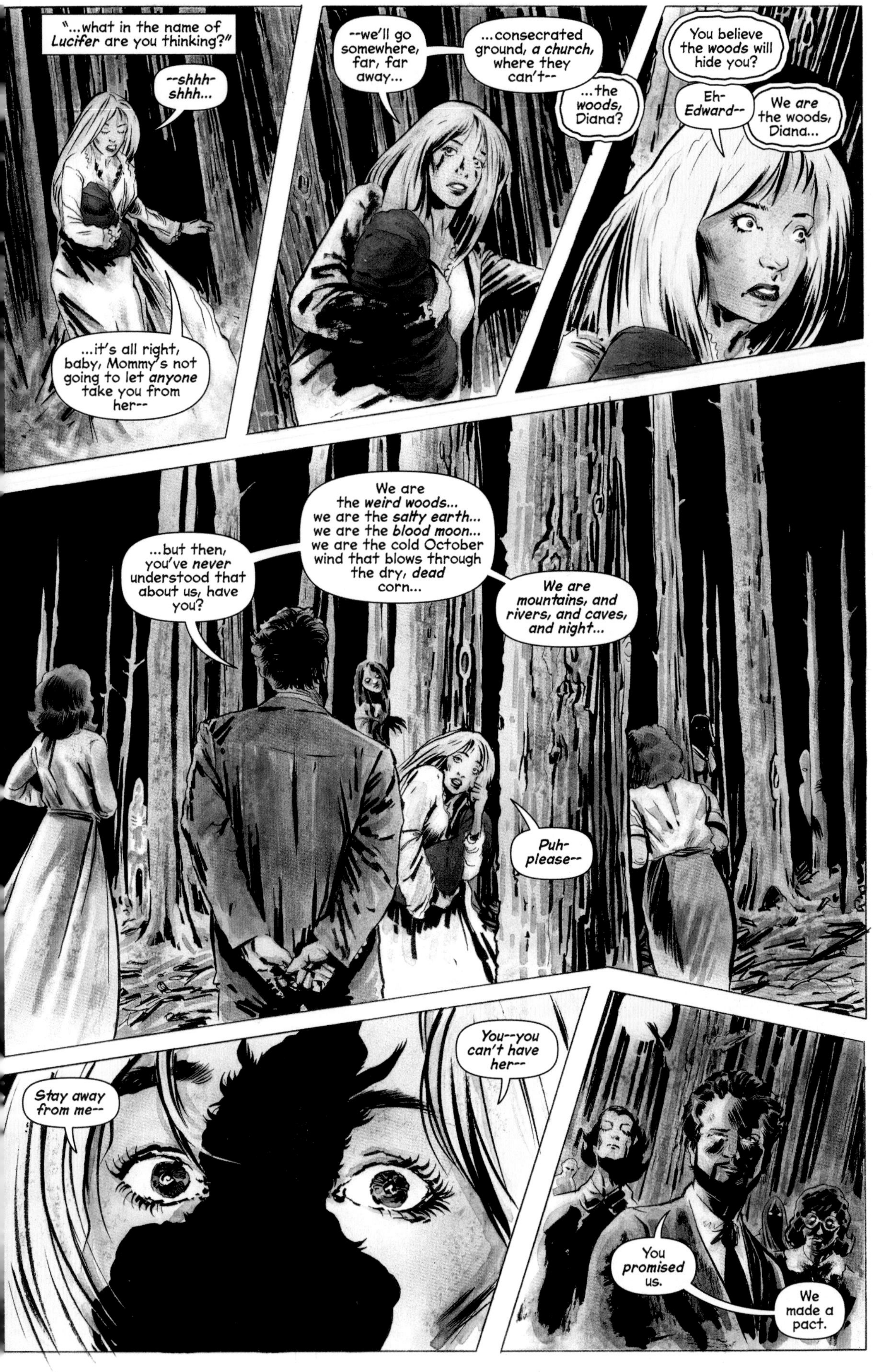
"...what in the name of Lucifer are you thinking?"
--shhh-shhh...
...it's all right, baby, Mommy's not going to let anyone take you from her--
--we'll go somewhere, far, far away...
...consecrated ground, a church, where they can't--
...the woods, Diana?
You believe the woods will hide you?
Eh-Edward--
We are the woods, Diana...
We are the weird woods... we are the salty earth... we are the blood moon... we are the cold October wind that blows through the dry, dead corn...
...but then, you've never understood that about us, have you?
We are mountains, and rivers, and caves, and night...
Puh-please--
Stay away from me--
You--you can't have her--
You promised us.
We made a pact.

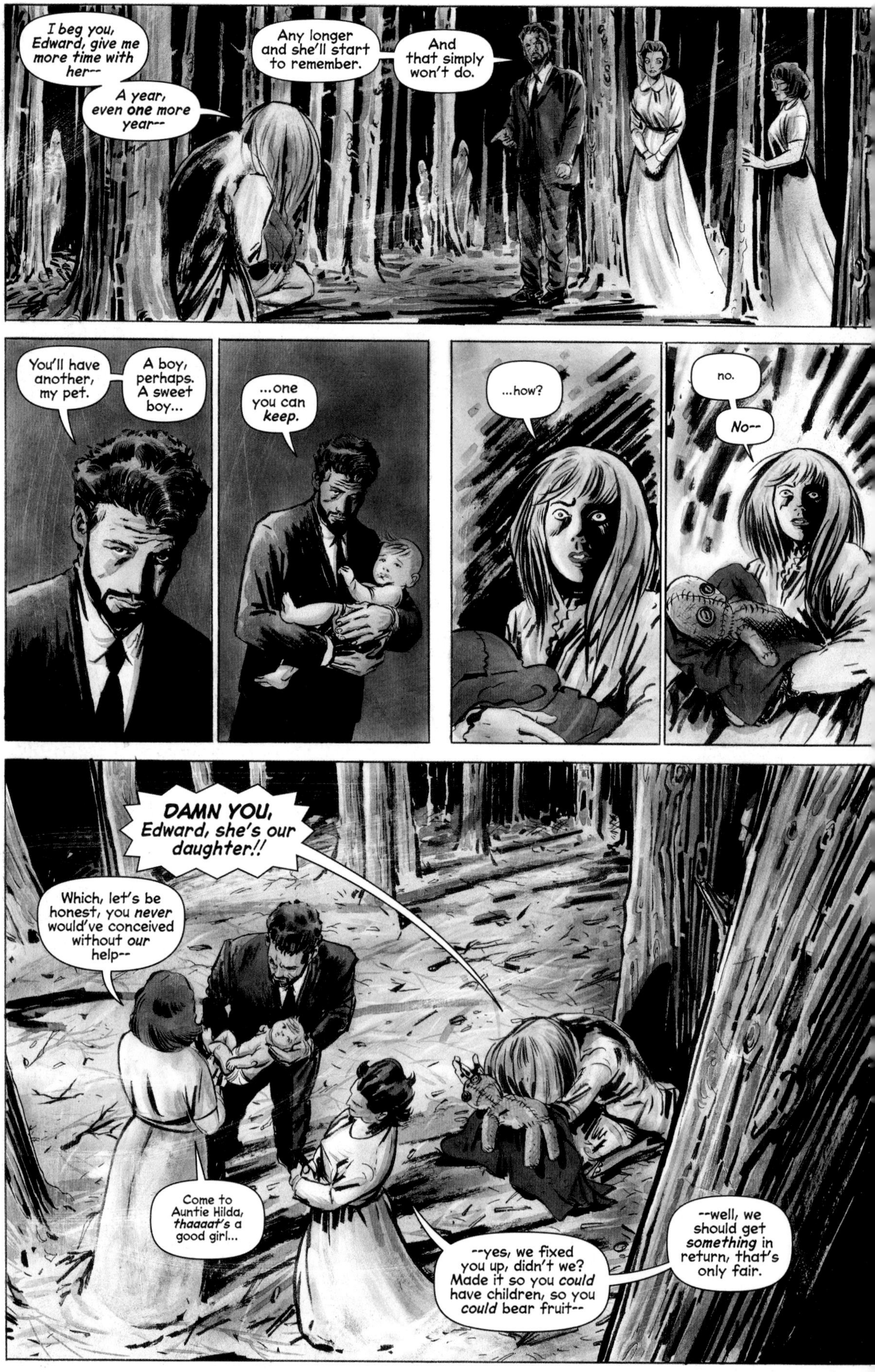
I beg you, Edward, give me more time with her--
A year, even one more year--
Any longer and she'll start to remember.
And that simply won't do.
You'll have another, my pet.
A boy, perhaps. A sweet boy...
...one you can keep.
...how?
no.
No--
DAMN YOU, Edward, she's our daughter!!
Which, let's be honest, you never would've conceived without our help--
Come to Auntie Hilda, thaaaat's a good girl...
--yes, we fixed you up, didn't we? Made it so you could have children, so you could bear fruit--
--well, we should get something in return, that's only fair.

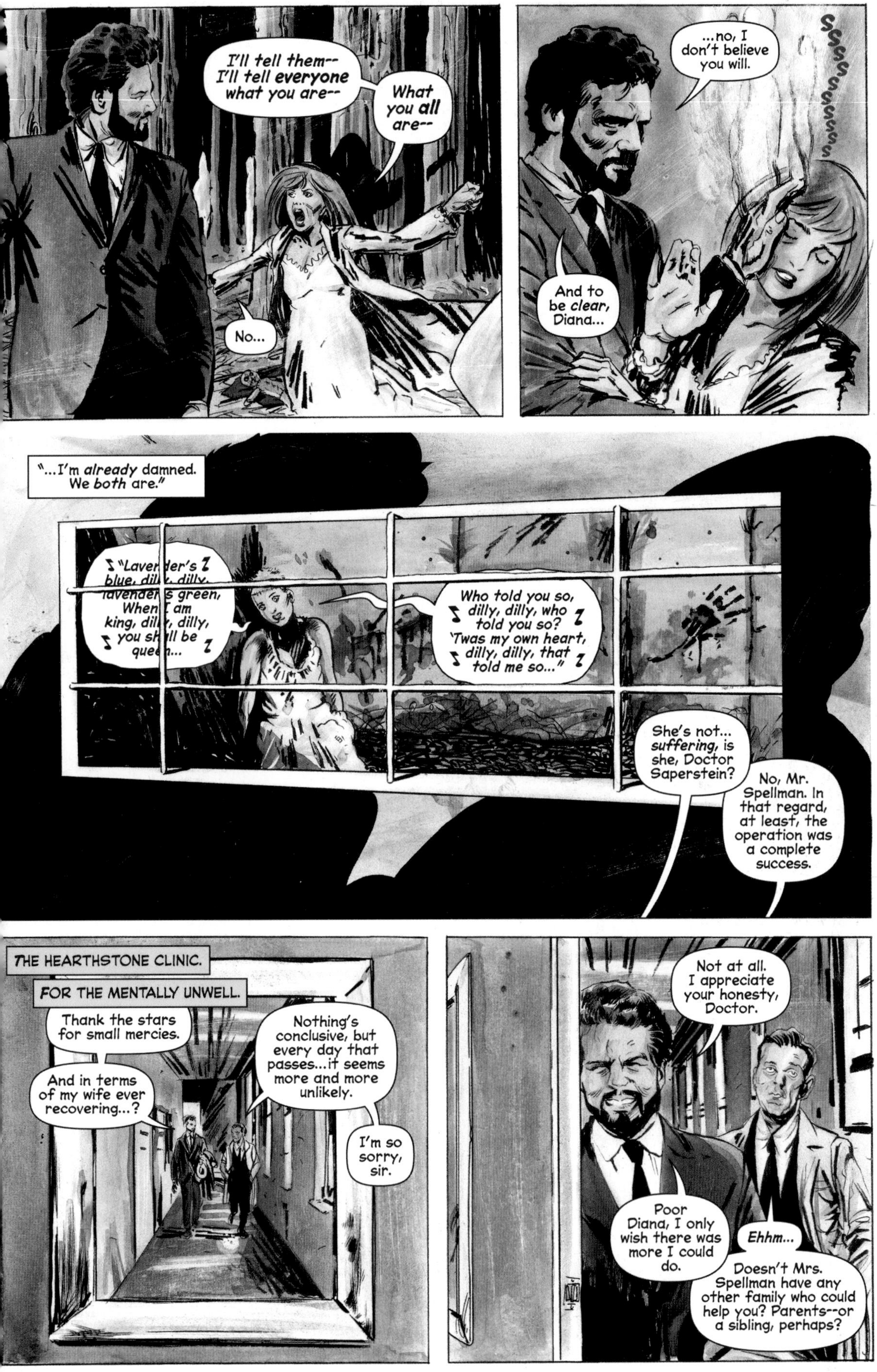
I'll tell them--
I'll tell everyone
what you are--
What you all are--
No...
...no, I don't believe you will.
SSSSSSSSSSSS
And to be clear, Diana...
"...I'm already damned. We both are."
"Lavender's blue, dilly, dilly, lavender's green, When I am king, dilly, dilly, you shall be queen...
Who told you so, dilly, dilly, who told you so? 'Twas my own heart, dilly, dilly, that told me so..."
She's not... suffering, is she, Doctor Saperstein?
No, Mr. Spellman. In that regard, at least, the operation was a complete success.
THE HEARTHSTONE CLINIC.
FOR THE MENTALLY UNWELL.
Thank the stars for small mercies.
And in terms of my wife ever recovering...?
Nothing's conclusive, but every day that passes...it seems more and more unlikely.
I'm so sorry, sir.
Not at all. I appreciate your honesty, Doctor.
Poor Diana, I only wish there was more I could do.
Ehhm...
Doesn't Mrs. Spellman have any other family who could help you? Parents--or a sibling, perhaps?

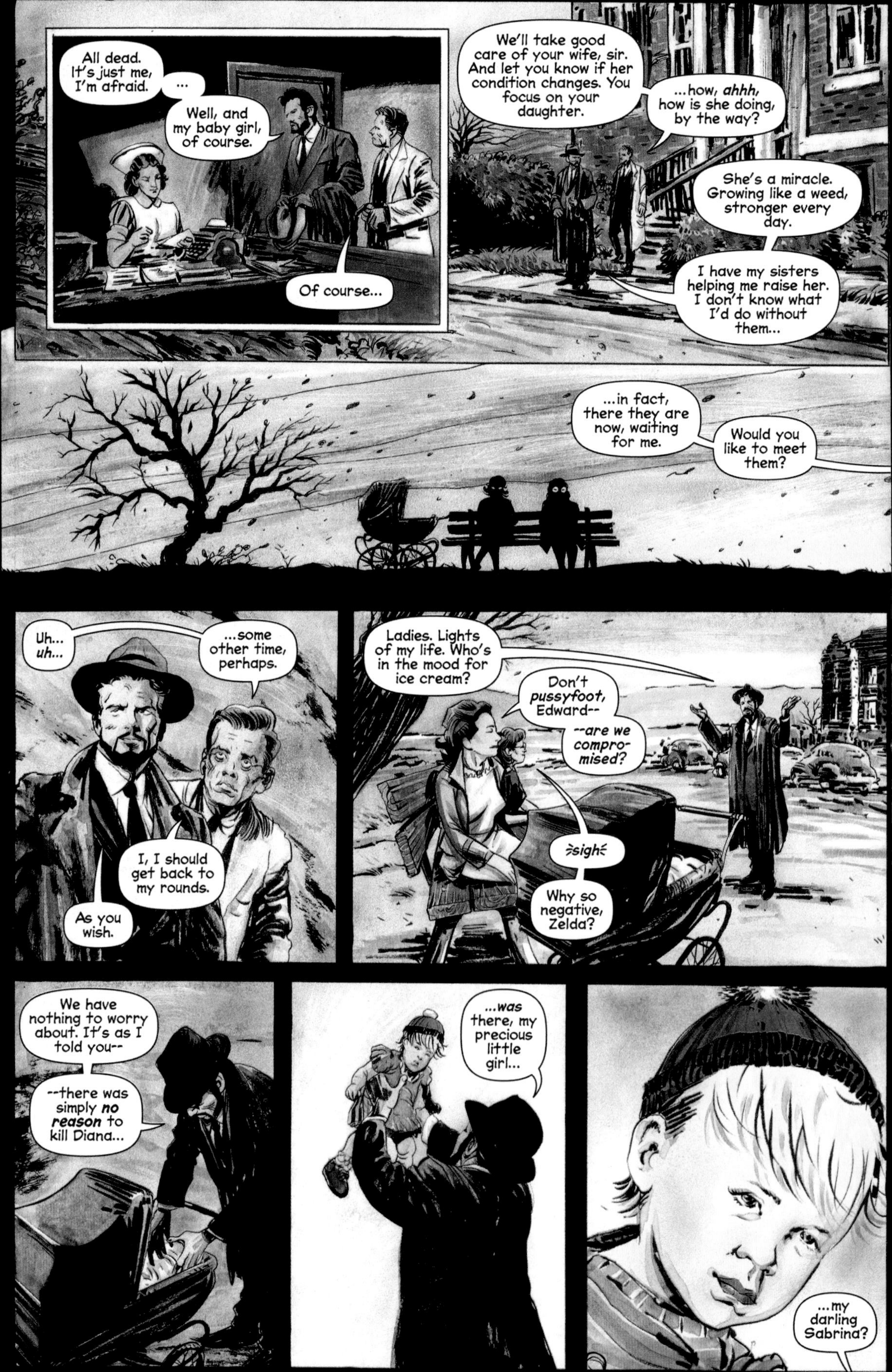

All dead. It's just me, I'm afraid.
...
Well, and my baby girl, of course.
Of course...
We'll take good care of your wife, sir. And let you know if her condition changes. You focus on your daughter.
...how, *ahhh*, how is she doing, by the way?
She's a miracle. Growing like a weed, stronger every day.
I have my sisters helping me raise her. I don't know what I'd do without them...
...in fact, there they are now, waiting for me.
Would you like to meet them?
Uh... *uh*...
...some other time, perhaps.
I, I should get back to my rounds.
As you wish.
Ladies. Lights of my life. Who's in the mood for ice cream?
Don't *pussyfoot*, Edward--
--*are we compromised*?
sigh
Why so negative, Zelda?
We have nothing to worry about. It's as I told you--
--there was simply **no reason** to kill Diana...
...*was* there, my precious little girl...
...my darling Sabrina?

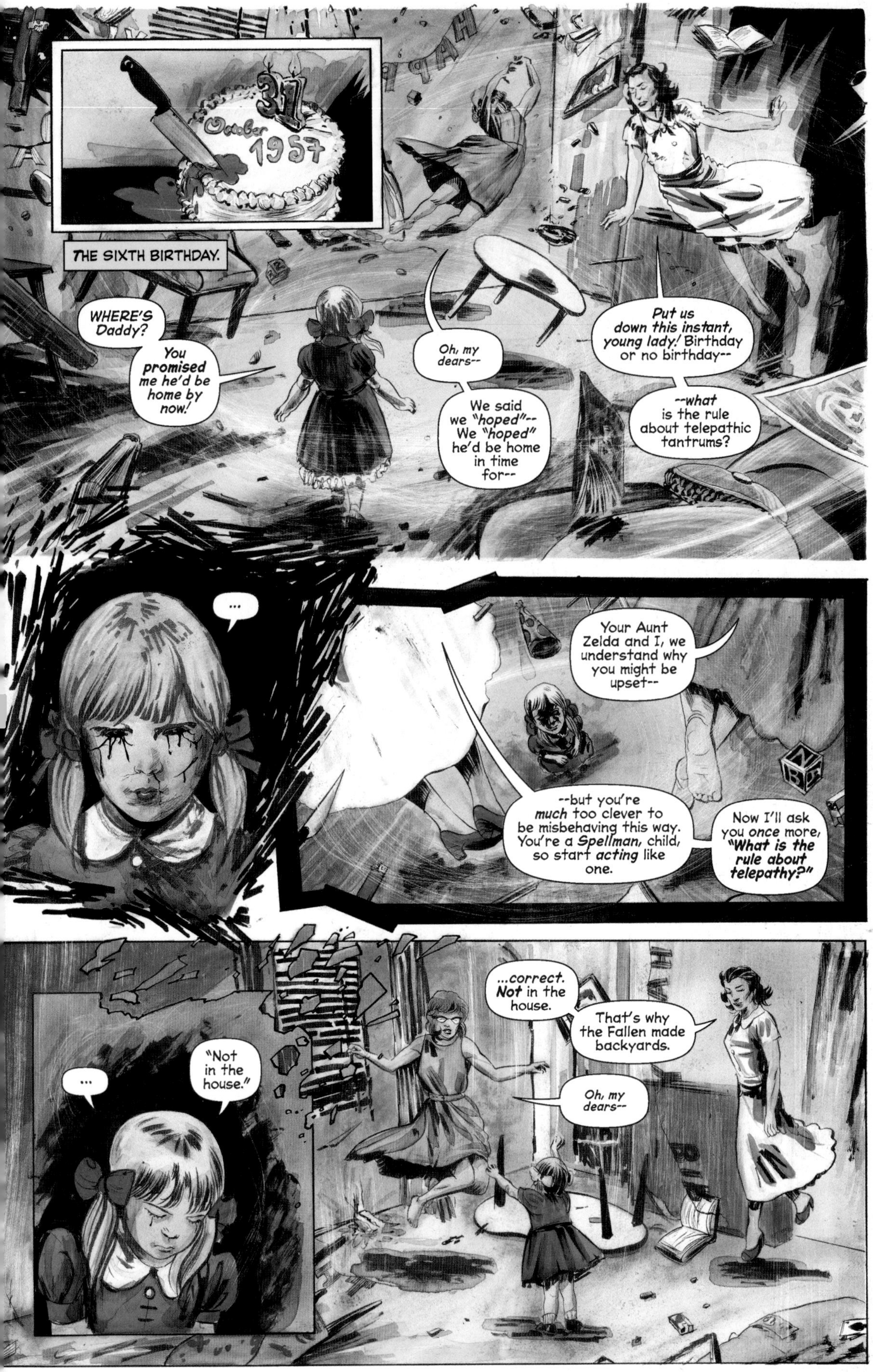
October 31 1957
THE SIXTH BIRTHDAY.
WHERE'S Daddy?
You promised me he'd be home by now!
Oh, my dears--
We said we "hoped"-- We "hoped" he'd be home in time for--
Put us down this instant, young lady! Birthday or no birthday--
--what is the rule about telepathic tantrums?
...
Your Aunt Zelda and I, we understand why you might be upset--
--but you're much too clever to be misbehaving this way. You're a Spellman, child, so start acting like one.
Now I'll ask you once more, "What is the rule about telepathy?"
...
"Not in the house."
...correct. Not in the house.
That's why the Fallen made backyards.
Oh, my dears--

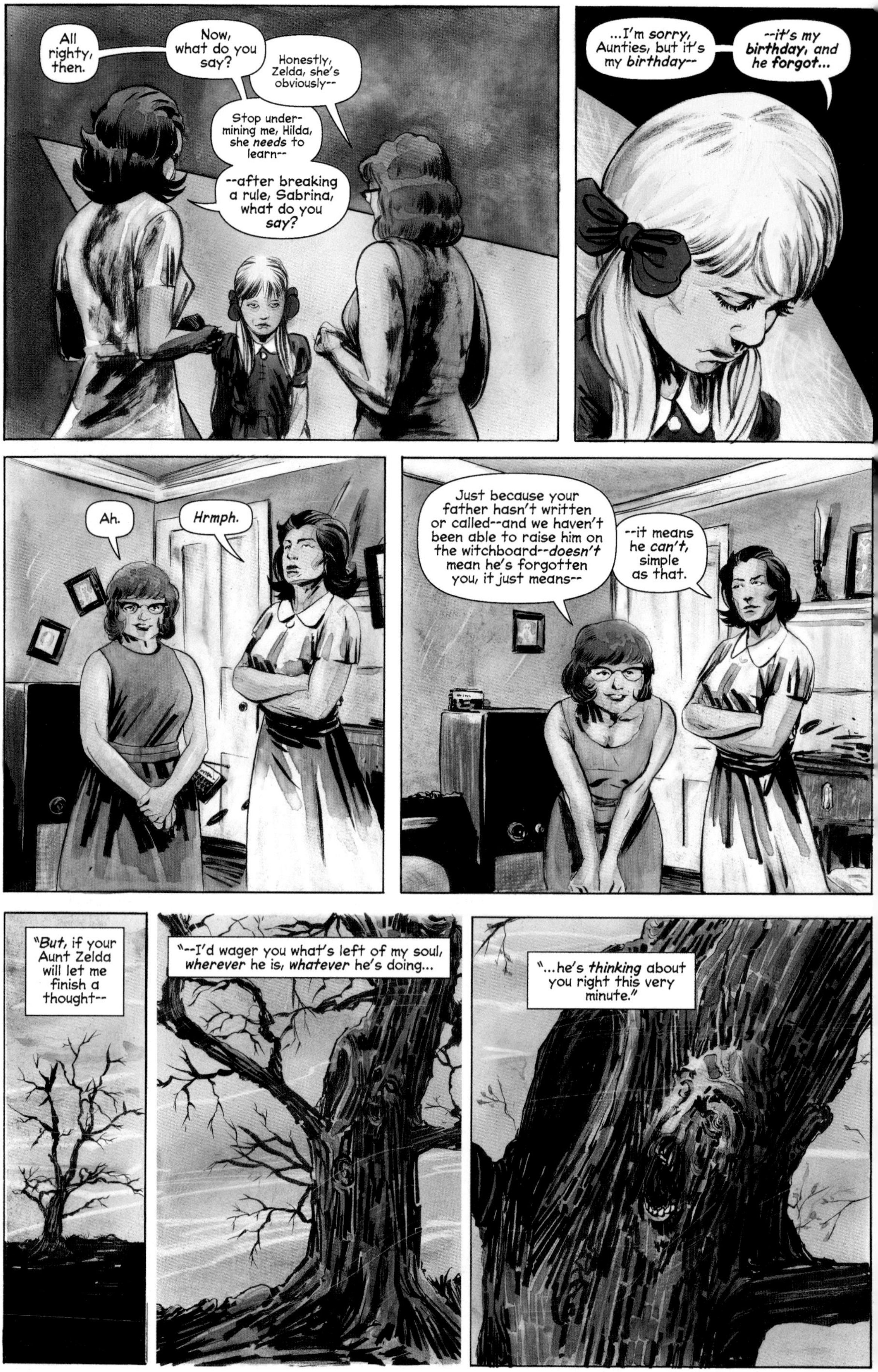
All righty, then.
Now, what do you say?
Honestly, Zelda, she's obviously--
Stop under-mining me, Hilda, she *needs* to learn--
--after breaking a rule, Sabrina, what do you *say?*
...I'm *sorry,* Aunties, but it's my *birthday*--
--*it's my birthday, and he forgot...*
Ah.
Hrmph.
Just because your father hasn't written or called--and we haven't been able to raise him on the witchboard--*doesn't* mean he's forgotten you, it just means--
--it means he *can't,* simple as that.
"*But,* if your Aunt Zelda will let me finish a thought--
"--I'd wager you what's left of my soul, *wherever* he is, *whatever* he's doing...
"...he's *thinking* about you right this very minute."

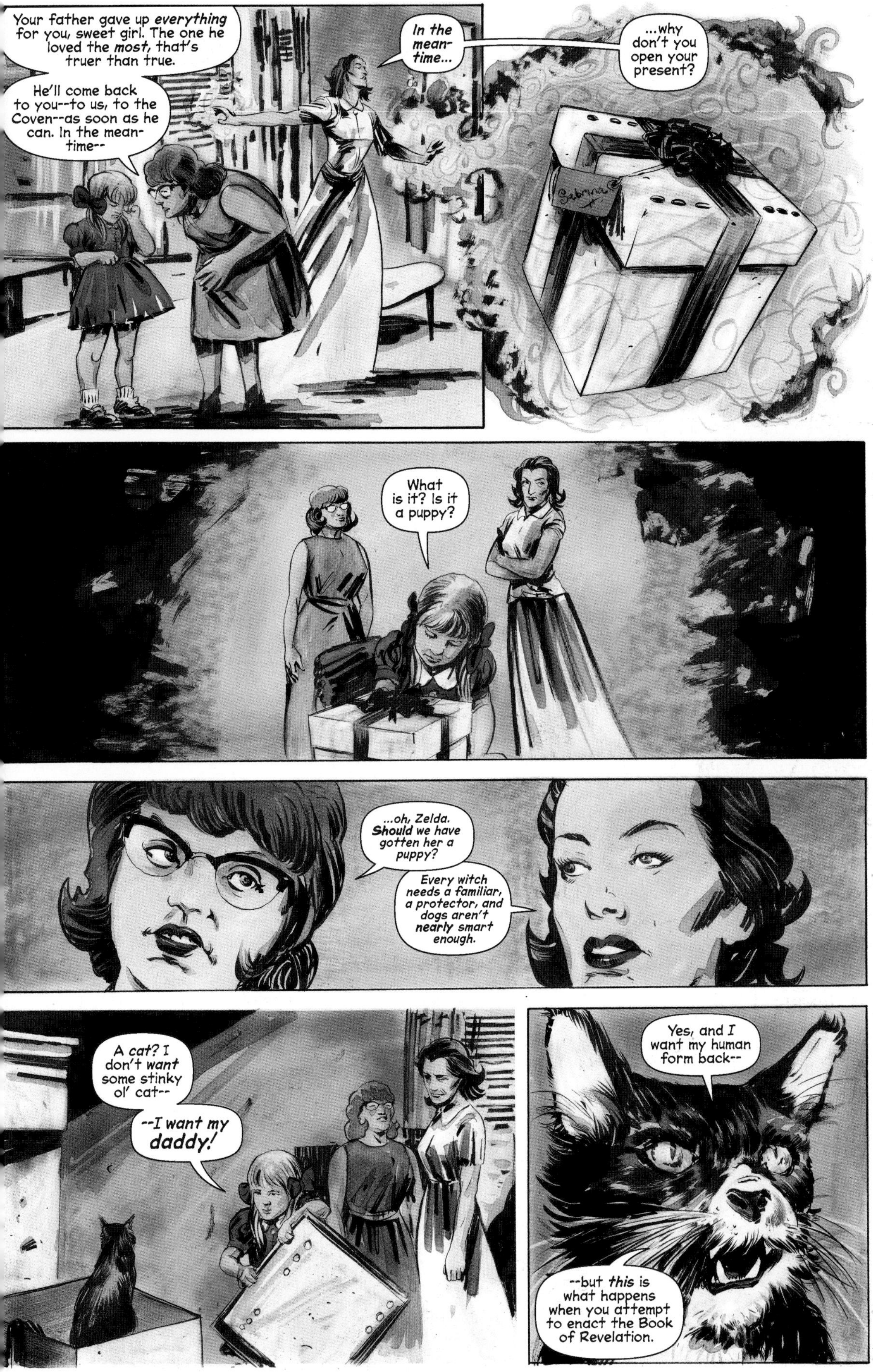
Your father gave up *everything* for you, sweet girl. The one he loved the *most*, that's truer than true.
He'll come back to you--to us, to the Coven--as soon as he can. In the mean-time--
In the mean-time...
...why don't you open your present?
Sabrina
What is it? Is it a puppy?
...oh, Zelda. ***Should*** *we have gotten her a puppy?*
Every witch needs a familiar, a protector, and dogs aren't ***nearly*** *smart enough.*
A *cat?* I don't *want* some stinky ol' cat--
--I want my ***daddy!***
Yes, and *I* want my human form back--
--but *this* is what happens when you attempt to enact the Book of Revelation.

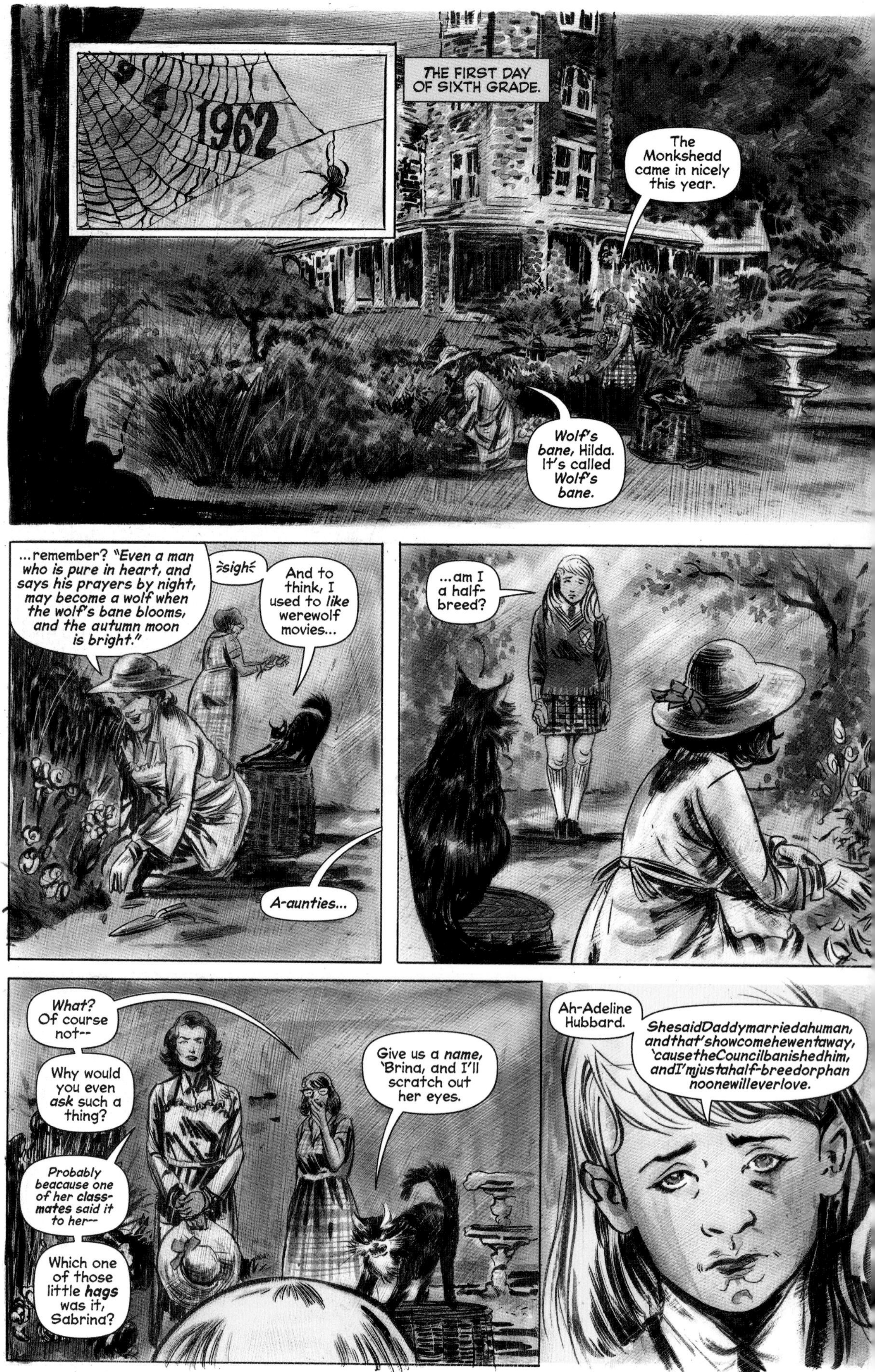
9 4 1962
THE FIRST DAY OF SIXTH GRADE.
The Monkshead came in nicely this year.
Wolf's bane, Hilda. It's called Wolf's bane.
...remember? "Even a man who is pure in heart, and says his prayers by night, may become a wolf when the wolf's bane blooms, and the autumn moon is bright."
sigh
And to think, I used to like werewolf movies...
A-aunties...
...am I a half-breed?
What? Of course not--
Why would you even ask such a thing?
Probably beacause one of her class-mates said it to her--
Which one of those little hags was it, Sabrina?
Give us a name, 'Brina, and I'll scratch out her eyes.
Ah-Adeline Hubbard.
ShesaidDaddymarriedahuman, andthat'showcomehewentaway, 'causetheCouncilbanishedhim, andI'mjustahalf-breedorphan noonewilleverlove.

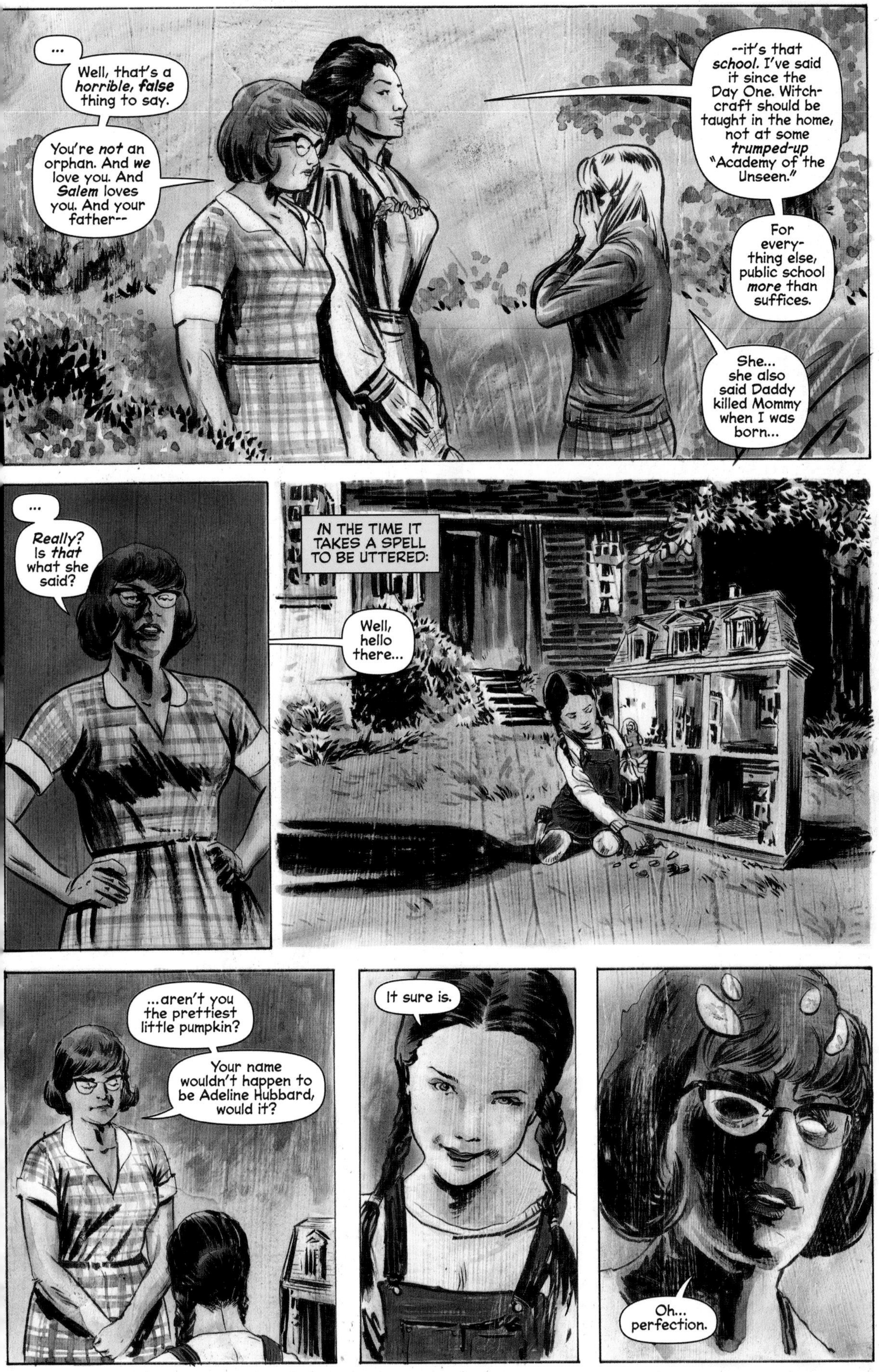
...
Well, that's a horrible, false thing to say.
You're not an orphan. And we love you. And Salem loves you. And your father--
--it's that school. I've said it since the Day One. Witch-craft should be taught in the home, not at some trumped-up "Academy of the Unseen."
For every-thing else, public school more than suffices.
She... she also said Daddy killed Mommy when I was born...
...
Really? Is that what she said?
IN THE TIME IT TAKES A SPELL TO BE UTTERED:
Well, hello there...
...aren't you the prettiest little pumpkin?
Your name wouldn't happen to be Adeline Hubbard, would it?
It sure is.
Oh... perfection.

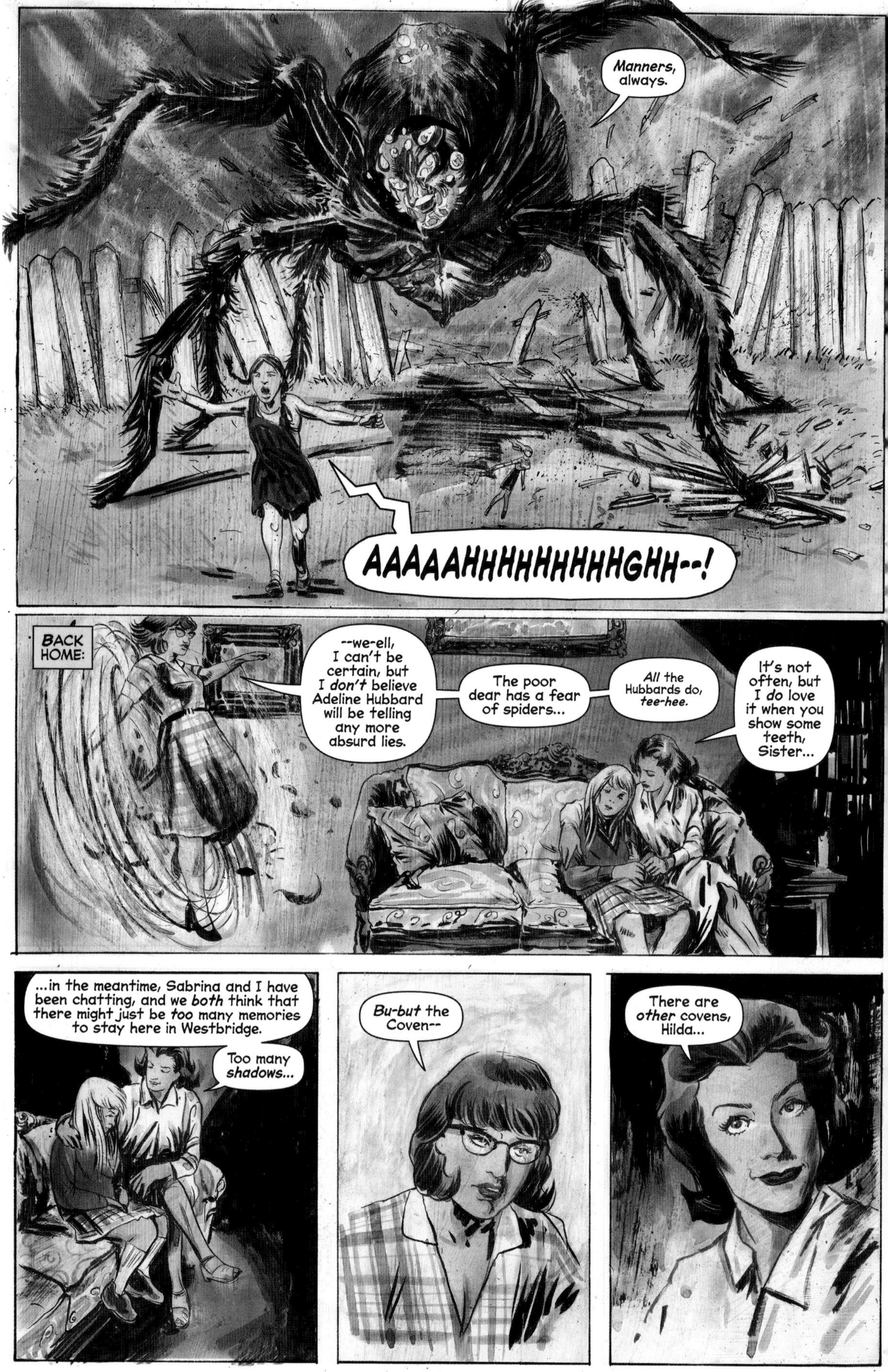
Manners, always.
AAAAAHHHHHHHHHGHH--!
BACK HOME:
--we-ell, I can't be certain, but I *don't* believe Adeline Hubbard will be telling any more absurd lies.
The poor dear has a fear of spiders...
All the Hubbards do, *tee-hee.*
It's not often, but I *do* love it when you show some teeth, Sister...
...in the meantime, Sabrina and I have been chatting, and we *both* think that there might just be *too* many memories to stay here in Westbridge.
Too many *shadows*...
Bu-but the Coven--
There are *other* covens, Hilda...

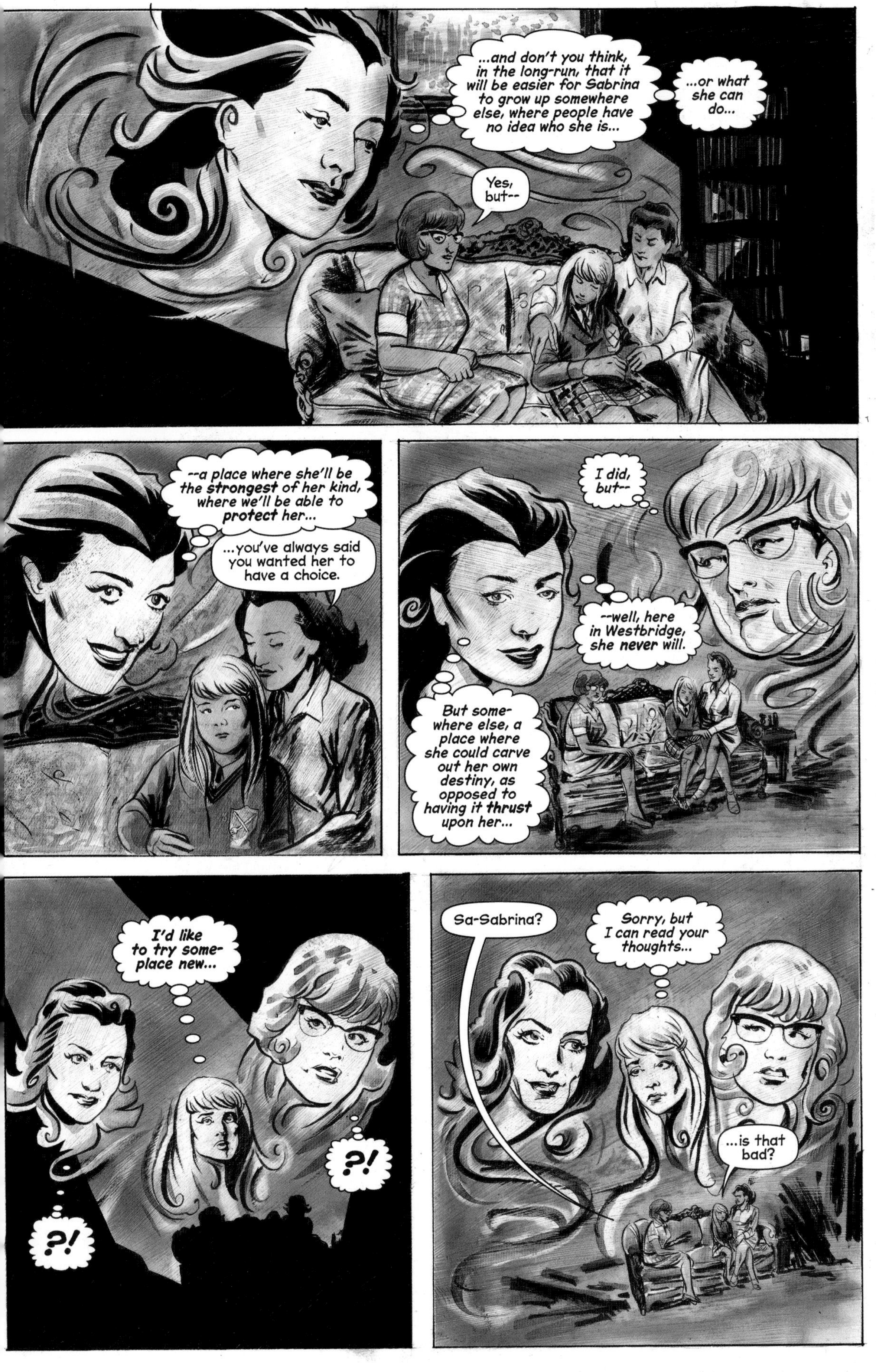
...and don't you think, in the long-run, that it will be easier for Sabrina to grow up somewhere else, where people have no idea who she is...
...or what she can do...
Yes, but--
--a place where she'll be the strongest of her kind, where we'll be able to protect her...
...you've always said you wanted her to have a choice.
I did, but--
--well, here in Westbridge, she never will.
But somewhere else, a place where she could carve out her own destiny, as opposed to having it thrust upon her...
I'd like to try someplace new...
?!
?!
Sa-Sabrina?
Sorry, but I can read your thoughts...
...is that bad?

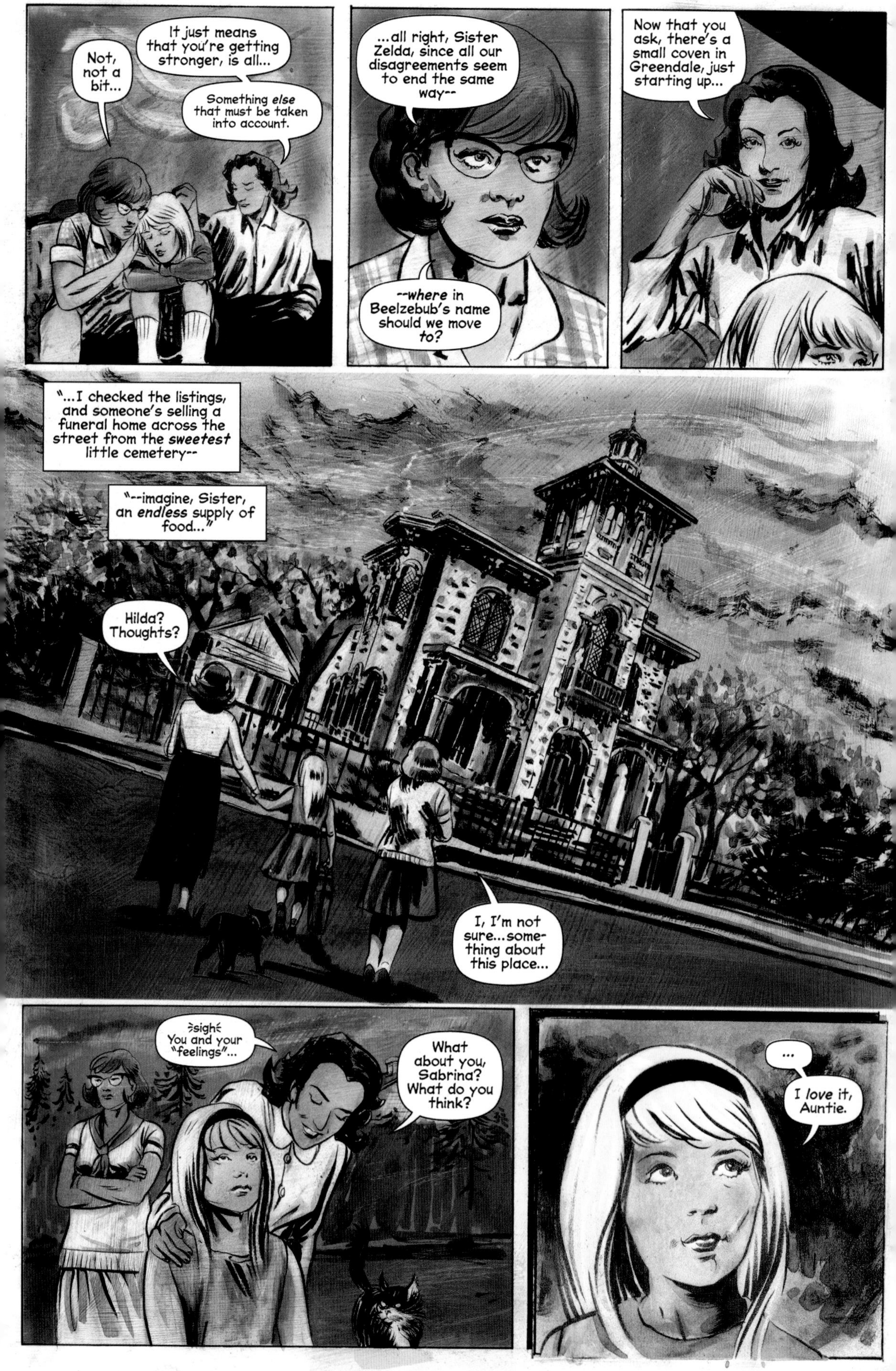
Not, not a bit...
It just means that you're getting stronger, is all...
Something *else* that must be taken into account.
...all right, Sister Zelda, since all our disagreements seem to end the same way--
--*where* in Beelzebub's name should we move *to?*
Now that you ask, there's a small coven in Greendale, just starting up...
"...I checked the listings, and someone's selling a funeral home across the street from the *sweetest* little cemetery--
"--imagine, Sister, an *endless* supply of food..."
Hilda? Thoughts?
I, I'm not sure...something about this place...
sigh You and your "feelings"...
What about you, Sabrina? What do you think?
...
I *love* it, Auntie.

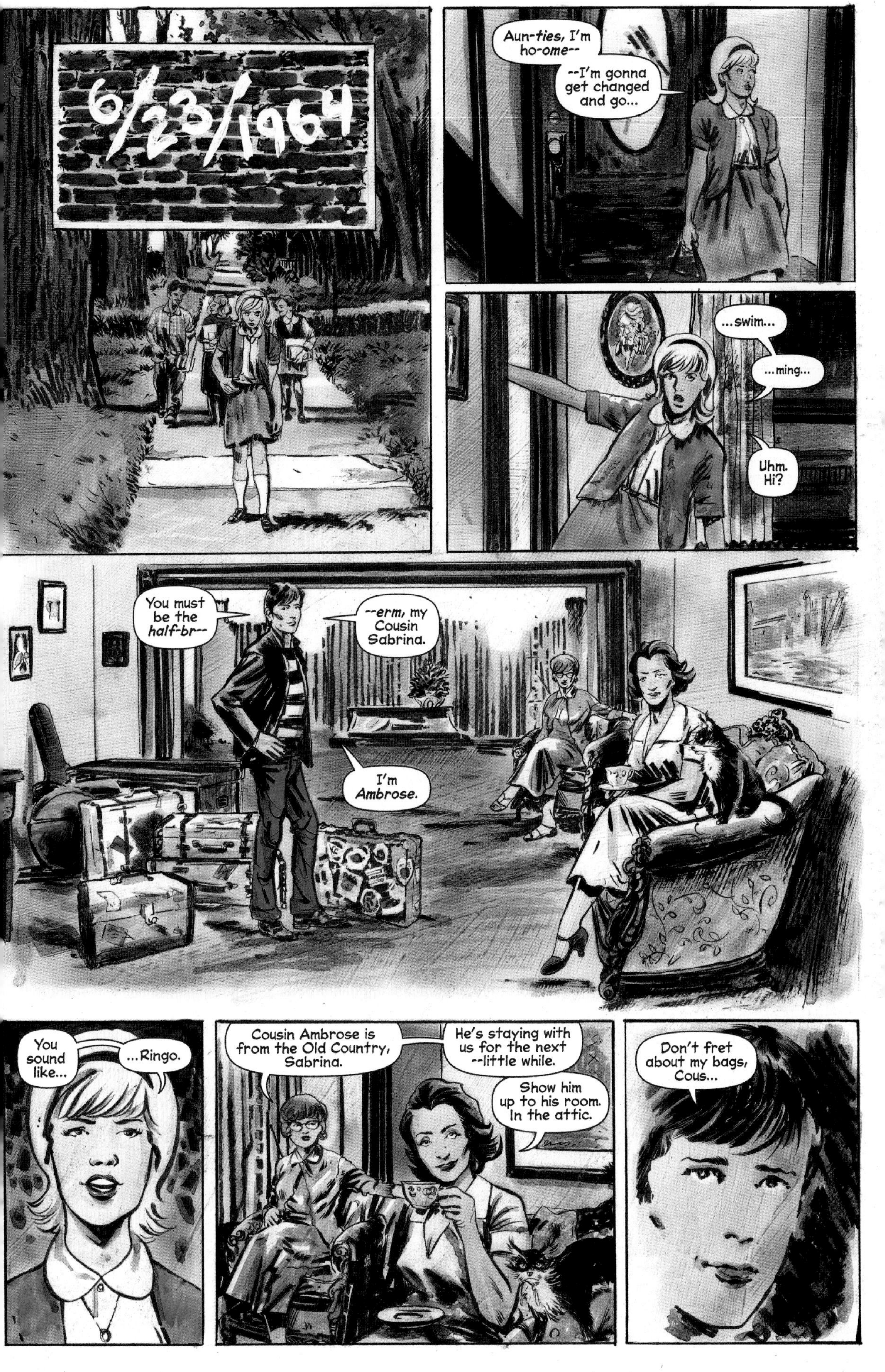

6/23/1964
Aun-*ties*, I'm ho-*ome*--
--I'm gonna get changed and go...
...swim...
...ming...
Uhm. Hi?
You must be the *half-br*--
--*erm*, my Cousin Sabrina.
I'm *Ambrose*.
You sound like...
...Ringo.
Cousin Ambrose is from the Old Country, Sabrina.
He's staying with us for the next --little while.
Show him up to his room. In the attic.
Don't fret about my bags, Cous...

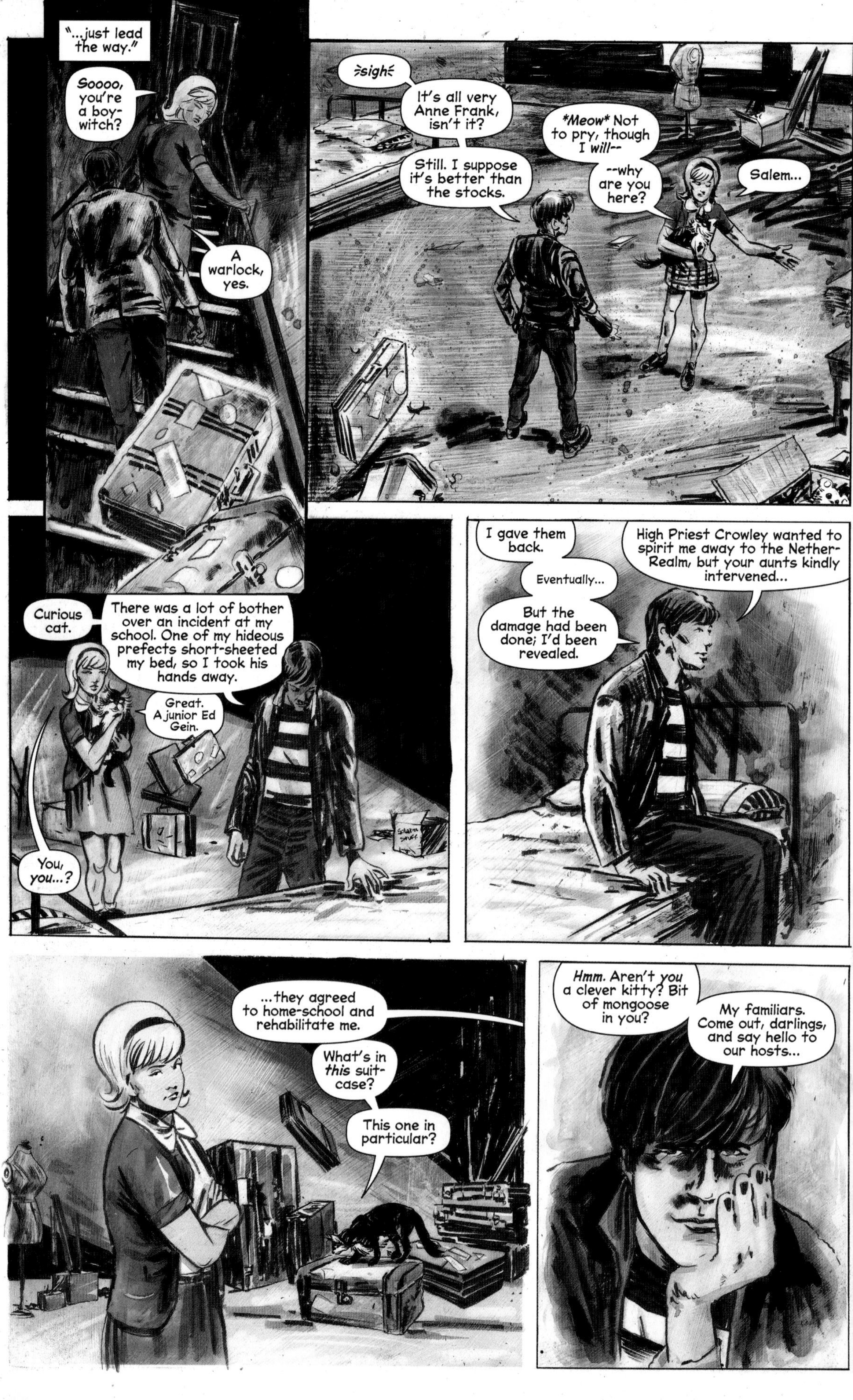
"...just lead the way."
Soooo, you're a boy-witch?
A warlock, yes.
sigh
It's all very Anne Frank, isn't it?
Still. I suppose it's better than the stocks.
Meow Not to pry, though I will--
--why are you here?
Salem...
Curious cat.
There was a lot of bother over an incident at my school. One of my hideous prefects short-sheeted my bed, so I took his hands away.
Great. A junior Ed Gein.
You, you...?
I gave them back.
Eventually...
But the damage had been done; I'd been revealed.
High Priest Crowley wanted to spirit me away to the Nether-Realm, but your aunts kindly intervened...
...they agreed to home-school and rehabilitate me.
What's in this suit-case?
This one in particular?
Hmm. Aren't you a clever kitty? Bit of mongoose in you?
My familiars. Come out, darlings, and say hello to our hosts...

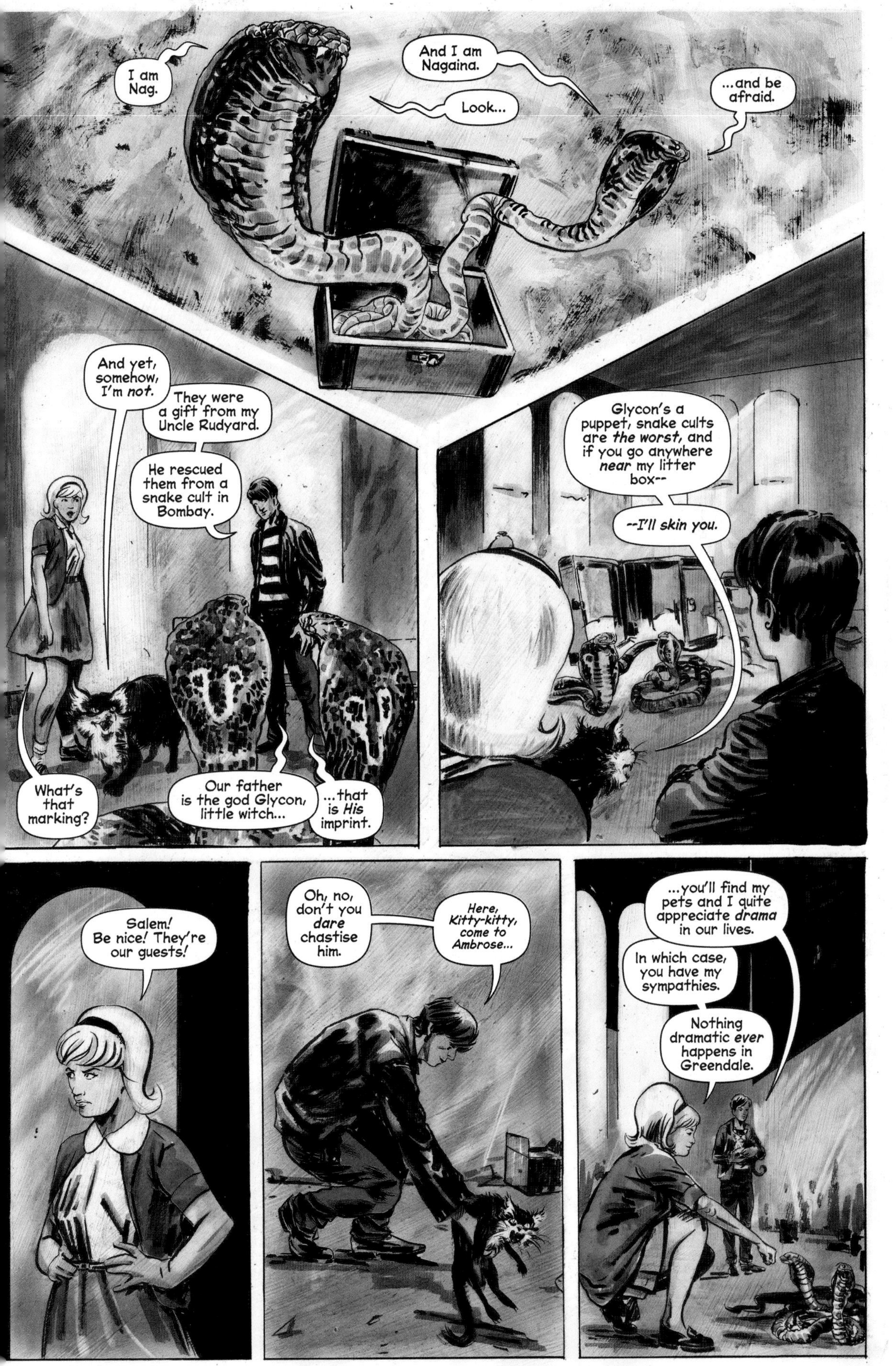
I am Nag.
And I am Nagaina.
Look...
...and be afraid.
And yet, somehow, I'm *not*.
They were a gift from my Uncle Rudyard.
He rescued them from a snake cult in Bombay.
What's that marking?
Our father is the god Glycon, little witch...
...that is *His* imprint.
Glycon's a puppet, snake cults are *the worst,* and if you go anywhere *near* my litter box--
--*I'll skin you.*
Salem! Be nice! They're our guests!
Oh, no, don't you *dare* chastise him.
Here, Kitty-kitty, come to Ambrose...
...you'll find my pets and I quite appreciate *drama* in our lives.
In which case, you have my sympathies.
Nothing dramatic *ever* happens in Greendale.

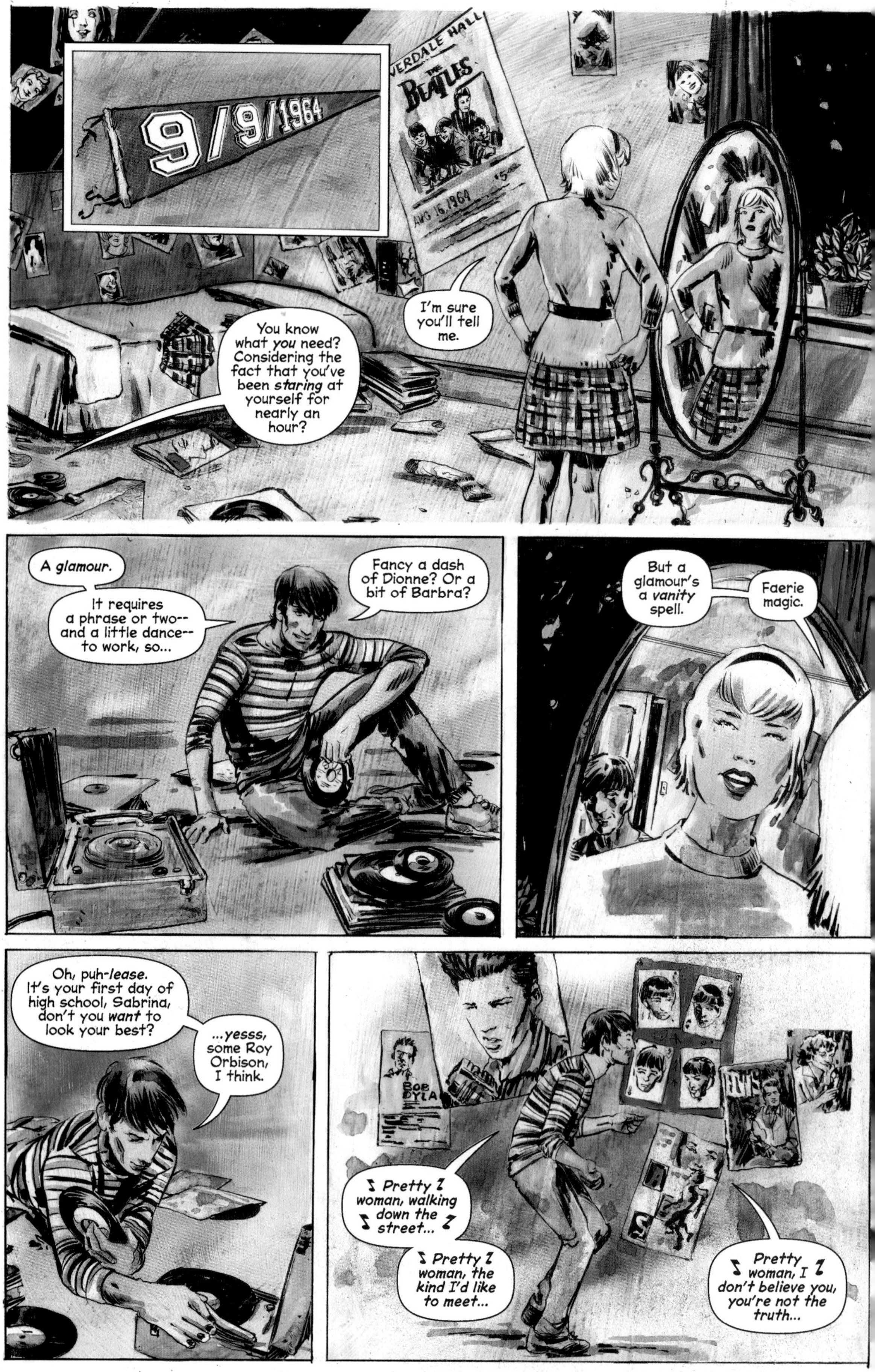
9/9/1964
RIVERDALE HALL
THE BEATLES
AUG 15, 1964
You know what *you* need? Considering the fact that you've been *staring* at yourself for nearly an hour?
I'm sure you'll tell me.
A *glamour.*
It requires a phrase or two--and a little dance--to work, so...
Fancy a dash of Dionne? Or a bit of Barbra?
But a glamour's a *vanity* spell.
Faerie magic.
Oh, puh-*lease.* It's your first day of high school, Sabrina, don't you *want* to look your best?
...*yesss,* some Roy Orbison, I think.
BOB DYLA
Pretty woman, walking down the street...
Pretty woman, the kind I'd like to meet...
Pretty woman, I don't believe you, you're not the truth...

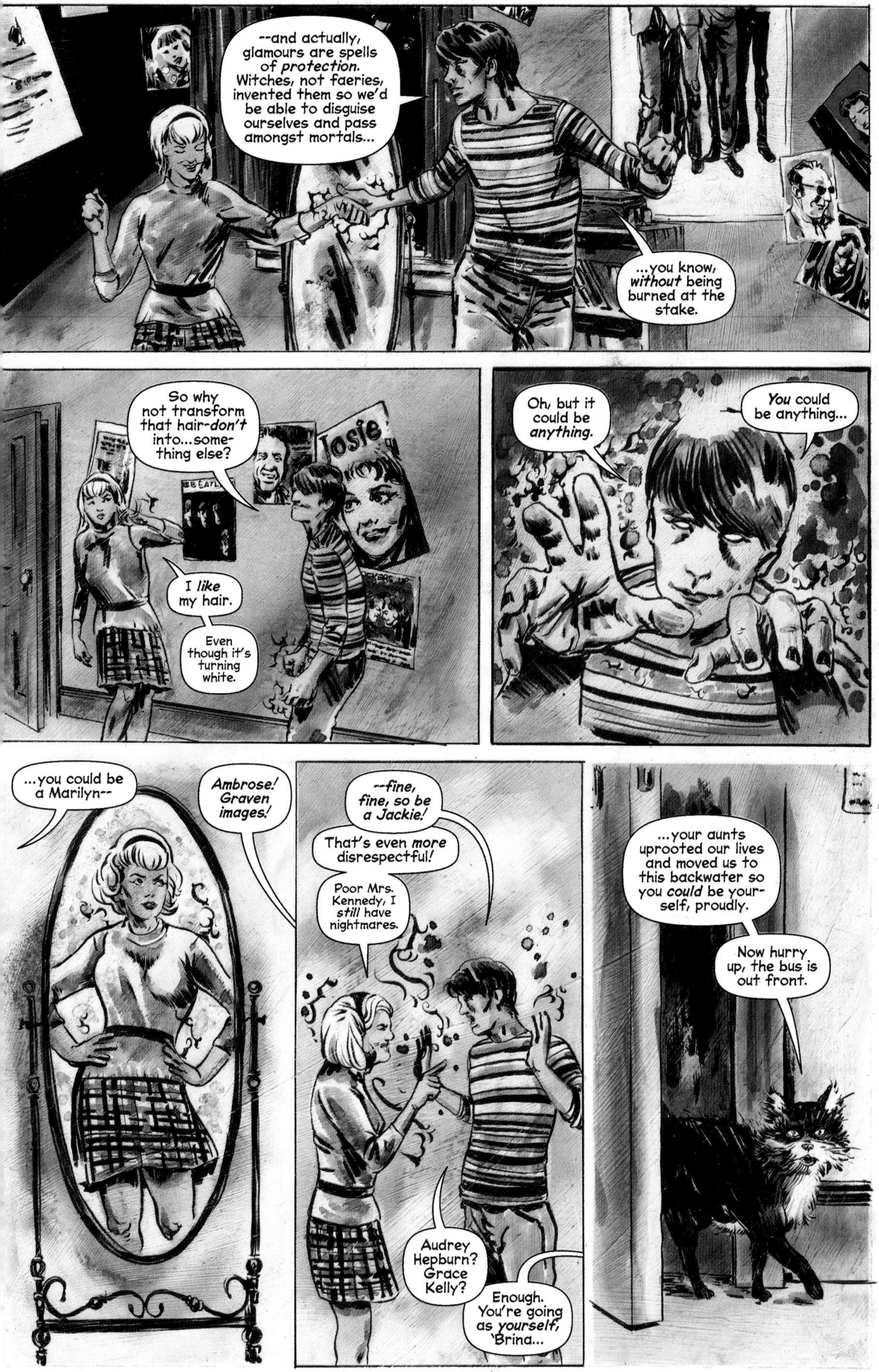
--and actually, glamours are spells of *protection.* Witches, not faeries, invented them so we'd be able to disguise ourselves and pass amongst mortals...
...you know, *without* being burned at the stake.
So why not transform that hair-*don't* into...something else?
Josie
I *like* my hair.
Even though it's turning white.
Oh, but it could be *anything.*
You could be anything...
...you could be a Marilyn--
Ambrose! Graven images!
--fine, fine, so be a Jackie!
That's even *more* disrespectful!
Poor Mrs. Kennedy, I *still* have nightmares.
Audrey Hepburn? Grace Kelly?
Enough. You're going as *yourself,* 'Brina...
...your aunts uprooted our lives and moved us to this backwater so you *could* be yourself, proudly.
Now hurry up, the bus is out front.

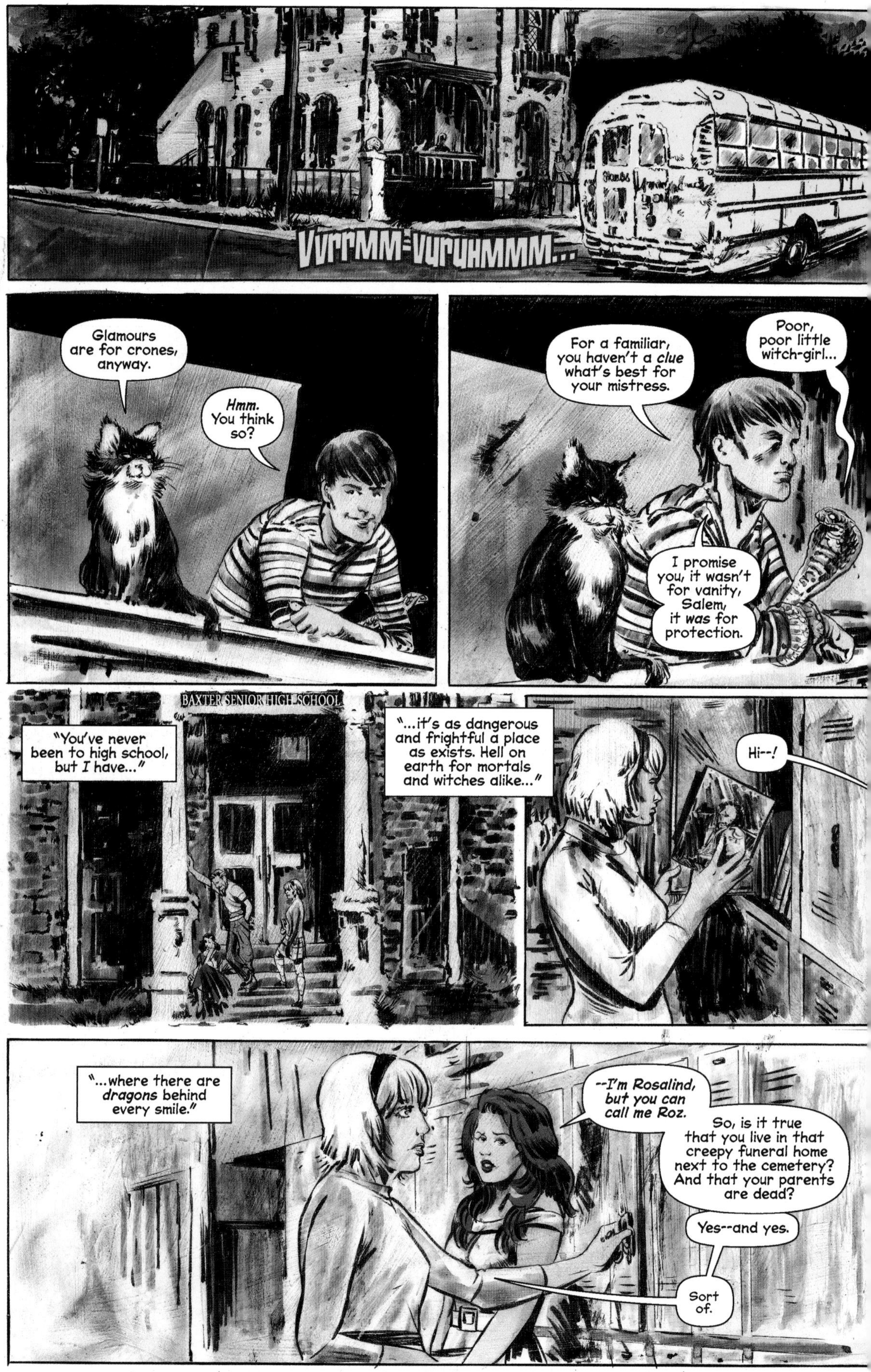

VVRRMM-VURUHMMM...
Glamours are for crones, anyway.
Hmm. You think so?
For a familiar, you haven't a clue what's best for your mistress.
Poor, poor little witch-girl...
I promise you, it wasn't for vanity, Salem, it was for protection.
BAXTER SENIOR HIGH SCHOOL
"You've never been to high school, but I have..."
"...it's as dangerous and frightful a place as exists. Hell on earth for mortals and witches alike..."
Hi--!
"...where there are dragons behind every smile."
--I'm Rosalind, but you can call me Roz.
So, is it true that you live in that creepy funeral home next to the cemetery? And that your parents are dead?
Yes--and yes.
Sort of.

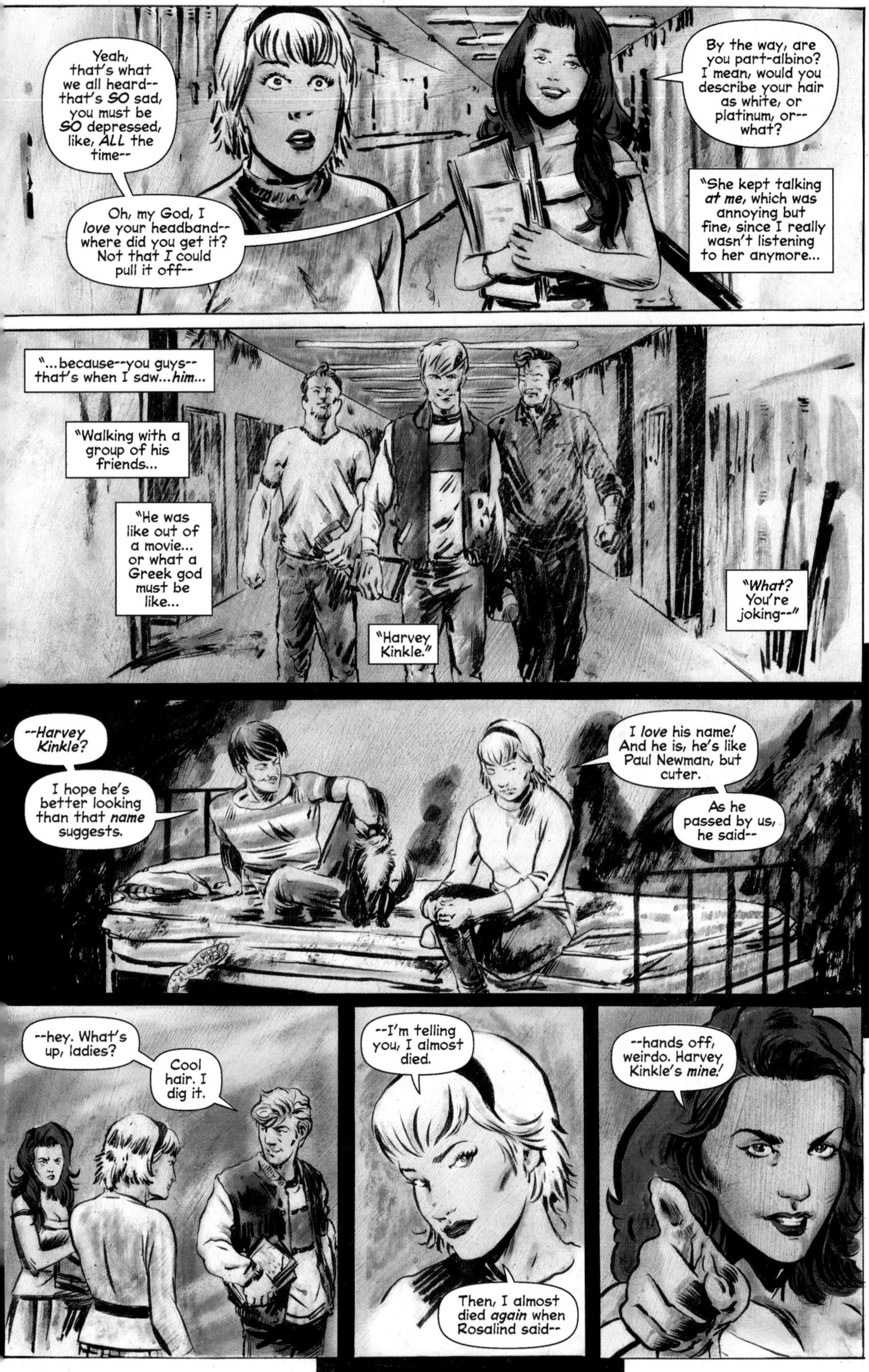
Yeah, that's what we all heard--that's SO sad, you must be SO depressed, like, ALL the time--
Oh, my God, I love your headband--where did you get it? Not that I could pull it off--
By the way, are you part-albino? I mean, would you describe your hair as white, or platinum, or--what?
"She kept talking at me, which was annoying but fine, since I really wasn't listening to her anymore...
"...because--you guys--that's when I saw...him...
"Walking with a group of his friends...
"He was like out of a movie... or what a Greek god must be like...
"Harvey Kinkle."
"What? You're joking--"
--Harvey Kinkle?
I hope he's better looking than that name suggests.
I love his name! And he is, he's like Paul Newman, but cuter.
As he passed by us, he said--
--hey. What's up, ladies?
Cool hair. I dig it.
--I'm telling you, I almost died.
Then, I almost died again when Rosalind said--
--hands off, weirdo. Harvey Kinkle's mine!

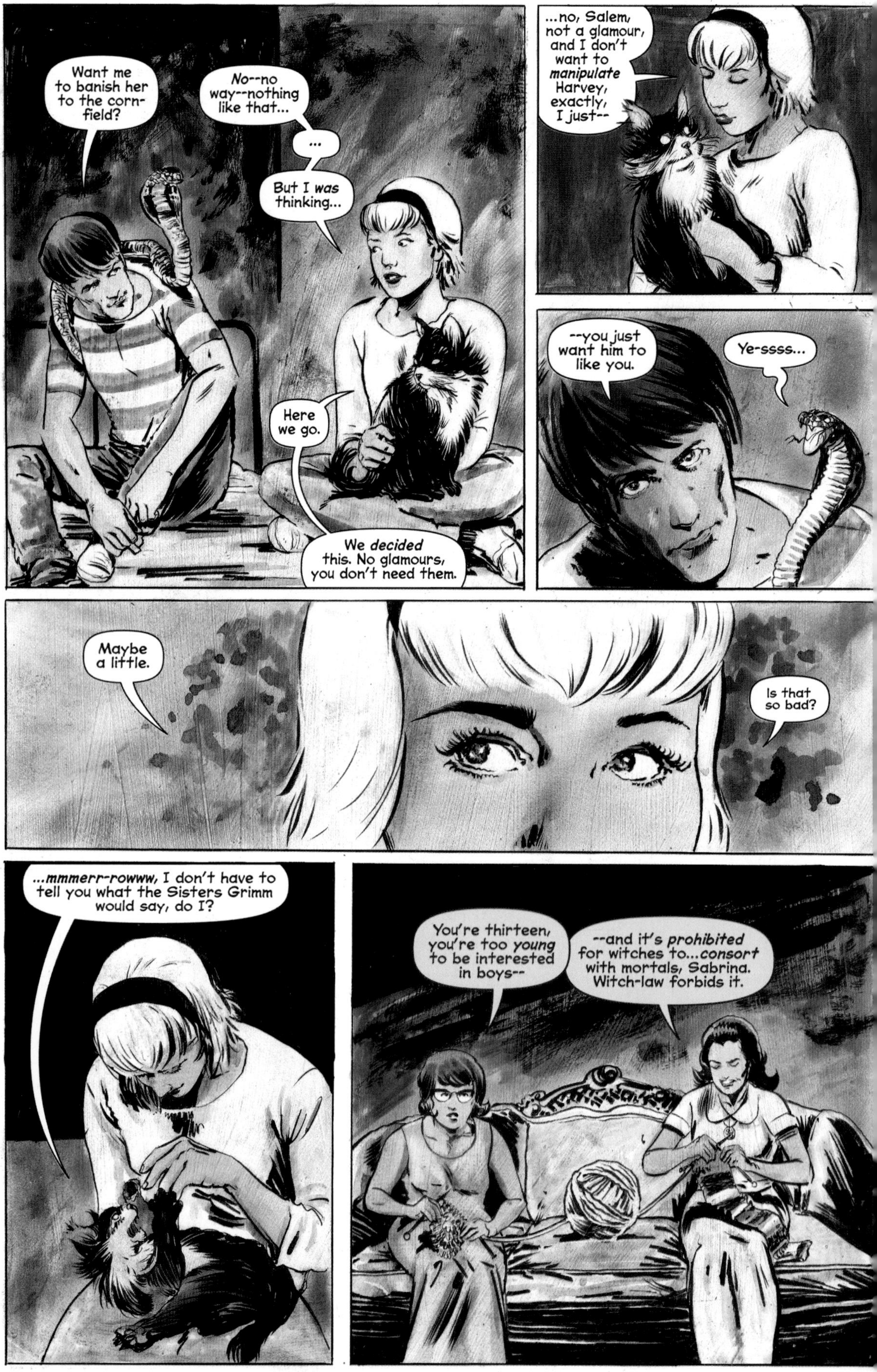
Want me to banish her to the corn-field?
No--no way--nothing like that...
...
But I *was* thinking...
Here we go.
We *decided* this. No glamours, you don't need them.
...no, Salem, not a glamour, and I don't want to *manipulate* Harvey, exactly, I just--
--you just want him to like you.
Ye-ssss...
Maybe a little.
Is that so bad?
...mmmerr-rowww, I don't have to tell you what the Sisters Grimm would say, do I?
You're thirteen, you're too *young* to be interested in boys--
--and it's *prohibited* for witches to...*consort* with mortals, Sabrina. Witch-law forbids it.

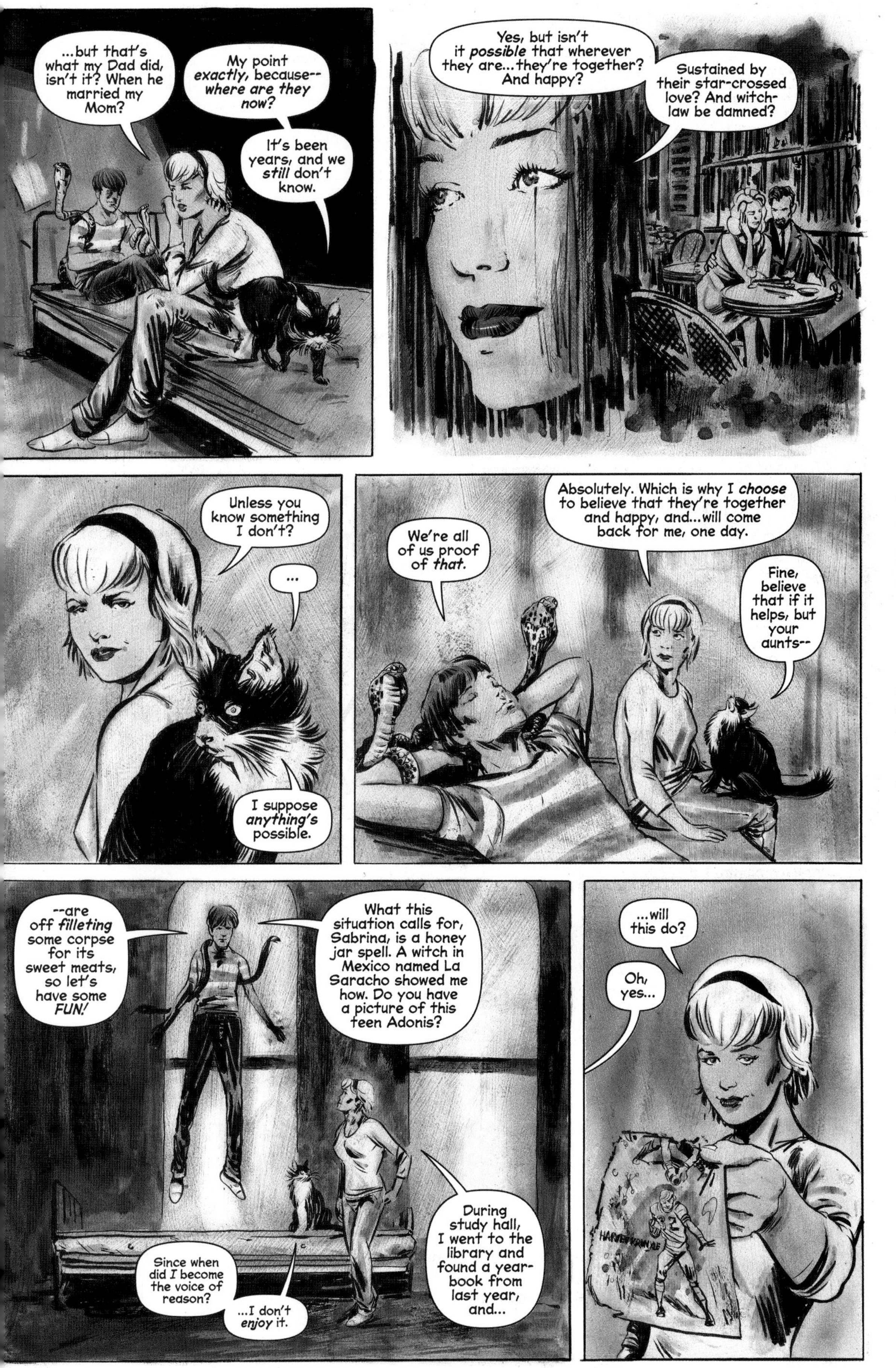
...but that's what my Dad did, isn't it? When he married my Mom?
My point *exactly*, because--*where are they now?*
It's been years, and we *still* don't know.
Yes, but isn't it *possible* that wherever they are...they're together? And happy?
Sustained by their star-crossed love? And witch-law be damned?
Unless you know something I don't?
...
I suppose *anything's* possible.
We're all of us proof of *that*.
Absolutely. Which is why I *choose* to believe that they're together and happy, and...will come back for me, one day.
Fine, believe that if it helps, but your aunts--
--are off *filleting* some corpse for its sweet meats, so let's have some *FUN!*
What this situation calls for, Sabrina, is a honey jar spell. A witch in Mexico named La Saracho showed me how. Do you have a picture of this teen Adonis?
Since when did *I* become the voice of reason?
...I don't *enjoy* it.
During study hall, I went to the library and found a year-book from last year, and...
...will this do?
Oh, yes...

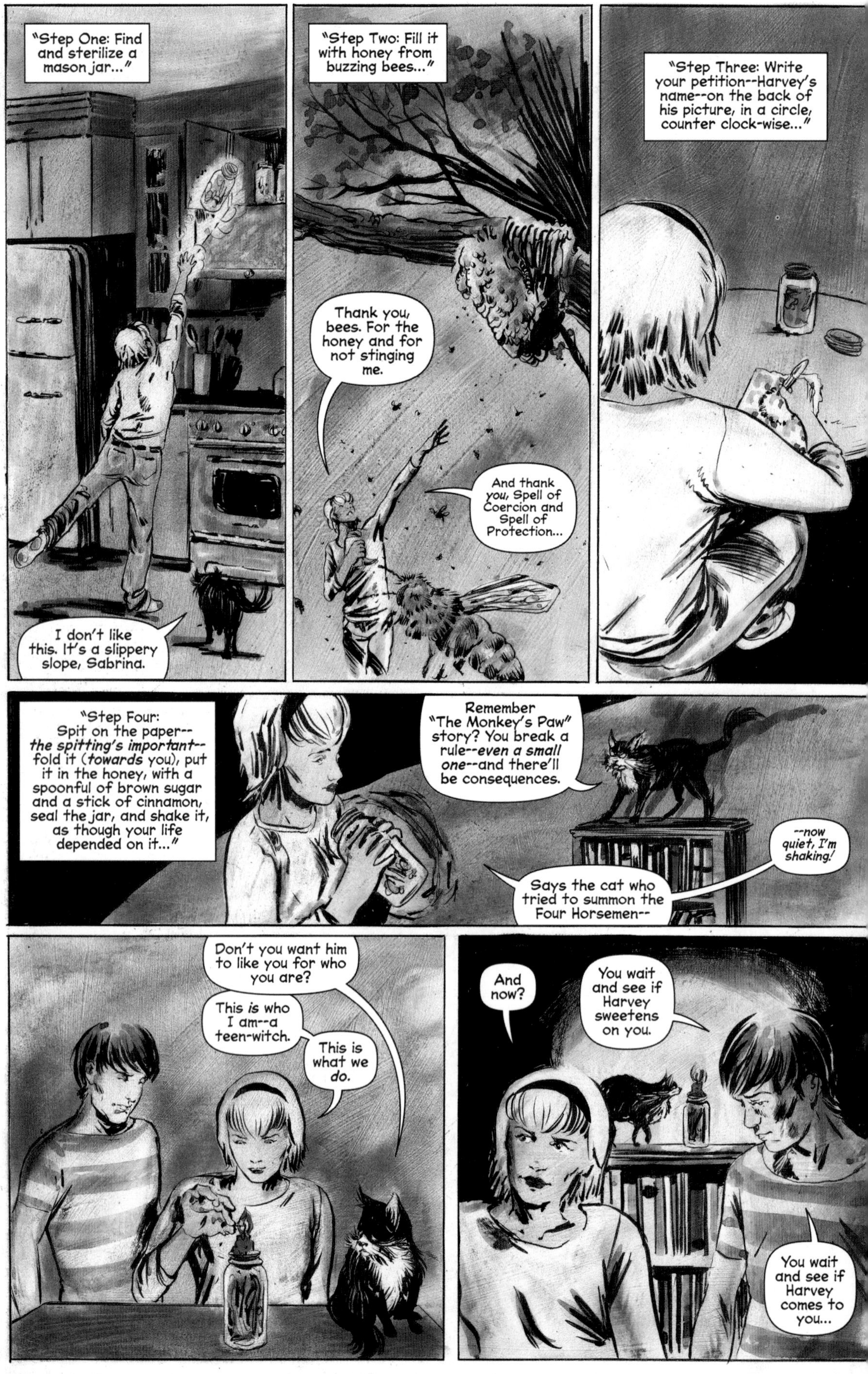
"Step One: Find and sterilize a mason jar..."
I don't like this. It's a slippery slope, Sabrina.
"Step Two: Fill it with honey from buzzing bees..."
Thank you, bees. For the honey and for not stinging me.
And thank *you,* Spell of Coercion and Spell of Protection...
"Step Three: Write your petition--Harvey's name--on the back of his picture, in a circle, counter clock-wise..."
"Step Four: Spit on the paper-- ***the spitting's important***-- fold it (***towards*** you), put it in the honey, with a spoonful of brown sugar and a stick of cinnamon, seal the jar, and shake it, as though your life depended on it..."
Remember "The Monkey's Paw" story? You break a rule--***even a small one***--and there'll be consequences.
Says the cat who tried to summon the Four Horsemen--
--now quiet, I'm shaking!
Don't you want him to like you for who you are?
This *is* who I am--a teen-witch.
This is what we *do.*
And now?
You wait and see if Harvey sweetens on you.
You wait and see if Harvey comes to you...

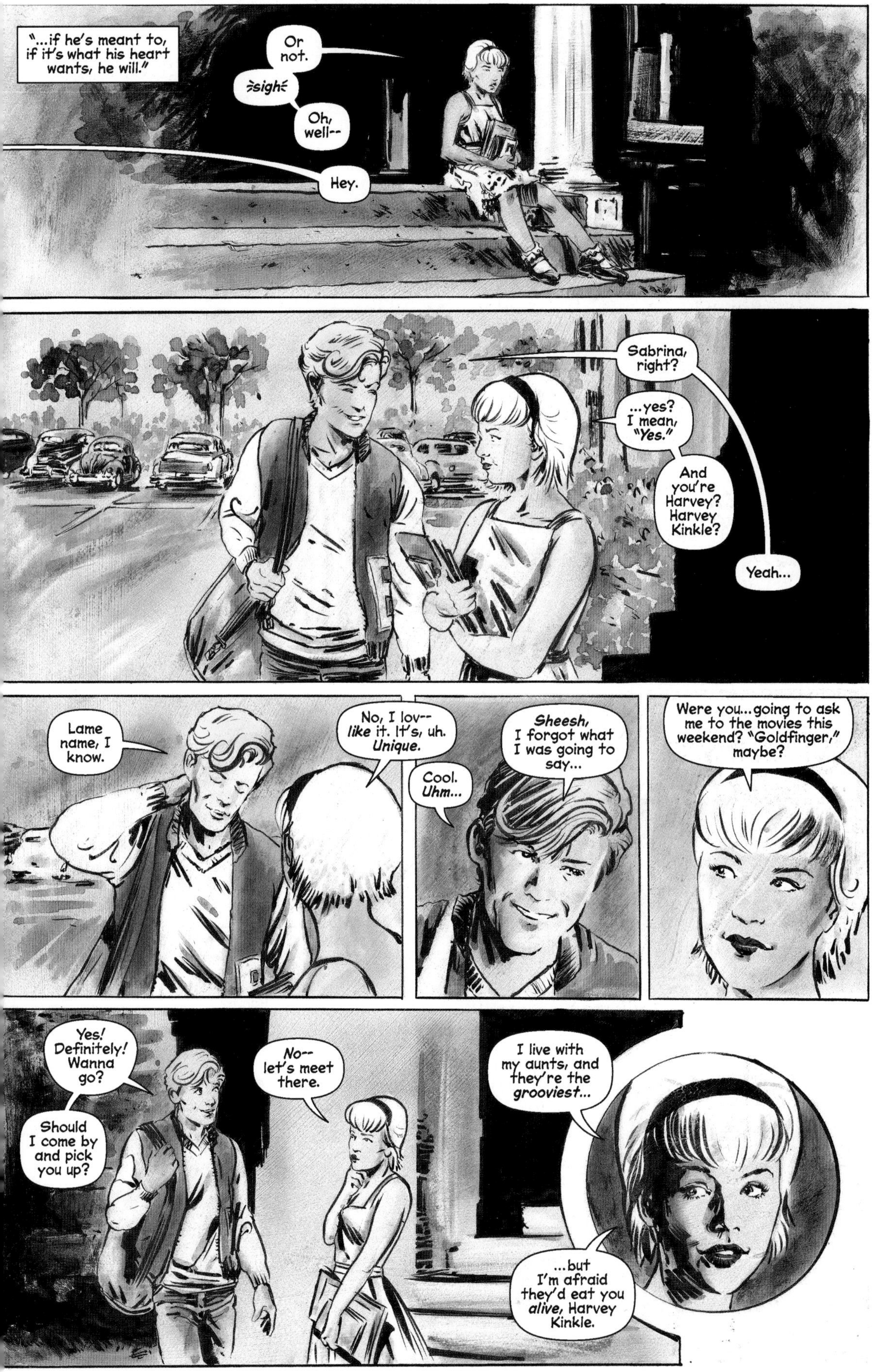
"...if he's meant to, if it's what his heart wants, he will."
Or not.
sigh
Oh, well--
Hey.
Sabrina, right?
...yes? I mean, "Yes."
And you're Harvey? Harvey Kinkle?
Yeah...
Lame name, I know.
No, I lov-- like it. It's, uh. Unique.
Cool. Uhm...
Sheesh, I forgot what I was going to say...
Were you...going to ask me to the movies this weekend? "Goldfinger," maybe?
Yes! Definitely! Wanna go?
Should I come by and pick you up?
No-- let's meet there.
I live with my aunts, and they're the grooviest...
...but I'm afraid they'd eat you alive, Harvey Kinkle.

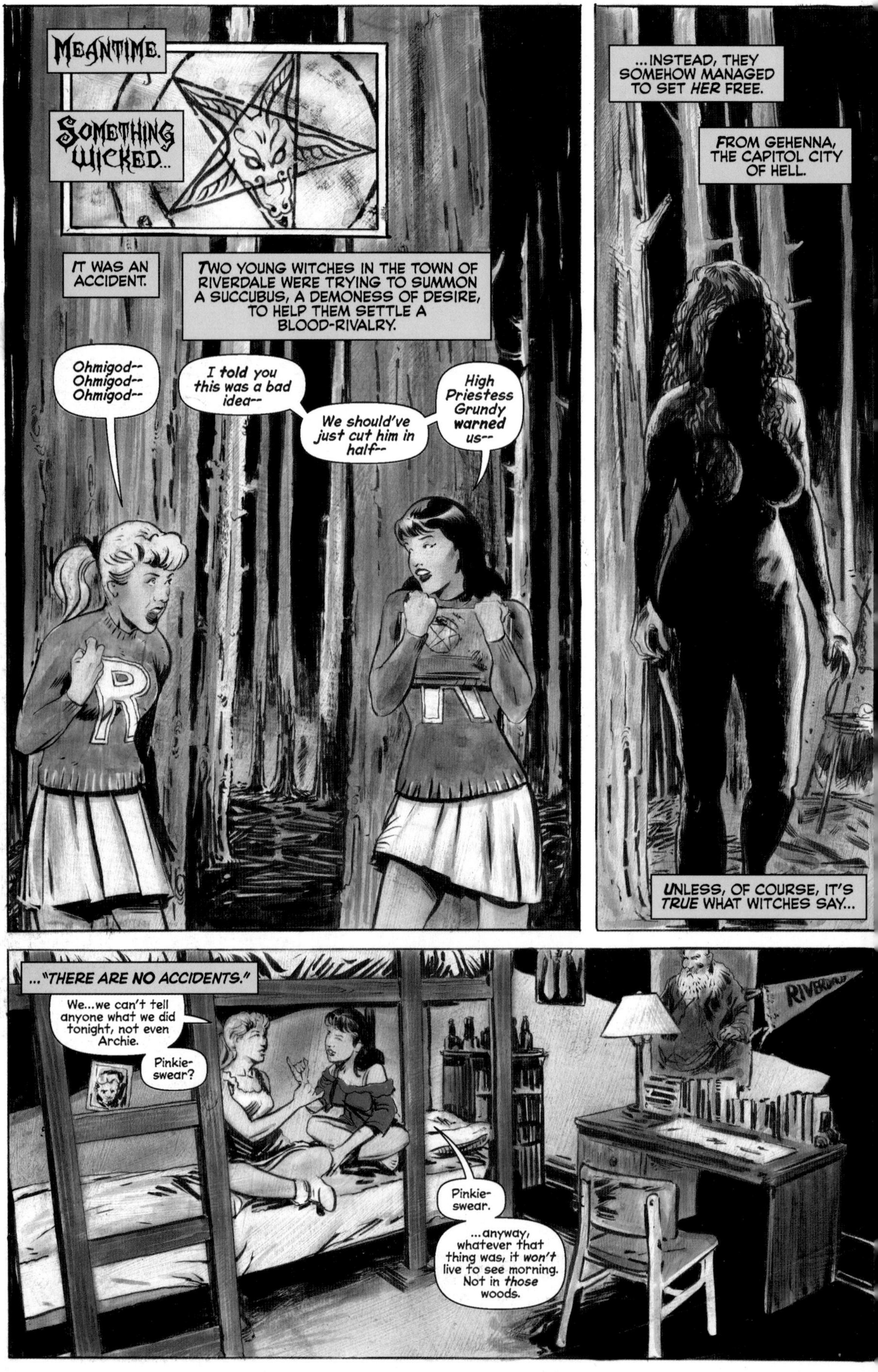
MEANTIME.
SOMETHING WICKED...
IT WAS AN ACCIDENT.
TWO YOUNG WITCHES IN THE TOWN OF RIVERDALE WERE TRYING TO SUMMON A SUCCUBUS, A DEMONESS OF DESIRE, TO HELP THEM SETTLE A BLOOD-RIVALRY.
Ohmigod-- Ohmigod-- Ohmigod--
I told you this was a bad idea--
We should've just cut him in half--
High Priestess Grundy warned us--
...INSTEAD, THEY SOMEHOW MANAGED TO SET HER FREE.
FROM GEHENNA, THE CAPITOL CITY OF HELL.
UNLESS, OF COURSE, IT'S TRUE WHAT WITCHES SAY...
..."THERE ARE NO ACCIDENTS."
We...we can't tell anyone what we did tonight, not even Archie.
Pinkie-swear?
Pinkie-swear.
...anyway, whatever that thing was, it won't live to see morning. Not in those woods.

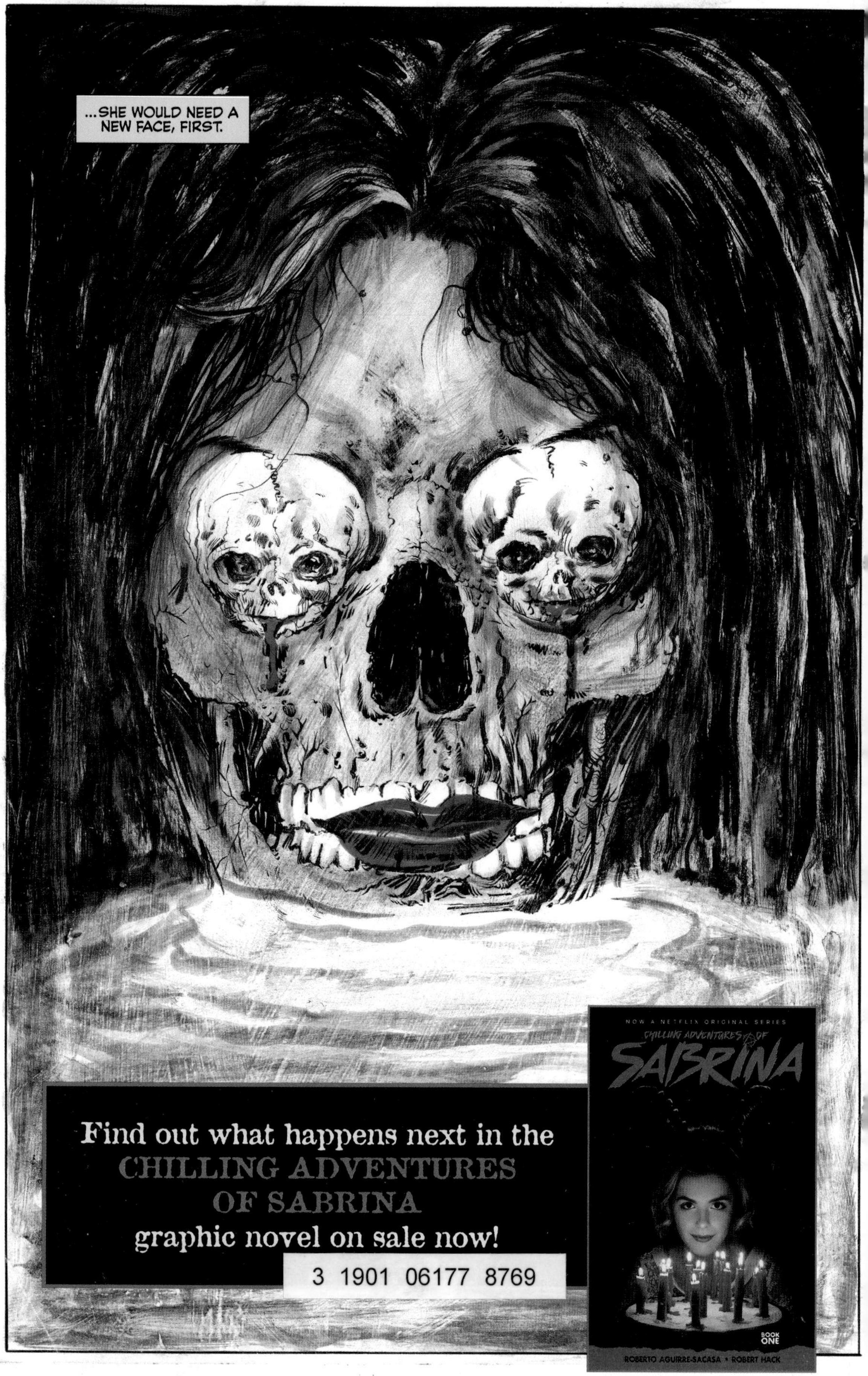
...SHE WOULD NEED A NEW FACE, FIRST.
Find out what happens next in the CHILLING ADVENTURES OF SABRINA graphic novel on sale now!
NOW A NETFLIX ORIGINAL SERIES
CHILLING ADVENTURES OF SABRINA
BOOK ONE
ROBERTO AGUIRRE-SACASA • ROBERT HACK

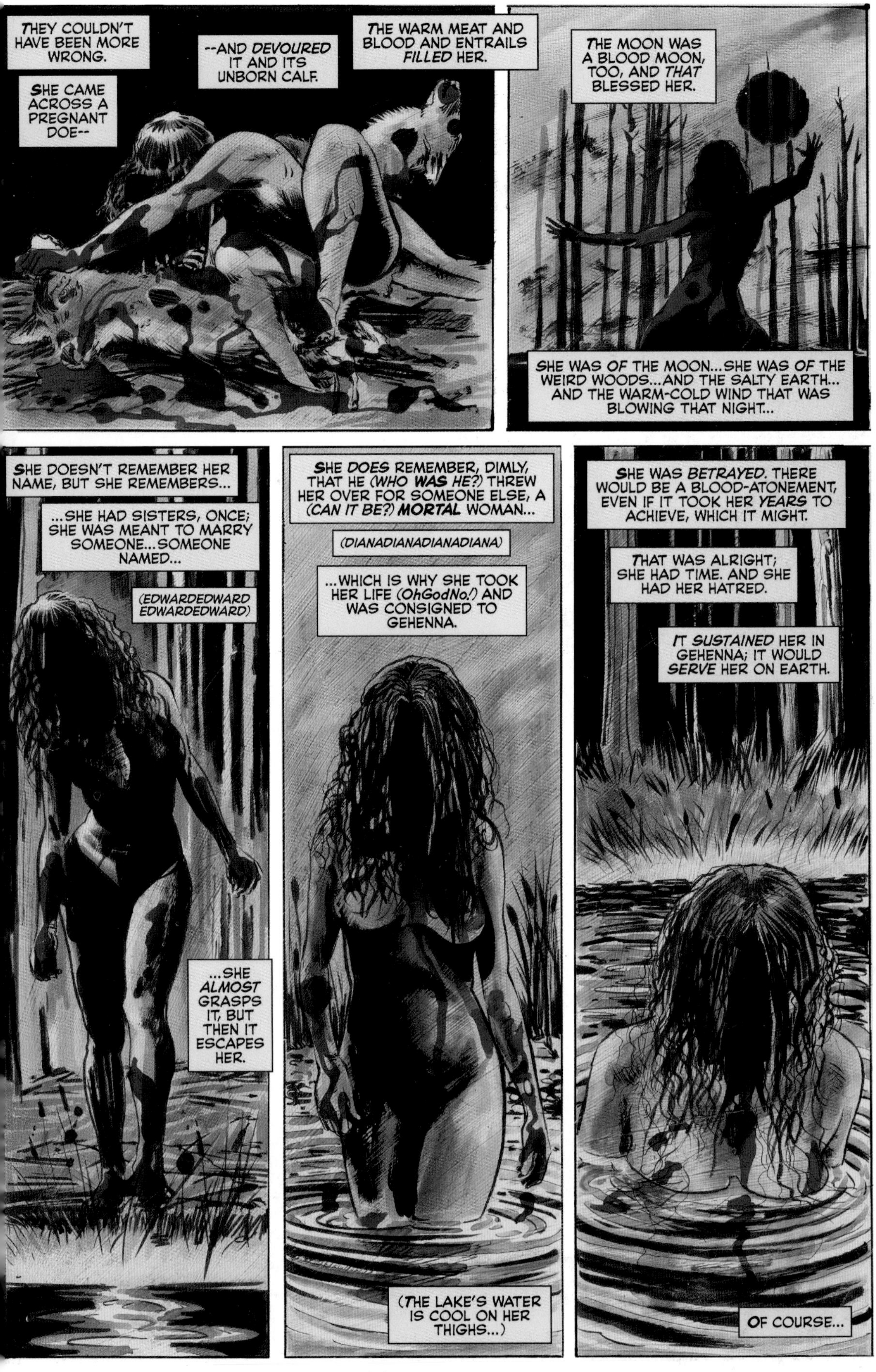

THEY COULDN'T HAVE BEEN MORE WRONG.
SHE CAME ACROSS A PREGNANT DOE--
--AND DEVOURED IT AND ITS UNBORN CALF.
THE WARM MEAT AND BLOOD AND ENTRAILS FILLED HER.
THE MOON WAS A BLOOD MOON, TOO, AND THAT BLESSED HER.
SHE WAS OF THE MOON...SHE WAS OF THE WEIRD WOODS...AND THE SALTY EARTH... AND THE WARM-COLD WIND THAT WAS BLOWING THAT NIGHT...
SHE DOESN'T REMEMBER HER NAME, BUT SHE REMEMBERS...
...SHE HAD SISTERS, ONCE; SHE WAS MEANT TO MARRY SOMEONE...SOMEONE NAMED...
(EDWARDEDWARD EDWARDEDWARD)
...SHE ALMOST GRASPS IT, BUT THEN IT ESCAPES HER.
SHE DOES REMEMBER, DIMLY, THAT HE (WHO WAS HE?) THREW HER OVER FOR SOMEONE ELSE, A (CAN IT BE?) MORTAL WOMAN...
(DIANADIANADIANADIANA)
...WHICH IS WHY SHE TOOK HER LIFE (OhGodNo!) AND WAS CONSIGNED TO GEHENNA.
(THE LAKE'S WATER IS COOL ON HER THIGHS...)
SHE WAS BETRAYED. THERE WOULD BE A BLOOD-ATONEMENT, EVEN IF IT TOOK HER YEARS TO ACHIEVE, WHICH IT MIGHT.
THAT WAS ALRIGHT; SHE HAD TIME. AND SHE HAD HER HATRED.
IT SUSTAINED HER IN GEHENNA; IT WOULD SERVE HER ON EARTH.
OF COURSE...